POLICE

&

THE EMPIRE CITY

RACE & THE ORIGINS OF MODERN POLICING IN NEW YORK

POLICE & THE EMPIRE CITY

MATTHEW GUARIGLIA

Duke University Press Durham and London 2023

© 2023 Duke University Press. All rights reserved
Printed in the United States of America on acid-free paper ∞
Project Editor: Ihsan Taylor
Designed by Aimee C. Harrison
Typeset in Garamond Premier Pro and Helvetica Neue Pro
by Westchester Publishing Services

Library of Congress Cataloging-in-Publication Data
Names: Guariglia, Matthew, author.
Title: Police and the Empire City : race and the origins of modern
policing in New York / Matthew Guariglia.
Description: Durham : Duke University Press, 2023. | Includes
bibliographical references and index.
Identifiers: LCCN 2023003684 (print)
LCCN 2023003685 (ebook)
ISBN 9781478025405 (paperback)
ISBN 9781478020622 (hardcover)
ISBN 9781478027546 (ebook)
Subjects: LCSH: New York (N.Y.). Police Department—History. |
Police—New York (State)—New York—History. | Law enforcement—
New York (State)—New York—History. | Racial profiling in law
enforcement—New York (State)—New York—History. | Discrimination
in law enforcement—New York (State)—New York—History. | Police
brutality—New York (State)—New York—History. | Police-community
relations—New York (State)—New York—History. | New York (N.Y.)—
Ethnic relations—History. | BISAC: HISTORY / United States / General |
SOCIAL SCIENCE / Criminology
Classification: LCC HV8148.N5 G83 2023 (print) | LCC HV8148.N5
(ebook) | DDC 363.209747/1—dc23/eng/20230714
LC record available at https://lccn.loc.gov/2023003684
LC ebook record available at https://lccn.loc.gov/2023003685

Cover art: Italians and police officers around a suspended bank in New
York City, circa 1907–14. Photo by Bain News Service, N.Y.C. George
Grantham Bain Collection (Library of Congress).

FOR MY FAMILY

CONTENTS

INTRODUCTION

Race, Legibility, and Policing
in the Unequal City

In 1906, the editors of Joseph Pulitzer's popular newspaper the *Evening World* proposed a plan they thought would finally allow police to get a foothold in New York's Chinatown. The proposal was to tear down sections of the majority immigrant neighborhood and turn it into a wide-open park. The headline "Tear Down the Dens of Chinatown and Make a Park of New York's Darkest Spot," sought to depict not just the densely inhabited tenements of Lower Manhattan but also their residents as dark and impenetrable. "Sightseers go through the streets and look at the silent Chinamen and think they have seen Chinatown," the article said, "but the mysteries hid behind those walls, the crime-polluted back alleys and cellars, the dungeon dives, the secret life of the thugs and thieves, and feuds, the slavery—these are not seen." To the working-, middle-, and even upper-class white readers of the *Evening World*, Chinatown, like many immigrant neighborhoods in New York at the time, was a shadowy spot on the map. It was a place unknowable and illegible to respectable white Manhattanites, even those predisposed to searching for the lurid and titillating and (often staged) slumming and tourism expeditions. The paper's editors and its readers were led to believe that because much of this world existed beyond the reach and gaze of the majority white and American-born police department, it was a place in which crime could flourish and even spread to other neighborhoods and threaten white communities.[1]

Officers and administrators of the New York City's police department, as well as the wider white public, were fed a steady diet of sensationalized reporting about Chinese immigrants. This reporting often played up the foreignness of the inhabitants of Chinatown to the point of racist caricature—especially when it came to depicting Chinese people as having a predilection for all manner of vice, including the seduction or sexual coercion of young white women. Stories of police liberating young white women from these supposedly unfindable basement dens would have been familiar to newspaper readers at the time. These stories slotted perfectly into the contemporary moral panic gripping politicians, police administrators, and the upper crust of New York society: fear that sexually predatory immigrant and nonwhite men were seducing and exploiting white women. These men would allegedly use affection, drugs, or force to profit from coerced prostitution. The panic weaponized xenophobic fears of interracial socialization and sexual interaction to criminalize and arrest immigrants and nonwhite men, and even to deport some of them.[2]

The *Evening World*'s proposal to turn spaces unknowable to police into a park reached beyond city planning—it was also an attempt to turn people who were supposedly so foreign as to be unknowable into something predictable and benign as well. "The criminals who infest the district," the editors wrote, "are forced to come together for mutual protection and concealment. . . . No one except those thoroughly afraid of them can understand their language." Consequently, because the only people who understood their language were also the same people who feared reprisals should they speak to law enforcement, "the police cannot get evidence of the conspiracy or of the murder when it is committed." The cultural gap between the alleged criminal and the police—the inability of police to gain cooperation from witnesses—conspired to make detectives believe the people of Chinatown were as incomprehensible as the dense urban landscape itself. As one officer said, "I'd be willing to wager a fair sum that a hundred murders have been committed in Chinatown, by Chinamen, without a word about such crimes reaching the ears of police." To some extent, these crimes were fantasies created by an American-born public eager to read criminality, deviance, and violence onto any cultures that seemed foreign or different.[3]

Arrests in the Progressive Era, especially in immigrant and Black neighborhoods, were not a clear indicator of the existence of crime. After all, police often used immigrants' inability to wield civic power, attract attention from municipal services, or communicate effectively with the government to extort money from the newly arrived and arrest those who protested. But police perceived their failures to solve those crimes that did exist as a manifestation of the cultural, linguistic, and even geographical unknowability of immigrants and the spaces they inhabited.[4]

This plan's apparent origin in the pages of a newspaper rather than from the mouth of a police administrator or legislator is also significant. During this period, police, commissioners, reformers, politicians, and even newspaper reporters and editors—commentators as lowly as beat cops and as elevated as renowned international intellectuals—dedicated considerable ink and intellectual labor to attempt to solve the problem of how to police a rapidly diversifying city. Through writings and policy proposals, they attempted to transform nineteenth-century-style policing into a modern science ready to tackle New York's new and more multiracial century. They were the producers, recyclers, and legitimizers of the knowledge on which racial violence and exclusion were built and justified. Throughout this book, I refer to this cohort of people who created knowledge about policing, whether they were detectives, politicians, or university scientists, as "police intellectuals." While I take the time to explore the mental work of police intellectuals, these actors can also be categorized as what Micol Seigel has labeled "violence workers." Although most of the people who created knowledge about policing never personally pulled a trigger or swung a club, they helped to build, justify, and legitimize a system of policing and power relationships that caused violence, not just on physical bodies but also on "discursive, epistemic, symbolic, psychic, and economic," levels. Although some of these people may have had limited contact with one another, they were all engaged in the project of trying to understand how police could exert power across the racial landscape and develop ways to make it more dependable and inescapable.[5]

The 1906 proposals about how to make Chinatown—and by extension Chinese—crime more visible to police were not by any means the start of the conversation. In the early twentieth century, there was a general understanding among the people who thought about crime in the United States that policing *did not work*. It was not that the system itself was flawed; after all, politicians and social scientists could always point to European police institutions that supposedly showed great results in managing crime. No, many believed that it was the American population itself that made policing ineffective.

Police and the Empire City

Police and the Empire City shows how race shaped modern policing and how, in turn, modern policing helped to define and redefine racial boundaries in New York. From its founding, the police department in New York had to organize in ways that addressed racial and ethnic difference. This meant recruiting certain kinds of officers, aggressively policing specific neighborhoods, and building a body of knowledge about the relationship between race and crime. By doing so, police became an engine of racial management and race-making. Not only did police administrators get to decide who was worthy of recruitment to the force—and thus eligible for inclusion in the project of racial state-building—they also got to decide which races were law-abiding and assimilable to American society, and which races were innately criminal and worthy of exclusion and violence.

By building a department that administrators, politicians, and social scientists thought capable of addressing crime in a diverse city, they allowed their engagement with race, perceptions about racial difference, and racisms to leave a tangible imprint on the shape and operations of modern police. In the first decade of the twentieth century, the NYPD explicitly recruited immigrants and created squads of multilingual officers to patrol specific neighborhoods. Police who served as anthropologists and translators gathering knowledge and making communities more knowable to the state were eventually eclipsed by more technocratic and academic ways of knowing. Technologies and filing systems that are now central to the bureaucratic operations of departments were integrated as a means to identify even those people who could not communicate with officers. By the mid-1910s, officer training and education included not just a physical, legal, and forensic curriculum, but also courses to provide linguistic and cultural knowledge. All of these innovations emerged in the early twentieth century as ways that the department could uphold its commitment to racial management in the city.[6]

I have chosen to write about the period between the NYPD's founding in 1845 and the 1930s because it encompasses the moment when police transitioned from a more informal collection of pugilists clad in wool coats to what we can recognize today as a modern professionalized police department. The desire to understand and subordinate immigrant and nonwhite communities catalyzed the rise of a technocratic and surveillance-based policing designed to know, document, and identify as many urbanites as possible—and forged connections between police and the federal immigration administration that endure to this day. This period also saw an acceleration of police departments' antagonistic and militarized posture against marginalized civilians as more technologies, tactics, and ways of racializing crime and violence from America's imperial projects traveled home. Progressive Era police laid the groundwork for the globalized and collaborative system of policing and surveillance so characteristic of international relations to this day. Those interested in the United States' commitment to training police abroad during the Cold War, or the NYPD's thirteen international outposts opened after the terrorist attacks of September 11, 2001, may find the earliest intellectual justifications of such connections not in 2001 or 1970, but in the State Department's 1910 plan to convene a World Police Congress to be held in Washington, DC, to establish international collaboration to combat Italian organized crime.[7]

The narrative in this book covers large demographic swings, the expansion of the US Empire, emancipation and Reconstruction, and the intellectual work and street-level experimentation by police as the fledgling institution navigated these turbulent changes. These national era-defining events sent waves of people, goods, and ideas to New York and forced the department to contend with their existence in the city. By experimenting with ways of exerting control over immigrant and Black communities—which the New York City Police Department believed to be hotbeds of crime—NYPD administrators and beat cops along with social scientists, politicians, racial scientists, early eugenicists, and a fearful, racist, and xenophobic white public all slowly and deliberately compiled the elements of the modern police department we still encounter.

This period also oversaw the nationalizing of local police problems. Feeling unable to control immigrant crime in New York and elsewhere, police intellectuals became outspoken advocates for using the federal levers of power to address their concerns. Federal immigration policy and deportations, culminating in the draconian immigration restrictions of 1921 and 1924, became vital tools to prevent immigration or remove immigrants from those demographics police believed were especially prone to criminality.

The intellectual history of policing New York City is also a global history. Excavating the history of how the NYPD adapted during the early twentieth century uncovers circuits of knowledge produced and exported to create racial boundaries and justify state violence around the world. These circuits do not exist purely because people proud to call themselves New Yorkers hailed from every corner of the globe, but also because its police department is itself a composite of pieces and tactics from around the world. Prominent figures in policing, as well as a good number of officers, had come to the profession as a result of the expansion of the US Empire in the American West, the Pacific, and the Caribbean. Tactics and mentalities of understanding race, insurgency, surveillance, and anticolonialist resistance all found their way into the structure and procedures of the NYPD, both in the minds of soldiers and through the books and academic studies that imperialism produced. The US occupation of the Philippines and other occupied colonies were, to use a phrase Alfred McCoy has popularized, a "laboratory of police modernity." European imperialism as well left its imprint on policing in New York. The first decades of the twentieth century were defined, in part, by the ready and continuous connection between the United States and Europe. As civil servants crisscrossed the ocean, and as police began to form an international community of law enforcement thinkers and practitioners, American police departments became frequent recipients of policing tactics and technologies in use in Europe. Many of these European technologies, fingerprinting chief among them, had been developed in colonies brutally occupied by Great Britain or France. Once in New York, these tactics, whether or not they had been tested on colonial subjects, were put to use to make a multiracial and multiethnic city more controllable by police.[8]

The Failures of Policing in a Multiracial Nation

From 1913 to 1917, Raymond Fosdick, a former NYPD administrator turned researcher, traveled the United States and Europe, visiting police departments in hopes of finding a solution to what he called the "American Problem." He declared it the defining difficulty of policing in the United States. It was, in his estimation, "this complex problem of nationality that the police are called upon to grapple with. They must enforce the same laws among a score of races and maintain a standard of conduct in a population coming from radically different environments." Europe, he argued, had the benefit of homogeneity, in addition to more advanced police procedures. Police there came from the populace they were policing, which meant, Fosdick presumed, they understood the people. American police simply weren't equipped to control "disorder" among so many different types of people perceived to have an innate propensity for crime. He believed that to handle immigrant crime, it was the near impossible duty of the police to make law-abiding Americans out of foreign, backward, or innately criminal Italians, Chinese, or Russians. But before they could do that, police first had to understand who these immigrants were.[9]

Even before the formal creation of the New York City Municipal Police Department in 1845, the police of the city—and before that its night watchmen—had been forced to contend with the city's multiracial and multiethnic residents. Irish, German, and Chinese immigrants, traders, and sailors from around the globe, formerly enslaved freedmen and women, descendants of original Dutch settlers—all of them lived, walked, ate, drank, socialized, and worked in the growing city, and all of them were subject to the growing power of the professionalizing urban police force.

The high number of Irish people employed as police may have helped to make the newly arrived seem a little less mysterious, but it did not offset decades of racialization, stereotyping, and discrimination by the city's Anglo-Dutch elite. Despite xenophobic stereotypes that the Irish had a propensity for violence and graft, Irish police were often useful and relied upon *for* their reputation as brawlers, not despite it. Likewise, the alderman of Tammany Hall—the Democratic Party's political committee that often used corrupt means to dominate city politics for a large portion of the nineteenth and early twentieth centuries—appointed a high number of Germans to the police force, which helped offset the language barriers that hindered many American-born officers as they patrolled German neighborhoods.[10]

The Municipal Police Department's early role in enforcing racial boundaries in the city also meant navigating various states of freedom and enslavement. Even in the urban North, where police departments can trace their direct origins more to London's metropolitan police than Southern slave patrols—the vestiges of slavery and the brutality of racial capitalism remained defining characteristics. Shortly after the 1845 founding of the NYPD, the federal government tasked police departments with enforcing the 1850 Fugitive Slave Act. Decades after New York had outlawed slavery, New York police officers were responsible for finding, capturing, and sending South self-emancipated African Americans who had risked their lives to make it to New York, hoping to find freedom. To say that all US police departments sprang from brutal slave patrols is not untrue—surveillance of Blackness in the North and South was a vital state and state-sanctioned function—but it also allows us to dismiss London-style policing as somehow more benign. It was not. Robert Peel, a founder of England's modern police system may have written in 1829 that police should maintain good public standing by "offering individual service and friendship to all members of society without regard to their race or social standing" but in the United States, early police were incapable of and uninterested in reconciling racial fairness with protecting the accumulation of capital. This was because Black people were themselves the capital being accumulated in the form of enslaved laborers. Even when the right of Black men to vote was affirmed by the Fifteenth Amendment to the US Constitution, plum police positions were not offered to members of New York's small Black community in exchange for their votes, as they were for other racial and ethnic groups in New York City.[11]

By 1904, the American Problem had already resulted in a majority monolingual police force ill-equipped for policing a diverse city. The model for ethnic policing emerged from this ad hoc place of need, and an inability to understand immigrant communities. In 1904, the NYPD officially appointed its first Chinese American officer and organized a German Squad and an Italian Squad, all in an attempt to correct the linguistic and cultural blind spots of a predominantly monolingual police force. These centralized squads tasked with patrolling and investigating specific racial groups were not the invention of the NYPD. Between 1900 and the 1920s, many police commissioners, administrators, and even beat cops had been involved in upholding the US imperial project in the American West and overseas. "Native policing," as it is called in a colonialist context, traveled home with police commissioners like Gen. Francis Vinton Greene or former assistant secretary of the Navy William McAdoo and found a place in New York's immigrant neighborhoods.

This attempt at ethnic policing was short-lived. Mounting hostility toward immigrants and a growing legislative movement to expand immigration restrictions that already depressed Chinese immigration to the United States sowed distrust even inside the now multiethnic NYPD. Between the end of xenophobic police commissioner Theodore Bingham's tenure in 1909, the rise of racial nationalism around World War I, and the eventual immigration restrictions of 1921 and 1924, immigrant squads were phased out. Police intellectuals lost interest in recruiting officers specifically for their language and cultural knowledge.

By the time Fosdick wrote in 1917 about the problem of policing immigrants, police in New York City were trying to catalyze a massive transformation—if not in function of the police, then at least in form. Technological advances in forensic science; presumptive racial science; mounting xenophobia; and a Progressive Era revolution that transformed, professionalized, and standardized municipal governance all collided in an attempt to change policing. Reformers hoped to transform the police from corrupt pugilists sicced on political rivals and opponents of the racial and economic status quo to a professionalized force that utilized legal, racial, and scientific know-how to solve and prevent crimes, maintain public health and safety, and build legal cases. Even under this aspirational regime police would still be called upon to enact state violence against those who represented a threat to "law and order." This included labor and civil rights activists, sex workers, people pursuing same-sex sexual and romantic relations, and racialized subjects whose assertion of the right to public space represented a threat to the white male monopoly on access to urban amenities. Standardizing police coverage over the entire city also meant finding ways for police to exert power over those people and spaces that, by virtue of their foreignness or distrust of police, had hindered police effectiveness and obscured the state's penetrating gaze.[12]

The problem of legibility—the idea that a government that understands the motivations, desires, and fears of its subjects can better govern them—is fundamental to Fosdick's formulation of the American Problem. As political scientist Hugh Heclo once wrote, the state must "puzzle before power." It must understand before it can subordinate. During the years of his investigation, millions of immigrants from around the world came to the United States in hopes of finding political and religious freedom and economic opportunity. During the high point of immigration in 1907, almost 1.3 million people arrived in urban and industrial centers in the United States. These people often spoke different languages from the government employees who registered their names and patrolled their streets.[13]

The American Problem was fundamentally an equation asking how the government might make immigrants more legible to police and, by subjecting them to more effective subordination, make them more reconcilable with life in white America.

On March 17, 1913, the same year Fosdick left for his tour of seventy-two police departments in the United States to find out how police could better patrol immigrant neighborhoods, Daniel Davis was shot six times by police on the corner of Lenox Avenue and 139th street in East Harlem. Davis, who was Black, had supposedly "molested" a white woman, Irene Leslie, as he walked by her on the street. Leslie summoned the police and the confrontation resulted in an officer shooting Davis to death. "The reports are confusing," the *New York Age*, the city's largest Black newspaper, reported. "What really happened will probably never be known."[14]

Although African Americans made up less than 2 percent of New York City's population in the years around the turn of the century, Black New

Yorkers like Davis were disproportionately represented in arrest records and anecdotes of police harassment and violence. The multiracial neighborhoods where the Black, immigrant, and native-born working classes cohabitated were among the most ferociously policed—both by uniformed officers and by white people looking to enforce the color line and forcibly distance themselves from those they perceived as below them on the racial hierarchy. Black women were often harassed and arrested on mere suspicion of being prostitutes simply because they were read by police as inherently deviant. Black men were equally labeled as biologically predisposed not just to crime but to other misdeeds as well because of assumptions about a lack of respectability stemming from sometimes precarious employment.[15]

Because of this supposed predisposition and the repetitive and time-flattening nature of state violence in Black communities, African Americans were often dismissed inside the police departments and in the writing of police intellectuals. While police were eager to recruit Italian or Chinese officers, administrators did not feel the need to appoint Black officers to act as translators. They saw Black criminality as a problem, to be sure, but not a problem in need of a solution—the solution to that problem was always violence. As Khalil Muhammad has written that in the wake of mounting panic about immigrant crime, the continued awareness of crime committed by Black Americans "would have sounded more familiar than alarmist." Any academic studies or attempts to find a solution or root cause of Black criminality were warped by notions of biological deviance and reified its permanence.[16]

The death of Daniel Davis, and the deaths of so many other Black New Yorkers at the hands of police, was understood with a different mental calculus on the part of police administrators and social scientists than the problem of immigrant crime. The police, Fosdick wrote,

> must be prepared to understand the criminal propensities of Sicilians and Poles, of Chinese and Russians. They must become expert in detecting crime characteristics as shown by twenty races. . . . To see the London "Bobby" at work, dealing with people of his race who understand him and whom he understands, is to learn a larger sympathy for his brother officer who walks the beat in New York, Chicago, or San Francisco.

But for Black men and women, there was almost always just "power" and never "puzzle."[17]

Policing, Police, and Race-Making

The language of race in the United States in the late nineteenth and early twentieth centuries was convoluted and situational. I often use "race" and "ethnicity" interchangeably. Ethnicity, as historian David Roediger argues, was a discursive creation of the mid-twentieth century that differentiated among types of white people after different immigrant groups had already been consolidated into a legally monolithic white race. Because in 1902 most New Yorkers would have understood the difference between Irish people and German people as being racial rather than ethnic, I endeavor to echo their language. However, there are moments when "ethnic" is useful because it connotes a process of racial formation that includes different European races and excludes groups like African Americans and Chinese New Yorkers. Therefore, I use "ethnic" to refer to white immigrants and their descendants who are still deemed a racialized other. I also use "Anglo-Irish" or sometimes "Anglo-German-Irish" to talk about these ethnic groups as a single consolidated unit of white New Yorkers who excluded new immigrants from Southern and Eastern Europe.[18]

Police departments served another important function in the maintenance of racial boundaries and racial capitalism: the consolidation of the social and economic mobility associated with whiteness around European immigrants. Scholars of race have debated whether European immigrants were technically "white" upon their arrival to the United States regardless of the legal and scientific consensus that they were a different race from Anglo-Americans. Despite the perceptions of *racial* differences between Jewish, Italian, Irish, and German immigrants, this book agrees that the presumption of eventual assimilability into white American culture came with social and economic mobility—in essence, whiteness—denied to Asian and African-descended Caribbean immigrants, as well as native-born Black Americans.[19]

In addition to showing how ethnic police officers led their communities into whiteness by participating in the project of racial state-building, it is also essential to acknowledge the role of anti-Black racism in allowing the formation of a more consolidated whiteness. Scholars have argued that European immigrants were able to prove their whiteness by forcibly emphasizing the difference between themselves and African Americans. This often took the form of refusing to work alongside or perform similar labor as Black workers, fighting over public space by enforcing uncrossable racial boundaries, and constructing moral and medical taboos around interracial socializing. By differentiating themselves from Black Americans, newly arrived immigrants attempted to prove their assimilability into whiteness—and their ascension to careers in the police department offered one such avenue.[20]

Immigrant men who served on the police force not only expedited the process of Americanizing their kin and neighbors but they also served as the vanguards of whiteness for their races. By taking on the shared obligation of policing their own communities and by contributing to the project of municipal governance, immigrant police officers were rewarded with social mobility often denied to their civilian peers. For instance, despite the intense racialization of Irish immigrants in the mid-nineteenth century, Irish officers who helped to beat back Irish rioters were both understood and visually depicted as more American and "whiter" than the countrymen they policed. Ethnic police were often among the first people in their racial categories to be treated with the deference usually reserved for white citizens.

But policing was not just about winning entrance onto the force: the key difference was *how* European immigrants were policed. For European immigrants in the United States, assimilation and whiteness became synonymous with the rights, privileges, and obligations of citizenship. *Police and the Empire City* argues that police viewed their presence in immigrant communities as an important engine of citizen-making. At all levels of the department, leaders and officers believed that the more communities of the newly arrived could be made hospitable to state control, the faster they would learn the legal and extralegal rules that dictated behavior in their adopted nation. In a sense, the NYPD's investment in policing a community often meant a vote of confidence in that community's assimilability. As New York City police commissioner William McAdoo said in 1906, police are doing "far more important work, so far as the future citizens are concerned, than probably any other officials in this land." In some neighborhoods police violence was inclusive, while in others it was intensely exclusive. [21]

Immigrants, however, were not the only racial others trying to carve out lives for themselves in diversifying and industrializing urban centers. Black residents were also living, working, and navigating the rapidly expanding city. But white thinkers of Fosdick's generation did not question how police could better "understand" Black urbanites. Black pacification was a central tenant of American governance and had been for centuries. African American brutalization at the hands of police in the name of order and safety went unchallenged and was expected even while Fosdick and his cohort agonized over making police departments more effective with immigrants. In the early twentieth century, European immigrants were treated as yet another challenge created as a byproduct of a modernizing society—a complication that could be solved by innovations in governance. Police treated Black New Yorkers, however, as a historical constant. Their perceived criminality was not a governance problem that police thought they could solve for good, but an immutable reality of American life.

When African American leaders sought to reduce police violence in Black neighborhoods, one of their most insistent requests was to desegregate the NYPD. Black officers, they claimed, would be more mindful of the needs of the neighborhood, less violent, and possess a better ability to discern the difference between troublemakers and respectable members of the community. Even though New York was behind Philadelphia, Chicago, and other cities in appointing Black patrolmen, advocates hoping for a Black NYPD officer often framed their request in comparison with the first generation of immigrant officers. After all, they argued, if the NYPD found it necessary to deploy Italians and Germans to their own neighborhoods, why shouldn't they do the same in majority Black neighborhoods? White administrators did not see any such need—but upon his appointment Samuel Battle, the NYPD's first Black patrolman, quickly felt the same way as many of the initial immigrant officers, that he was acting as a translator and anthropologist helping the department to decode and understand his community.[22]

Black officers received access to some levers of social and economic mobility. Samuel Battle climbed the ranks to become an NYPD lieutenant, and later the New York City parole commissioner. But he also occupied complicated and fraught territory, by grappling with racism aimed at him by white officers and civilians while being expected to mete out racist violence on behalf of the police department. He could not bestow whiteness and belonging on himself or his community in the same way that white ethnic officers could, but he did help to enforce the color line in New York by serving the NYPD project of racial management.

Chinese immigrants inhabited a liminal space between European immigrants, who could eventually be assimilated into whiteness, and Black Americans who were forcibly and permanently excluded. Chinese immigrants were subject to entwined racialization and criminalization that was simultaneously similar to that faced by other immigrants but also different. While there were some aspects of Italian or Jewish culture that may have seemed familiar to American police, assumptions about Chinese culture shaded them to appear more alien—sometimes to the point of novelty. While some upwardly mobile immigrants dared not visit working-class multiracial neighborhoods for fear of socially self-demoting, many upper-class New Yorkers enjoyed "slumming" in ethnic enclaves, especially Chinatown. The financial incentive to cater to amusement seekers meant Chinese business owners often exaggerated their foreignness in order to "manufacture" the performance of race expected by white customers. While this created economic possibilities and social mobility for Chinese New Yorkers, it also reinforced stereotypes that were the basis of public opinion and often policing.[23]

Unlike European immigrants, the Chinese had already been the subject of punitive and xenophobic enforcement. The US government had enacted the Chinese Exclusion Act in 1882, which prohibited Chinese laborers without immediate family in the United States from immigrating, with a few notable exceptions. This already distinguished them, both racially and in a sense of national belonging and citizenship, from European immigrants who did not encounter substantial restrictions barring them from the United States until 1921. Decades before the Progressive Era politicians argued over whether restrictions on immigration from some regions of Europe might decrease urban crime and improve the health of the body politic, they had already made the determination on Chinese immigrants.[24]

Xenophobic presumptions about criminality and economic adaptability warped the way that police intellectuals and other social scientists understood racial difference. In a society broken into "good" and "bad" minorities, goodness and badness were determined by who could *act* the most like white New Yorkers and thereby assimilate into their way of ordering society. Immigrants, especially nonwhite immigrants, had to overcome not just systemic repression and a lack of economic opportunity extended to white native-born Americans but also the preconceived notions about a group's ability to assimilate. They did this by developing language skills, changing styles of dress, and sometimes even converting to predominant religions.[25]

The racial formation Chinese immigrants underwent on US soil did not occur in a vacuum but as part of a process of race-making that unfolded throughout the urban landscape. The growth of Chinese and Japanese immigrants in the United States both complicated and reinforced the Black/white color line. On the one hand, over the better part of a century, a mountain of case law was developed to determine where Asian immigrants belonged within a society built upon a racial dichotomy. Would they attend segregated schools or ride segregated public transit? In some ways, it forced legal, political, and cultural institutions to grapple with a group of people who were not Black but also not white. In other ways, however, it strengthened the racial divide as Asian Americans in New York achieved more economic power and opportunity by the 1940s, even as Japanese Americans on the West Coast were subject to imprisonment during World War II. Their economic and social mobility in New York, like the Irish or Italian immigrants before them, bolstered preconceived police and upper-class white notions about Blackness, just as they challenged notions about Asian-ness. Despite the state's understanding and enforcement of racial hierarchy, the intellectual work of policing was not always perceivable from the street level.[26]

While the police department's forceful treatment of immigrants, Black people, and working-class New Yorkers of all stripes often looked similar on the ground, how police *thought* about each group and their ability to participate in American society reflected their slow accumulation of economic and political power in the city.

Building the Early Carceral State

Even though NYPD officers seemed to have treated pedestrians and residents differently depending on the community they were patrolling, we must understand these various modes in relation to one another. Authors and historians have produced thorough and illuminating bodies of literature exploring policing of Black Americans or in predominantly immigrant neighborhoods.[27] Other indispensable histories written in recent years have been dedicated to the policing of gender and sexuality.[28] Still more plumb the depths of the police department's place within electoral and party politics.[29] This books builds on that necessary and paradigm-shifting work by considering the varying functions of the department as happening in the context of others. I take up the call that historians must, as Kelly Lytle Hernández has written, "suture the split" that has cleaved the history of deportation and immigrant policing from the history of incarceration and brutalization of Black people. Suturing this split shows how the various shades of racialization and criminalization that affect immigrants and Black Americans in different ways belong to the same process of racial capitalist state-building and settler colonialism.[30]

Administrators in the NYPD spoke about the necessity of recruiting Chinese-speaking officers as they simultaneously brutalized Black women for asserting their belonging in public life. Officers clubbed Yiddish strikers as they simultaneously built a departmental library that included scientific texts about the "Italian temperament." Police interaction with each of these communities deserves scholarly attention—especially in the case of those groups that have been subjected to untold violence and trauma at the hands of the racial state. But behind each of these specific examples was a unified and hierarchical system of policing simultaneously informed by—and informing—scientific and political understanding of crime, violence, and national belonging in a patriarchal and white-dominated nation. As Ruth Wilson Gilmore reminds us, "People who enliven the agencies, policies, and institutions that we call the 'surveillance state,' are thinking about all of us all the time together. And yet, in many cases, we think of ourselves separately, in isolated struggles that at best join together as alliances rather than a unified movement."[31]

Policing does not happen in a vacuum. It exists on a continuum in which the perceived necessity of policing in one neighborhood affects how police behave elsewhere. To understand how police learned to patrol communities differently at the beginning of the twentieth century is to begin to unravel how racial formation shaped the state and how the state shapes race. Racialization is a shared process, in which different groups share common stimuli, historically contingent social and economic factors, and are acted upon by a range of state and individual actors. "Whiteness and blackness, as well as other modern racial forms, emerge as subject positions, habits of perception, and modes of embodiment that develop from the ongoing risk management of settler and slave capitalism, and more generally racial capitalism," writes Nikhil Pal Singh. The ongoing and changing positionality of racial groups in regards to their relationship with policing, police, and criminality, dictates their racial and economic mobility. By incorporating Natalia Molina's notion of *racial scripts*, or the connections and mutual constructions of racial formation, we can begin to understand policing as a common factor that acts upon many groups in the same city in the same historical moment. "A racial scripts approach," she writes, "pulls the lens back so that we can see different racial projects operating at the same time, affecting different groups simultaneously."[32]

This book relies upon the methodological and political framework of the many Black, immigrant, queer, and activist scholars who have heeded the urgency of our moment and painstakingly built our growing literature on the carceral state. Although most of their scholarship and research has focused on uncovering the bipartisan, imperialist, and cultural roots of our current moment of mass incarceration, I am interested in widening the scope to show the slow buildup of carceral capacity. By carceral capacity I do not mean, as other scholars have, the enormous increase in the construction of cells or the frequent passage of statutes stemming from the war on crime, the war on drugs, and quality-of-life policing. I mean instead the growing capacity of the state to exert power over a diverse multiracial and multiethnic populace. In the case of Chinatown, and by extension the Chinese community dispersed across the city, the expansion of carceral capacity meant exerting control over terra incognita, unknown and unmappable territory. It was not always a given that police could traverse dense immigrant neighborhoods to locate and apprehend a single person. In the late nineteenth century there were large swaths of ethnic and nonwhite New York believed to be unpoliceable. Over time, departments needed to build the capacity to identify, track, and apprehend even those people attempting to be illegible to the state. Before the state could imprison millions of people, it first had to build a punitive system capable of exerting control over large areas of the nation.[33]

My contribution to our understanding of the late twentieth- and early twenty-first-century carceral state comes from excavating the relationship between policing, racial formation, the state's project of subjection and subordination—and the impact of this project on shaping our institutions. Specifically, I am interested in merging studies of global circuits of knowledge and imperial power with domestic race and ethnic formation and policing's role in the hardening of Black/white racial boundaries. By integrating my study of the entwined processes of racialization and criminalization in Black and immigrant communities with the shared knowledge of colonial race-making and governance, a clearer picture emerges of a global collaborative system of racial state violence. The police department did not appear one day, a fully functioning institution with a set of tactics and philosophies. It emerged slowly over time and carried a deep intergenerational institutional knowledge. Despite modern police intellectuals' assertion of "color blindness" in their procedures, these contemporary departments inherited and still use tools developed when the consideration of race was explicit and integral to policing.

For police intellectuals, the integration of tools like the criminal file and the filing cabinet meant people could be sorted by criminal history, by name, or even by skull circumference—whatever simplified the process of identifying a person. The retention of this information, combined with the NYPD's heavy investment in statisticians at the turn of the century, laid the foundation for a technocratic model of policing in which harassment of the same racialized communities was no longer justified by racial and biological characteristics but by data. It was the same racial profiling, now cloaked with the veneer of objectivity. Police make arrests, arrests generate statistics, and statistics then justify police presence in a neighborhood. This is part of the meaning of carceral capacity. Turning arrests into data points—like seeing a forest solely as feet of sellable lumber—allowed the police to think of the city on a much larger scale and more easily write off entire neighborhoods as requiring harassment and constant surveillance. In this approach, we see the origins of police gang databases and machine-learning predictive policing that rely on police statistics to inscribe people as inherently criminal in a way purported to be "color blind."[34]

Likewise, NYPD administrators in 1915 stocked the department's library with the work of criminal anthropologists who believed they could predict criminal behavior in people based on their race and upbringing. They laid the groundwork for current racialized attempts to deploy officers based on data-driven and predictive policing algorithms. These are just two of many examples. Studying the professionalization and solidification of policing in the Progressive Era holds many keys to understanding why the carceral state functions as it does. It opens the US police's shallow toolbox and shows the racial history of many tools that purport now to be "color blind."[35]

Chapters and Organization

This book is split into eight chapters that trace the evolution of the NYPD more or less chronologically. It is difficult to write a book that considers policing as not simply directed against one community or another but applied both simultaneously and unequally on various groups. While individual chapters trace different threads—Black activism against police brutality, panic over Italian crime, the development of new technologies and methodologies of policing—many occupy the same chronological territory. The NYPD relied heavily on German-speaking officers in 1904 even as administrators attempted to develop new ways of policing that no longer required immigrant or first-generation personal knowledge. It is not my intention to create a clean narrative of change over time, but rather show that competing visions of policing existed simultaneously, sometimes in contention with one another and sometimes in harmony.

What follows is an attempt to balance this commotion with a readable narrative that engages the major hegemonic trends in policing—from Anglo-Irish dominated patrol to ethnic policing, followed by the rise of technocratic and standardized policing.

Chapter 1 explores how the police department in New York City, from the time of its founding in 1845, was immediately enmeshed in the project of racial management and an active engine of race- and citizen-making. Politicians attempting to exchange police appointments for votes all but ensured an ethnically diverse police force from its very inception. Critics of Irish and German immigration to the United States voiced their concerns that these early immigrant police were biologically susceptible to graft and brutality in ways the Anglo-American officers were not. These often violent debates about good policing, embodied traits, and ethnicity usually spilled out of the halls of government and into the streets. One way that immigrant police officers felt they could Americanize—and by the same token consolidate their "whiteness"—was in their participation in racial state-building. Reinscribing racist notions of inherent Black criminality, enforcing anti-Black policies like the Fugitive Slave Act of 1850, and even putting down Irish-involved urban disorder all allowed immigrant police officers a way to prove their belonging and differentiate themselves as being racially different from Black New Yorkers and less Americanized immigrants.

After several late nineteenth-century reform movements attempted to break up Irish influence within the department, chapter 2 argues that the evolving understanding of race, civilization, and the role of police in society changed to accommodate some immigrants. Serving from 1895 to 1897, police commissioner and future US president Theodore Roosevelt argued that the supposed natural fighting ability of Irish men made them invaluable to a style of policing predicated solely on pacifying urban unrest by force. Their embodied traits, which had once supposedly made them a liability to the force, now made them essential. Irish and German police had found their racial and national inclusion at the expense of Black New Yorkers, nonwhite immigrants, and newly arrived foreigners.

Chapter 3 traces the career of Gen. Francis Vinton Greene as he furthered the US imperial project in the Philippines and Cuba, returning to become the NYPD's police commissioner in 1903. This chapter argues that ethnic squads, which police administrators developed in 1904 to deploy multilingual immigrant officers into their own communities, were a direct transplant from the US Empire. A tactic already common in European empires, "native policing" became essential in the Philippines as the US colonial government grappled with how to subdue such a diverse archipelago. Back in New York, the years between 1898 and 1904 saw an unprecedented uptick in the arrival of European immigrants, turning it into one of the most diverse cities in the world. During Greene's tenure as commissioner, he confronted police problems that looked like those he had faced as a colonial administrator. Chapter 4 explores the afterlives of Greene's career and the problem posed by diverse, multilingual populations that became acute during the 1904 *Slocum* disaster. When the ferryboat carrying over one thousand German New Yorkers caught fire in the East River, NYPD Inspector Max Schmittberger organized over one hundred German-speaking officers into a "German Squad" to deal with the investigation and manage the angry grieving families.

Chapter 5 traces the rise and fall of the NYPD's "Italian Squad" between 1904 and 1909. Starting with six Italian-speaking officers and growing until the group had over one hundred members, the Italian Squad represented the high-water mark of ethnic policing in New York. Learning to police Italians in the United States became a national agenda as police intellectuals around the country dedicated a multitude of resources to the dilemma of organized crime and political radicalism associated with Southern Italians and Sicilians. The NYPD's Italian Squad was the largest of these endeavors and often served as a model for other cities. Although there were several practical reasons for the group's dissolution in 1909, including the assassination of the squad's leader, Joseph Petrosino, I argue that Police Commissioner Theodore Bingham's increasing skepticism toward immigrant officers made the NYPD inhospitable to ethnic policing.

Chapter 6 explores how police practices in Black communities diverged from those employed in immigrant neighborhoods. Starting in the wake of the riot of 1900, in which police and white pedestrians unleashed a multiday reign of terror on a Black neighborhood, community members intensified their calls for police reform. Activists like Rev. Reverdy Ransom made the appointment of Black police officers a central demand in those years because they believed it would curb police brutality as well as make Black neighborhoods safer. After ten years of escalating calls in the Black press, Samuel Battle became the first African American NYPD officer in 1911. Although his status as a "Black first" has put Battle in the pantheon of civil rights notables, it has also meant that popular historical narratives about his appointment tend to ignore the complex multiracial context in which he lived. This chapter demonstrates how Black activists understood the first Black officers as an extension of ethnic policing, often citing the Italian Squad as justification for the integration of the NYPD. It also makes a larger argument about the uneven development of the NYPD archives and what its absences suggest about racial citizenship in New York and the United States at large.

Chapters 7 and 8 explore the NYPD after the dissolution of the Italian Squad as the NYPD turned to technocratic and European methods. Rather than being dependent on immigrant officers, NYPD administrators like Commissioner Arthur Woods created a rigid regime of training that they believed would produce officers who were skillful, adaptable, and interchangeable. This involved starting a training school, a library, and partnerships with institutions like Columbia University to provide classes in law, forensic science, and foreign languages. Making officers interchangeable also meant that the NYPD needed to assure that all their officers were physically prepared to handle any situation. In the years following 1914, the NYPD took a renewed interest in the bodies and hygiene of their officers. Following in the footsteps of Taylorism, Fordism, eugenics, and other scientific discourses that sought to increase the efficiency and effectiveness of laborers, the NYPD began a campaign to break down policing into its component movements and re-teach officers how to do them correctly. Teaching officers how to chew properly and what to eat became a major theme in police publications of the period as NYPD administrators attempted to discourage the presence of overweight police officers among the ranks.

In addition to creating rather than finding more effective police, the NYPD also increasingly relied on European techniques of information management and investigative science to make subjects on the street more understandable and policeable. These techniques were part of a concerted effort to learn from and communicate with municipal police authorities and criminologists overseas. At the center of this transatlantic exchange was Raymond Fosdick, a lifelong bureaucrat by then on the payroll of the Rockefeller-funded Bureau of Social Hygiene. By importing and integrating new technologies such as the fingerprint, files, filing cabinets, and border controls, NYPD administrators hoped that all subjects, no matter how foreign, could be easily indexed and thus identifiable in the paperwork. The type of expertise valued in police work shifted—in essence, the necessity of police intellectuals was overtaken by the growing value placed on police scientists.

Archives, Storytelling, and Police Power

The belief in the power of records has had profound implications for historians of policing in New York City. Since its creation, the NYPD has been a diligent destroyer of its own archive and so has no central repository teeming with documents, case files, or criminal records. Following the threads of the intellectual and racial underpinnings of the NYPD's operations and their changes in this period requires analyzing the existing personal papers of commissioners who served between 1850 and 1920. As records of the men's previous military service and roles in colonial governments, the commissioners' papers are also valuable for understanding the effects of the US imperial project on domestic policing. The sprawling collections of the Municipal Archives of the City of New York provide a back door into the NYPD's records and everyday operations by means of the records of its frequent contact with other municipal departments including the Office of the Mayor. Published materials, including departmental reports, training manuals, and police publications, have also been central to exploring how and where the priorities of the department shifted over time. Like the personal papers of commissioners, the published memoirs of close to a dozen immigrant and native-born patrolmen and detectives from this era provide a window into the mindset of police, albeit a limited and highly managed one. Police wrote many of these memoirs in the years immediately following Prohibition, and they are drenched in nostalgia for the days before criminals supposedly wielded machine guns and presided over multimillion-dollar bootlegging operations. The voices of citizens who routinely wrote to newspapers and organized rallies to protest police violence in those same years temper the quaint ways that police memoirists describe "harmless" street brawls and laughably inept criminals of the period between 1880 and 1920. The archive created by the policed represents an alternative to the NYPD's diffuse collection of documents and presents the most complete challenge to the worldview of the punitive racial state.

The NYPD's total control over its archives—in the past through destruction and in the present through classification—has also meant an ability to control historical knowledge production about the department. In the late twentieth and early twenty-first centuries, department administrators could give new meanings to people and events from the department's past when they became politically expedient or could even erase them entirely. The recycling, retrofitting, and rebranding of historical events and actors happened regularly with the help of websites, exhibits, an internal magazine, memorials, statues, and renaming ceremonies that enforced and disseminated the NYPD's narratives.

Policing is a machine. Its product, the brutalization and subordination of working-class people and racial minorities, the protection of profits, and the enforcement of gender roles and sexual relations, have remained virtually unchanged for centuries. But the machine itself is very different now than it was in 1860. It looks different. Some mechanisms inside have changed—for instance police are expected now to serve more roles traditionally filled by other municipal services and to handle more daily tasks than ever before. But, as scholar Dennis Childs writes about survivors of the racial capitalist misogynist state, "conditions that render the differences between past and present modes of domination [are] virtually indecipherable, if not completely nonsexist." This is the "time-bending power of the racialized carceral." So why study the machine if its product has remained so similar? Showing the simultaneous change over time and continuity in the history of policing and state violence is explicitly an argument that the machine cannot be rebuilt. No matter how many changes one makes to the interior or exterior of the machine, if it is designed to create a single product indefinitely, it will continue to do so no matter how many alterations it undergoes.[36]

Policing the multiracial city took a lot of work, both intellectual and physical. Police intellectuals wrote books and articles. They traveled. They held hearings about crime and criminality. All this labor informed, and was informed by, what police did on the street. This book endeavors to show the work of racial state violence. To quote Stuart Hall, "Hegemony is hard work." By prying open the policing machine to show its moving parts, how they function, how they change, who designed its gears, and for what purpose, I hope to expose some of that work.

BECOMING BLUE

1

New York Police's Earliest
Encounters with Race
and Ethnicity, 1845–1871

Although Arthur Carey joined the New York City Police Department in
1889, he spoke of the department's forty-four-year history as if it was part of
his religion, his race, and his sole inheritance. Toward the end of his career,
Carey's retelling of the 1845 origin of the police department took on the gravi-
tas of a mythological origin story. "I recall hearing a tale about this when I
was a boy," he wrote in 1930. "In 1844 Mayor Harper of New York City went
to England. He was much impressed by what he saw of the London police,"
and so he brought back a single copper star-shaped badge. When the mayor
returned, Carey says, he pinned that badge, and many based on it, onto the
first Irish patrolmen: his ethnic and professional forefathers.[1]

"Here in America the opportunity opened up to them, starting with policy
duty. They were equipped by nature, too for the job." With this statement,
Carey summed up the complicated relationship between race, immigration,
bodies, and politics in New York City in the nineteenth century. Carey's assertion that people of Irish descent were naturally and biologically inclined
to be police was central to the question of what qualities made someone a
good patrolman and how the Irish came to make up almost half of the new
police force. What types of people made effective police? What constituted

good policing? What was the relationship between the racialized body of the officer and the blue uniform that housed it? What role did police have in mediating racial formation and belonging? These questions were hotly and even violently contested in the years following the 1845 creation of the New York Municipal Police Department.[2]

This chapter explores the police in New York City as they first encountered racial difference, both at the station house and on the street. Policing in the United States never existed outside of the currents of racial politics and racialization. White politicians, police administrators, and journalists high and low manufactured and perpetuated links between certain racial groups, morals, criminality, and even physical ability. This meant that all New Yorkers were judged on a spectrum of racial difference. The Irish and German immigrants who came to New York in large numbers and became an important voting bloc, political force, and a large part of the police department did not exist in a vacuum. They arrived in a city already being shaped by people of African descent, born free or into slavery. Police attempts to patrol the city, to form and consume popular knowledge about different groups, and to protect the existing racial and gendered hierarchies helped to give purpose and an institutional shape to the fledgling department.

Earlier generations of historians debated what served as the catalyst for politicians in the United States to import British-style policing and form professionalized municipal police departments. While some argued that police departments became a necessity with the rise of capitalist wealth accumulation and the growth of property crimes that allegedly followed, others claimed that it was the reoccurring riots and urban disorder, or even the exponential growth of "dangerous classes" of industrial workers and immigrants in the early nineteenth century that necessitated the first police departments. Historian Eric Monkkonen however, argues convincingly that it was the rise of civil services and the professionalization and bureaucratization across a number of civic institutions in both the United States and Europe that led to the creation of a municipal organization tasked with handing civil disorder and public safety.[3]

From its earliest iteration, however, the police department in New York was far from a color-blind civic institution. Early stories of the department's founding, including Arthur Carey's, rely heavily on the myth that the institution it was modeled on, London's Metropolitan Police, imbued its offspring with a modern way of maintaining order without racial bias or consideration. Nothing could be further from the truth. The municipal police force was in the business of racial management, which ranged, as Nikhil Pal Singh writes, "from biopolitical inclusion (an ever-graduating whiteness) to necro-political destruction of entire communities (genocide)." This was true in New York just as it was in other US cities. In Philadelphia, municipal politicians formed one of the nation's earliest police forces explicitly to appease native-born residents' anti-Irish sentiment and the riots and ethnic violence it engendered. From the 1840s onward, police were on a knife-edge of forcibly creating and reinscribing racial difference by presuming the criminality of some races and punishing their demands for public space, leisure, and civil rights. However, the department itself also served as an engine of race-making. A job on the force served as an important crucible in which Irish immigrants and their descendants could prove their belonging, and slowly lose the stigma and racial consequences of foreignness by taking part in the project of racial management and enacting violence against Black New Yorkers.[4]

Mired in party politics, a well-entrenched spoils system, judicial impunity, and the manly sporting culture of the era, the Anglo and Irish uniformed bodies of policemen often elicited as much fear and anxiety in New Yorkers as they did feelings of safety. Without oversight, civilian protection, or any mechanism for accountability, police were free to take bribes, brutalize, and act arbitrarily in pursuit of their own whims or of maintaining the status quo in the city. During the 1850s and into the early 1860s, police not only harassed and arrested Black New Yorkers on charges of public intoxication or vagrancy, they were also obligated to return people who had escaped from enslavement in the South back to their former life in bondage. Enduring accounts of the New York City police during the nineteenth century are overwhelmingly stories of brutality, graft, corruption, and state authority run amuck. During the 1880s and 1890s, politicians from both the Democratic Tammany machine and the "good government" reformers associated mostly with the Republican Party struggled to distance the department from its sordid past and redefine the role and makeup of the New York City Police Department.[5]

The Tammany system had relied for decades on powerful ward bosses providing plum police appointments to loyal neighborhood residents. At a rate of twelve dollars per week, these were lucrative and secure jobs that could provide a modicum of social mobility. Under Tammany control of New York City, with ten consecutively elected Democrat mayors between 1875 and 1894, the party's electoral base of Irish and German working-class immigrants and their descendants shaped the demographics of the police department and built strong public associations between immigrant men, corruption, and police work. As a counter to the appointee system, reformers in both parties advocated civil service exams that would remove the police department from the purview of party politics, and in the minds of some, loosen the close ties between policing and the proclivities for vice and violence supposedly demonstrated by immigrant Irish and German officers. It is not surprising, then, that during this period explicit and implicit anti-Irish and anti-Catholic sentiment became one of the prevailing discourses through which Anglo-Protestant and Republican reformers critiqued police corruption and the failures of policing.[6]

The dual and seemingly contradictory associations between the police and foreignness, particularly Irishness, and between foreignness and criminal violence, developed slowly over time between the 1840s and the 1890s. Specifically, three pivotal and well-publicized moments of violence, the police "civil war" of 1857, the infamous Draft Riots of 1863, and the Orange Riots of 1871 served to reinforce associations of the ferocity of Irish people, and especially of Irish police.

Race and Power in Nineteenth-Century New York

In the decades leading up to the Civil War, immigration to New York City grew exponentially. In 1825, there were 166,086 white residents of Manhattan, 18,826 of whom were foreign-born. Only 850 immigrants lived in Brooklyn at the time. That made the foreign population of New York City in 1825 about 11 percent. By then, immigrants already outnumbered Manhattan's 12,559 Black citizens, and the foreign-born would soon surpass the 1,542 Black Brooklynites. By 1860, the number of foreign-born people living on the island of Manhattan would increase almost eight-fold. Irish immigrants, fleeing famine, disease, and oppressive colonial rule arrived in increasing numbers during the 1840s. By 1845, one estimate puts the number of city residents born in Ireland at approximately 70,000, and by 1860, that number would be 203,740, over half of the foreign-born population in the city. By the start of the US Civil War in 1861, close to one-fourth of all New York City residents had been born in Ireland.[7]

Germans were the other major group traversing the Atlantic and coming to rest on the East Coast of the United States during the 1840s. Often referred to as the "forty-eighters," these immigrants were cast as liberal and radical sympathizers fleeing German-speaking nations after the violent state suppression of the 1848 revolutionary movement. They hailed from several preunified German states and regions but came overwhelmingly from Bavaria, Prussia, Baden, and Wurttemberg. During this period the German-speaking population of New

York City quadrupled from its pre-1848 number of 24,416, to a staggering 118,292 in 1860.[8]

Both the Germans and the Irish struggled to find their place in a rapidly expanding city, and a nation cleaved in two by war. Arriving in large numbers and settling in one region of Manhattan's Lower East Side, historians have described Kleindeutschland, or Little Germany, as the first massive foreign-language enclave in the diversifying city. Stretching from the docks on the East River to the active social scene of the Bowery to their west, it incorporated what would become the majority Jewish Lower East Side. Kleindeutschland soon became one of the most densely populated German-speaking neighborhoods in the world, peppered with German theaters, beer halls, and churches. To the south and west of the insular Little Germany, hundreds of thousands of Irish New Yorkers inhabited more multiracial neighborhoods. In the years leading up to and during the Civil War, both Irish-born and first-generation Irish American New Yorkers shared the sidewalks and alleyways of the infamous Five Points neighborhood and the vast territory between the Bowery and the Hudson River, now known as Greenwich Village and the West Village, with an Anglo working class, a slowly growing Black population, and an emerging Chinatown.[9]

Visiting New York City for the first time in 1842, English author Charles Dickens recorded in his diary that while Manhattan was not as clean as Boston, it was more colorful and almost shimmering. From his vantage point on the upper floor of the Carlton House Hotel, close by what is now the foot of the Brooklyn Bridge in Manhattan, Dickens admired the way the city itself seemed to sparkle, "the pavement stones are polished with the tread of feet until they shine." But leaving the gilded business district of Broadway, full of shops and theatres, Dickens encountered another side of the city. Some parts of the glittering metropolis were far more impoverished and far more diverse than he had imagined—and Irish immigrants were the heart of this other New York. "Poverty, wretchedness, and vice, are rife enough where we are going now. This is the place: these narrow ways, diverging to the right and left, and reeking everywhere with dirt and filth. Such lives as are led here, bear the same fruits as elsewhere.... Debauchery has made the very houses prematurely old. See how the rotten beams are tumbling down, and how the patched and broken windows seem to scowl dimly, like eyes that have been hurt in drunken frays."

Descending into the unsavory Five Points, a multiracial neighborhood made up mostly of Irish immigrants and African Americans, Dickens translated and flattened the diverse New York into images he was more familiar with: a homogeneous and gritty London in the midst of the Industrial Revolution.[10]

Although slave labor and Southern agriculture continued to grow the United States economy and by extension the New York economy throughout the 1840s, it was in Five Points that Dickens's English eyes saw what he believed was the secret behind New York's success. Seeing two Irish laborers walking the neighborhood, Dickens remarked, "It would be hard to keep your model republics going, without the countrymen and countrywomen of those two laborers. For who else would dig, and delve, and drudge, and do domestic work, and make canals and roads, and execute great lines of Internal Improvement!" These racialized working classes not only provided much of the labor required to build the growing city but they also, as described above, inhabited some of the city's most densely crowded areas.[11]

Starting in the 1840s, and continuing long after Dickens left New York, the Irish made up the lion's share of residents in multiracial working-class neighborhoods like Five Points. Here, "street meeting," everyday interaction among Black, Irish, Chinese, German, and Anglo pedestrians, was commonplace and fostered a familiarity between the groups, even if that familiarity was riddled with stereotypes, racial tension, and occasional violence. It was also from their interactions that, as historians like James Barrett and Noel Ignatiev argue, the Irish were able to model Americanization and racial mobility for other immigrants through civic engagement and the forceful, often violent, assertion of the racial superiority of Irish immigrants over Black and Chinese New Yorkers.[12]

In the 1850s, the native-born Anglo population of the city began to fear that they would soon be outnumbered on the street, in sites of manual labor, and in the voting booth. According to the anxieties of one physician writing in 1856, roughly 33,000 foreign-born eligible male voters would soon outnumber the 40,000 native voters. The "immigrant," he continued, "cannot understand the theory of a free government, because he is destitute of the knowledge sufficient to comprehend its objects, purposes and blessings." The perceived lack of knowledge or comprehension of a free liberal democracy among Irish and German New Yorkers raised nativist concerns that immigrant power at the ballot box would shift the mechanisms of patronage and corrupt the conduct of municipal life. "By this it will be seen that not only may aliens control the local elections, and thus secure themselves a large part of the corporation patronage . . . with this astounding proportion which the alien bears to the native population, it is not surprising that the watchmen, police officers, and other subordinate officers, should be filled chiefly with men who have too recently arrived in the country to comprehend or care for its interests." To the nativist, foreign votes and foreign electoral victories meant the slow erosion of the municipal and civic fabric of the city.[13]

Where the mayor's mansion went, so too did the police go, and if the people who served in these roles had no honest or accurate grasp on the necessities of an Anglo-American population, how then could they be expected to fulfill their duties? Police presented a special concern because of their monopoly on the legitimate use of violence. Republicans and other Anglo New Yorkers feared Irish control of the police department would mean a regime of policing based solely on clubbing and a full subversion of democratic principles. For Republican politicians in New York, changing demographics seemed to justify their anxieties.

By the mid-1880s, local Democratic aldermen organized by the Tammany political machine promised enough police appointments in exchange for immigrant votes that over one-third of the police department was of Irish descent. Concern grew in the Republican-dominated state legislature in Albany over the Municipal Police Department's increasingly full ranks of immigrant Democratic loyalists. Rather than attempt to drive out almost 40 percent of the police force, the state government tried to legislate away the problem by subverting growing Irish control over the city, its streets, and its politics.[14]

The Police Civil War

In 1857 the state legislature created a second police department: the Metropolitan. For a few months that year the Municipal Police drew its authority from the city and the Metropolitan drew theirs from the state, but both vied for legitimacy within the confines of Manhattan. In May of that year, the State Supreme Court sided with the legislature and legitimized the gambit. The legislation that had created the Metropolitan Police Commission also sought to change another rule that state officials thought would break up the Democratic monopoly on police power: They ended the requirement that police officers had to serve in the ward where they lived. This meant that power could be less easily consolidated within certain communities and neighborhoods but would also have longer-term consequences as the police department struggled in the 1900s to exert control over immigrant enclaves with native-born English-speaking patrolmen who commuted in from other wards.[15]

Quickly, the political and demographic divides between the two departments became abundantly clear as the Irish and German Democrats held strong in support of the Democratic mayor Fernando Wood's Municipal Police, and native Anglo and Dutch police resigned and enlisted with the new Metropolitans. Around 850 patrolmen and fifteen captains stayed in the Municipal department and around three hundred officers and seven captains migrated to the Metropolitans. Chaos and violence ensued as two police departments attempted to patrol a racially and politically divided city. One captain at the time reported: "Thus there were two complete sets of policemen on duty, covering the same beats throughout the city. Collisions were frequent." Although both the majority Irish Municipal Police and the majority Anglo-American Metropolitan had their respective neighborhood strongholds, the situation was increasingly untenable.[16]

Wood's tenure as mayor and his closeness with immigrant-dominated Democratic machine politics made him sensitive to the plight and needs of the recently arrived. Historian Brendan O'Malley has written about how the mayor's attempts to take a more active role in immigration management in the city led him to expand an early "Emigrant Squad" of the police department under the direction of immigrant police officer Ludwig Semler. The squad's role was to handle complaints from immigrants, but also to undermine attempts to control immigration bureaucracy from Albany. The two police departments were another front in this same partisan war.[17]

July 4, 1857, a day rife with patriotic celebrations, was also one of the most violent nights during the war between the two police departments. "At about 5 o'clock five members of the Metropolitan Police in the Seventh Ward were surrounded in Jackson Street near Cherry, by several hundred of the Irish occupants of the tenant houses thereabout and men went to the Tenth and Thirteenth wards for help."[18] One recently sworn-in Metropolitan Police officer, Thomas Slowey, was patrolling the heavily German Tenth Ward, Kleindeutschland, when a mob formed. A "party of loafers were going into the Tenth Ward and would kill all the Metropolitan Police they could find; when I got to Chatham square they were cheering Mayor Wood, and were armed with clubs and revolvers." The incident spilled into the Five Points, where the factional conflict between the two police departments extended to their street gang counterparts. As the crowd cheered for the Irish gang, the Dead Rabbit Club, the Anglo-nativist Bowery Boys rescued the embattled Metropolitans. Barricades went up and projectiles flew. Enmeshed ethnic, religious, and political factional differences divided not only one police department from the other, but also street gang from street gang. For the moment, the difference between the two sides was far more important than any rift between police and civilians.[19]

The Metropolitan Police attempted to quell the disorder by arresting the insurgent mayor, who had resisted the orders to dissolve the Municipal Police and rejected the authority of the state's new department. But his impending arrest did little to stanch the violence. Under the headline "The Mayor's Rebellion," the *New York Tribune* announced that the Metropolitan Police had arrested Mayor Wood for "resisting service of a criminal process." In a later recollection, one captain described Wood telling the Metropolitan officers who had come to arrest him, "I do not recognize the legality of the service or the existence of the Metropolitan police." After a tense standoff, Wood went peacefully and the violence that had consumed the city streets since May subsided, but the tension between immigrants and native-born New Yorkers persisted. Days after the action of Independence Day, on July 12, German immigrants marched through Kleindeutschland carrying the body of a neighborhood resident killed during the riots. Above him, marchers and mourners flew the banner "OPFER DER METROPOLITAN-POLIZEI," or "Victim of the Metropolitan Police." The violence may have subsided and the department that would eventually become the modern New York City Police Department had emerged, but it was decidedly in opposition to many of the politically engaged immigrants in the city.[20]

On December 2, the day the results of the mayoral election were announced, street violence was minimal. Daniel Tiemann of the American Party became mayor by beating Wood by almost three thousand votes. The newly solidified Metropolitan Police, who had absorbed most members of the Municipal, was able to maintain the Election Day peace. If sectarian differences caused major rifts within station houses, it was not as readily apparent or violent. Thus the NYPD was born. The police department itself, in its current institutional iteration, was born out of a struggle for Anglo-American domination of an increasingly immigrant and ethnically diverse city. The Metropolitan department won the battle and with it, the system absorbed many, if not most, of the Irish police, making them contributors to a system of Anglo domination of the city and starting a long process of the formerly foreign subject being absorbed into whiteness and belonging.[21]

On the day that Albany decreed that Mayor Wood should be arrested, Captain George Walling was dispatched to do the deed. Born to a Welsh-descended family in New Jersey in 1823, Walling was quick to join the other American-born officers transferring to the Metropolitan Police after May 1857.[22] Climbing through the ranks in the years following the police riot, Walling went on to serve one of the longest terms as the superintendent of the

New York Police, helming the department from 1874 to 1885. But during the chaos of 1857, he was the captain responsible for the Eighteenth Ward, overseeing the territory between Fourteenth Street on the south and Twenty-Fifth on the north, and between the East River and Second Avenue. His officers policed the densely packed Gas House District, which contained crowded tenements interspersed with large warehouses filled with tanks for storing the gas necessary to illuminate the city.[23] Although Walling was forced to wait for reinforcements after his first unsuccessful attempt to arrest the mayor, the conflict ended and interpolice violence subsided. Walling's long career in a diversifying city forced him to learn and relearn that policing in New York was entwined with freedom, privilege, and race-making.

New York Police and Black New Yorkers

Despite the interdepartmental conflict, the freedom and livelihoods of Black New Yorkers on a daily basis remained at the mercy and whim of Anglo and Irish police. The very same year as the war between New York's two police departments, the Supreme Court decided the infamous case *Dred Scott v. Sandford*. Dred Scott, who was held in bondage in Missouri by Dr. John Emerson, traveled north to Illinois and the Wisconsin Territory, both free regions. In Wisconsin he met and married his wife, Harriet Robinson. After their return to Missouri, the Scotts sued for their freedom on the grounds that they were free by virtue of having lived in the North. The 1857 decision dictated that Scott's status as an enslaved person superseded his residence in the free North. Scott's case strengthened the precedent set by the 1850 Fugitive Slave Act, which required self-emancipated individuals caught anywhere in the country to be returned to the people who had kept them enslaved. This federal policy created a new role for fledgling local police departments: slave catchers.[24]

Police in New York had a new reason to regard Black people as potentially criminal. Although the Fugitive Slave Act provided a new justification for police to stop and question African Americans, many documented cases from the era show that police often discovered that a person had escaped from slavery after apprehending them for unrelated petty or invented wrongs. After fleeing bondage, one young man stepped off a boat in New York City "weak from confinement and insufficient food," only to be arrested on a charge of public intoxication. While at the police station awaiting a judge to rule on a charge of drunkenness, the man confessed to the arresting officer that he had escaped slavery. The arresting officer took it upon himself to run to a local US marshal, but the marshal was too late. By the time he asked the judge to hold the prisoner for rendition to the South, local abolitionists had already paid his drunkenness fine and spirited him away.[25]

Police did not always wait to find escaped enslaved people during a chance encounter within the small and disproportionately policed Black community. With a large portion of the force loyal to the proslavery Democratic Party, many police were all too happy to work directly with Southern slaveholders to find escapees in New York. For Irish police, this transcended party politics. In the case of one woman who had escaped to New York in June 1852, her enslaver, who was also her father, offered a large reward to a police officer to discover where she lived. When abolitionists learned of the attempt to locate her, they raised the alarm and allowed her to escape. Being commissioned in this manner could be a way to further differentiate racialized Irish officers from people of African descent. After all, even in abolitionist literature writers could invoke a comparison between enslaved people of African descent and recent immigrants. A report of the American and Foreign Anti-Slavery Society called attention to "immigrants of every complexion, condition and religion from the old world, many of whom possess less Anglo-Saxon blood than do our proscribed fellow countryman." Although abolitionists could make a case against chattel slavery by invoking the freedom of recent immigrants, recent immigrants enforcing the Fugitive Slave Act might have helped to break that comparison. The widening chasm between Black Americans and recent white immigrants was particularly hostile in cities like Baltimore or on the docks of Brooklyn, where a large number of Black freedmen were often forced into competition with Irish and German workers for jobs. Thus policing allowed the Irish to declare superiority over the people they were capturing and returning to slavery, as well as taking a stand against any competition African Americans might pose to the white working classes on the labor market.[26]

There were those within the police department who opposed the use of officers for federal slavery enforcement. In 1860, a Republican faction on the Police Board of Commissioners put forward a resolution that would exempt officers from arresting fugitive slaves. The resolution failed. At that same meeting, however, the board did finally pass a resolution that would fire police found drinking when in uniform.[27]

Black New Yorkers and abolitionist allies also resisted police both as agents of enslavers, as well as violence workers. The abolitionist Samuel May diligently argued against slavery by laying out hundreds of examples of those who fell victim to and resisted fugitive slave policing. New York's widespread network of freedmen, freedwomen, and white allies attempted to thwart police wherever they could by helping people escape police custody, flee, seek legal writs of freedom, or raise money to purchase back the people who could not be saved before being sent South. Abolitionists rallied, for instance, after James Hamlet became the very first person to be apprehended in New York under the 1850 law. After he was apprehended his enslaver, Mary Brown of Baltimore, put him up for auction, at which abolitionists from New York City raised the $800 necessary to purchase him from bondage and bring him home. Horace Preston of Williamsburg, Brooklyn, was similarly rescued after being arrested by a municipal police officer known to be in league with Southern enslavers. Allies raised $1,200 to pay his Baltimore enslaver for his freedom. Abolitionists did more than raise money to save people. Before the *Scott* decision, eight Black men and women brought to New York by a Texas slave owner sought legal counsel and procured a writ of habeas corpus, which allowed them to win their freedom because they were not fugitives but had been brought to a free state. Similarly, when sailors discovered a "nearly white" man living as a stowaway on a ship heading to New York from Savannah, Georgia, they summoned police to meet them at the dock. While the man slept under guard in a house near the Red Hook docks, Lewis Tappan, the famed lawyer who argued the *Amistad* case, was summoned to corral a judge and constable to free him.[28]

Of course, not everyone could be saved. No matter how much money could be raised to pay off owners or how many kidnappers could be charged, there were some New Yorkers who were taken back into a life of bondage. Fearing re-enslavement and tired of the threat of police harassment, some African Americans fled Manhattan altogether. Those who remained in the city, however, were subject not only to the regular inhumanity of policing but also to incidents of mass upheaval and racial violence. Whether motivated by racial animus or by large bounties offered by slave owners, police were an integral part of the power structure that governed freedom and captivity in the city. Just five years after the department's formal founding, officers' awareness of race and knowledge of the small Black community in New York was precisely what made them valuable in the pursuit of self-emancipated individuals. Even the officers who refused to become paid informants in the pursuit of fugitive slaves unavoidably understood the racial boundaries and animosities that animated the city, especially in moments of disorder.[29]

Six years after the dissolution of the Municipal Police, and thirteen years after police in New York began enforcing the 1850 Fugitive Slave Act, Captain Walling and the Metropolitan Police came into conflict again with what appeared to be Democratically aligned, proslavery Irish New Yorkers during the antidraft riots of 1863. Unlike the 1857 police riot, which pitted Irish against American-born police, during the disorder of 1863 the police proved a unified front against a working-class mob out to brutalize African Americans and their Republican defenders. Walling's landmark book *Recollections of a New York Chief of Police* provides a romanticized, if not at times totally fabricated, view of life in a department attempting and often failing to modernize and professionalize—and provides one of the more detailed firsthand accounts of police activity during the riots.

For nearly a week that summer, from July 13 through July 16, working-class and immigrant New Yorkers rioted to protest the March 1863 announcement of a military draft and to assert fears that emancipation would jeopardize poor whites' racial superiority and job prospects. Mob violence broke out in every corner of the city as groups of marauders, motivated by racial hatred, politics, graft, or all three scoured city streets attacking African Americans, laying siege to police and municipal buildings, and looting well-to-do homes. When the violence subsided, chroniclers estimated that across the city, eighteen people had died, eleven of them Black victims of the mob, many of whom had been hung from lampposts or murdered while attempting to defend themselves and their communities. Police who rallied to protect Black New Yorkers and the property of wealthier Manhattanites from the mob also suffered the consequences, with untold injuries and the complete incineration of two police stations. "The immediate actors in the late riots in this city, got up to resist the draft and to create a diversion in favor of the southern rebellion, were exclusively Irishmen and Catholics," recalled one writer describing the uprising and violence directed at Union soldiers and Black residents across the city. As the violence broke out, around four thousand police and "specials" rallied to the newly built police headquarters at 300 Mulberry Street. The large building not only became the center of operations to quell the riots, it also housed seven hundred "refugees" fleeing the violence and hundreds of prisoners apprehended in the mayhem. The Draft Riots reinforced the prevailing and now decades-old concern among upper-class Anglo New Yorkers that Irish immigrants could not comprehend or appreciate the duties and obligations of liberal citizenship—exemplified at this moment by their ongoing campaign of terrorizing Manhattan's Black population as a way of signaling their opposition to the martial effort to end slavery.[30]

Captain Walling, working within a police force that was largely made up of Irish Americans, avoided engaging with explicitly racialized anti-Irish critiques of the crowd. He described the makeup of the mob by saying, "Aside from the strictly criminal classes—always ready to take advantage of any local troubles in order to carry on their peculiar vocations—there is a large body of idle persons, with no interests at stake, who amalgamate with the thieves for purpose of sharing plunder." Perhaps by virtue of his proximity to Irish police participating in the daily project of racial governance, he chose to see or portray the crowds in a less decidedly racialized way. Even though many police on duty during the riots were Irish, not everyone was as willing to disaggregate race and disorder.[31]

Many writers in the moment and in the years that followed wrote detailed accounts of those tumultuous days. Writing as an anonymous "Volunteer" because "no adequate account of the Draft-riot of 1863 has ever been printed," William Osborn Stoddard, an author and former assistant to President Abraham Lincoln, wrote one of the most popular volumes on the topic. Published in 1887, *The Volcano under the City*'s epigraph, a quote from executed anarchist George Engel, makes clear that Stoddard's concern was with the fast-spreading fear of "disorder" and chaos that accompanied social and immigrant upheaval in a rapidly urbanizing nation. Although the book was written close to thirty years later, the retroactive framing of the riot as a result of mass immigration and a failure of those newcomers to grasp the etiquette of American civic life was as central to nativist rhetoric in 1887 as it had been in 1863. *The Volcano under the City* drew a strong line of continuity from the alleged Irish draft dodgers in riots of the 1860s to the Central, Eastern, and Southern European anarchists of the 1880s. Both represented a racialized and foreign threat of urban upheaval and violence.[32]

Describing one scene during the riots, Stoddard depicted a torch-bearing mob marching on a hospital for wounded Union soldiers at the corner of Forty-First Street and Lexington Avenue. For many upper-class nativist New Yorkers, the wounded soldiers convalescing in the hospital served as the very symbol of everything Irish immigrants were not. Despite the many majority Irish units that served in the war, Stoddard saw those who had sacrificed for their country as a testament to the natural reverence of native-born Americans for civic duty and the American project. Of the soldiers, Stoddard wrote: "The cardinal sin of these men was that they dared to suffer for the country which their would-be destroyers had invaded by way of the immigrant station at Castle Garden. It was a sin requiring that they should be burned alive if possible."[33] Here, Stoddard portrayed Irish and German immigrants as an invading unpatriotic horde and entirely responsible for the riot. Accounts immediately following the incident had reported that on Tuesday morning, downtown near the Bowery, Inspector Carpenter of the Metropolitan Police led two hundred officers to confront rioters attempting to sack the mayor's house. At the front of the mob the marchers flew a large banner that read "No Draft" and an American flag. When the two sides began to brawl, police seized and destroyed the banner and the Stars and Stripes were taken as a prize "and carried in the ranks of those who, by word or deed, would never dishonor them."

The perceived inability of immigrants to serve as trustworthy, reliable, and reverent police was again reinscribed by the nativist perception that immigrants were lashing out at the wounded soldiers because of the soldiers' patriotism.[34]

The Irish rioters became one of the most visible and lasting images of nineteenth-century urban upheaval, reinforcing the mounting association between violence and Irishness. As Stoddard noted, although the New York City press universally condemned Irish involvement in the riots, statistically speaking, the police combating those rioters were also Irish.

The riot of 1863, as well as Irish involvement in the Civil War, marked an early turning point after which some chroniclers extended a degree of acceptance and inclusion to Irish police and soldiers because of their willingness to beat back other Irish people. Just years after the supposed "death" of anti-Irish sentiment in New York as a result of their heroic involvement on the side of the Union during the Civil War, subsequent riots, like the Orange Riots of 1870 and 1871 brought that prejudice back to the forefront. As Stoddard noted decades later, "heavy clubs of Roman Catholic and Irish policemen" met their kin. With one pen stroke he demonized Irish rioters because of their foreignness, and with the next praised the police despite it. In one scene Stoddard depicted an, "excellent body of trained militia . . . composed exclusively of Irishmen," as a way to defend Irish police. In opposition to the trained bodies of the Irish police were their ethnic kin, made foreign by their Catholicism and unproductive violence. Once again, even though many of the police themselves would have identified as Catholic, by virtue of their blue uniforms and their productive violence they escaped the descriptor of being practitioners of "some sort of inbred superstition." One chronicler writing in 1863 went so far as to describe one rioter as "crazy for riot and blood . . . he literally exhibited demonic rage." The rioters were not only racially and religiously different from the Protestant upper classes, they were described as coming from hell.[35]

There was, however, one indication that without their uniforms and obligations, the police were themselves not that different from the rioters. The detective force of the Metropolitan Police, led by officers Young, MacDougal,

Farley, Dusebury, Slowey, and others infiltrated the mob in an effort to feed information back to headquarters. "They went disguised in all ways, now as laborers and again as rioters, sometimes on horseback, sometimes driving hacks and carts, and often were part and parcel of the lawless." Only Detective Slowey was eventually identified as an infiltrator and beaten by the crowd—an indication of how easily most of the officers would have blended into that specific crowd while undercover.[36]

Having served with Irish police for decades, most of George Walling's writing ran counter to the well-circulated depictions of the Irish rioters as small and bestial. Instead, his recollections focused on the bodies of the defenders and victims of the Draft Riots. On July 13, a mob of around three thousand surrounded the Colored Orphan Asylum on Fifth Avenue and Forty-Third Street to burn and raze the building. Its inhabitants, "two hundred colored children" as well as matrons and attendants, were spirited away under police protection and sheltered in police stations. When those still were threatened by mob violence, "the poor creatures were almost crazed with terror." Throughout his chapter on the Draft Riots, Walling conjures images of small and defenseless people when depicting the riot's Black victims, despite well-documented but often failed attempts of Black New Yorkers to defend themselves and their neighborhoods. Through this discursive device, more boundaries are created between Blackness and shades of whiteness. Blackness is portrayed as both without agency and as an obligation or burden that liberal society must protect. It allowed Irish immigrants willing to use a type of violence that upper-class New Yorkers would have recognized as valuable and productive to preserve order to be the bearers of that burden—while their kin on the other side of the batons represented a threat to that order and a type of violence that was burdensome and unproductive. The Irish could rise to the challenges of American society or threaten its existence, but people of African descent were permanently relegated to remain outside it.[37]

Amid the stories that emerged of African Americans being murdered, tormented, and brutalized, many police accounts of events reflect a number of stories of people who had defended themselves and their communities. On Tuesday morning at 2 a.m., police on Clarkson Street were finally able to return to the site where a Black man had been murdered and recover the body. Two hours later on Leroy Street, Captain Dickinson watched a man use his fists to defend himself from a white assailant before finally being beaten in the head with a blunt object. Many accounts describe Black neighbors arming one another with carts full of bricks, sticks, and other impromptu weapons, while at least one told of police arming Black residents so that they could assist officers in their defense. For every moment when police defended African Americans from rioters, there were many when police looked on as murders took place.[38]

Despite the visible evidence and recorded testimony about Black defensive action, Walling's association of size, whiteness, and bravery led to the deputizing of a number of working-class white men to aid in the defense of the police station. "'Captain Walling, I've seen a big, rough-looking fellow peeping through the window. He's done it three or four times,'" one man shouted during the riot. The rough-looking man was discovered to be Leonard, a ship carpenter and Walling's own brother. "He told me his fellow workmen had struck and wouldn't let him work. 'Well, if you can't work, can you fight?' 'Try me,' he replied. I immediately had him sworn in, gave him a club, and had no occasion to feel ashamed of my unexpected recruit. He served under me the whole week, and took an active part in all that occurred."[39] Walling's decision to deputize strong men, making "can you fight?" the only prerequisite to act on behalf of the police, reveals that on the hierarchy of policing skills, fighting was number one. Although the willingness of Irish officers to fight their kin and the beginnings of a meritocratic police force based on racialized understandings of fitness helped some people to disaggregate Irish police from Irish rioters, it could not erode xenophobia overnight. Some people may have literally fought their way into a contingent whiteness, but others remained foreigners.

Irish Rioters, Irish Police

Ethnic and racial tensions flared up again in the 1871 Orange Riots when 1,500 police and the National Guard, on edge after the Draft Riots, were in place to guard a parade of Irish Protestants. Irish Catholic and city officials, including Archbishop John McCloskey, had hoped that the parade would be canceled, perhaps out of both sectarian animosity and a fear of the inevitable violence, but the parade went on in the early hours of July 12.

As the Catholic crowd collected around the march, "stones and other missiles were now thrown from rooftops," and when a shot was fired from an unknown source, "the Eighty-fourth regiment, without waiting for orders, fired upon the crowd," leaving dozens of men, women, and children dead. The event became known as the Great Orange Massacre. In the days that followed, Irish Catholics met to mourn and reflect on the fact that a heavily

Irish police force along with the military had clubbed and shot a crowd of their own Irish-Catholic kin hoping to interrupt the parade of Protestants.[40]

This episode confirmed the loyalty and American-ness attributed to Irish men in uniform. With the exception of two officers who refused to fight fellow Irish Catholics and were imprisoned, the Irish Catholic police earned the respect of many that day for their willingness to beat back a mob with whom they shared a culture and religion. The Orange Riots proved that the Irish could serve simultaneously as an embodiment of how a foreign-born person could conform to American ideals, and also the ways that their bodies and culture would confound assimilation.[41]

Throughout the nineteenth century, according to eyewitnesses and later chroniclers alike, the bodies of Irish rioters often served as the ultimate distillation and truest indicator of their ferocity. One writer for the *New York Times* described a rioter bragging about the murder of a Black man as an "obese, small, villainous-looking Irishman." Again, African Americans were the anvil on which Irish people could make or unmake their belonging in the United States by proving themselves to be capable of productive—or unproductive—violence in the preservation of order and social status in the city. Stoddard as well, writing from firsthand accounts, newspapers, and speculation, described the rioters at various moments as "savage," "bestial," "cloudy-faced," "black of heart," and having a "barbarian zest worthy of the Huns of Attila." By comparing the Irish to Huns, the author meant explicitly to show the Irish as an invading force—one whose growing presence would displace, if not destroy, Anglo-American culture as it had supposedly existed. This metaphor also served the dual purpose of presenting the 1880s, when Stoddard was writing, as another moment when the fabric of American life was under attack from immigration and urban disorder.[42]

The famous political cartoonist Thomas Nast, publishing frequently in *Harper's Weekly*, often depicted the Irish as small and apelike. Even though many of the officers quelling the riot were undoubtedly Irish, in his 1863 cartoon, "Charge of the Police on the Rioters at the 'Tribune' Office," Nast depicts the shriveled, hunched rioters being surprised by stoic officers almost twice their size, many of whom appear to have avoided so much as a wrinkle in their uniforms.[43]

Nast's depictions of the 1863 Draft Riots serve as an early visual indicator of the consolidation of whiteness around immigrant and immigrant-descended police officers. While working-class Irish men and women were still being

CHARGE OF THE POLICE ON THE RIOTERS AT THE "TRIBUNE" OFFICE.

1.1 Thomas Nast, "Charge of the Police on the Rioters at the 'Tribune' Office." *Harper's Weekly*, August 1, 1863.

depicted as apelike and treated as racially and behaviorally dissimilar to Anglo-New Yorkers, police began to experience a type of social and even racial mobility denied to their peers. Nast's later cartoons show that he did not treat most Irish New Yorkers with the generosity he extended to the Irish police. In an 1871 cartoon entitled "The American River Ganges," Nast depicted Irish Catholics as crocodiles with large crosses on their backs and long snouts, shaped like papal miters, and filled with sharp teeth. On the shoreline, Tammany associates toss terrified, praying Protestants into danger.[44]

Wearing the blue uniform, however, seemed to allow Irish police and their immediate descendants access to more social mobility and respect. For Irish New Yorkers, policing often became a family business, spanning two or more generations. The Irish detective Arthur Carey recalled the sense of duty and family obligation that led many Irishmen in the mid-nineteenth century to join the police. "Family tradition always has insisted that I was born a policeman," he wrote in 1930, two years after his retirement.[45] Carey recalled wearing clothes made of similar fabric to the patrolman's blue uniform from a very young age and standing "in front of our home in lower Manhattan swinging a policeman's club, reduced size." The dual signifiers of the club and the blue uniform—one a symbol of the state's monopoly on violence and who has the power to wield it, and the other the transformative agent that turned foreign Irish bodies into bodily representations of the state, operated in tandem as a promise of young Carey's rights and obligations as an Irish American New Yorker.

The desire to become an officer was implanted in him from a young age by his father, who joined the NYPD after emigrating from Ireland. When considering why Irish police were so prevalent on New York's force, he considered that in Ireland, the working-class was so thoroughly left out of the process of governance that they "wanted a chance to try their hand at governing," and the first available opportunity was the police force in New York.[46] More than that, however, Carey seems to suggest that the drive behind Irish participation in the police force was something more bodily and innate. "So I say that deep down my father's desire to make me a policeman was ruled by the Irish blood in his veins, even when I lay in my cradle."[47] The desire, according to Carey, and the perceived inheritance of policing was as ingrained and biological as the genetic traits and attributes that made Irish people exceptional patrolmen.

In the first half century after the founding of modern American police departments, patrolmen and administrators were forced to think about race constantly. When patrolling the street, while deciding whom to give commissions and promotions to, and in deciding what good policing looked like— race was the terrain on which policing was founded and governed. Carey may have thought that being Irish meant he was genetically and historically predisposed to being not just a police officer, but a *good* police officer, and he was hardly alone in this racial fantasy. In the later decades of the nineteenth century, as racial science, criminal anthropology, and proto-eugenics percolated and spread around the northern Atlantic, it sank into the very foundations of police departments.

RACIAL HIERARCHIES OF CRIME & POLICING

2

Bodies, Morals, and Gender

in the NYPD, 1890–1897

In the nineteenth century, bodies, race, masculinity, and morality became the entwined currencies of policing. The administrators of the Metropolitan Police Department of New York and the politicians who oversaw it were forced to grapple with sometimes paradoxical choices created by their understanding of race and policing. Recruiting police who could fight well often meant recruiting from segments of the population they saw as more racially disposed to graft, corruption, and unsanctioned violence. But the continued reverence for a policeman's ability to fight put a higher value on Irish police *because of,* and not *despite,* their perceived penchant for violence. After decades of attempts to wrest control of the New York City Police Department from Irish officers and the corruption that they and other racialized Democrats evoked, the nineteenth century ended with a momentary synthesis as Anglo and Irish officers consolidated their shared identity and police power just in time to address the new wave of immigration from Southern and Eastern Europe. Despite all this, the general battle between good government reformers and the coalition of racialized white working-class New Yorkers that made up Tammany supporters continued, and the very bodies of policemen emerged as an important battleground in this fight.

This chapter covers the final decade of the nineteenth century as entwined discourses about bodies, race, and gender informed police administrators and politicians about who might be susceptible to criminal behavior and who might make a good police officer. Dominant ideas in white society about Black, Chinese, and other working-class criminality continued to dictate where police invested their concern and investigatory resources. Patrolmen themselves, however, could not avoid the scientific and moral gaze of reformers and politicians. Racialized police, especially those of Irish-Catholic descent, were both revered and reviled for their hypermasculinity, which Protestant reformers saw as a liability and moral threat to the city. Some bodies, administrators believed, were better suited to American-style policing than others, and early social scientists and politicians encouraged the department to organize accordingly. Anticorruption reformers, skeptical of both the Irishness and belligerent manhood of the police, were especially concerned about their ability to protect, rather than hurt, white women in the city. Even as upper- and middle-class white women rallied to the cause of appointing women police officers and women prison matrons who they believed would be more nurturing and discerning, Black women and the larger Black community were left to their own devices to oppose police brutality and the particular criminalization imposed on Black New Yorkers in public.[1]

Bodies as Signifiers of Good Policing and Criminality

George Walling, the New York police commissioner from 1874 to 1885, knew that when it came to the development of a rough-and-tumble American style of policing by force, bodies mattered. He wrote extensively on the topics of good policing, crime, and criminality in the late nineteenth century, and his writing provides a useful window into the thinking of police and politicians of the era. "The police force of New York City is without doubt the finest organization of its kind in the world. The men composing it are finer looking, better paid, more vigilant than the protectors of any other large city. No organization is more effective either; and even if our police do not exercise that perpetual espionage over individual citizens that the Parisian gendarmes exercise, they are better trained, more athletic, more resolute and hardy." The value of New York City's police officers was, according to Walling, their strength, their athleticism, and their hardiness—put plainly, their manliness. Discussing manliness and the entrenched prizefighting culture of the era, historian Gail Bedermen writes: "Late Victorian culture had identified the powerful, large male body of the heavyweight prizefighter (and not the smaller bodies of the middleweight or welterweight) as the epitome of manhood." European gendarmes, deployed throughout the countryside of France and Germany, were a force whose primary function was intelligence-gathering as a way of rendering inaccessible regions more amenable to state control. Walling's comparison pits the nonconfrontational and therefore less manly style of policing prevalent in Europe, against the hypermasculine prizefighting aesthetic of New York patrolmen.[2]

Sometimes Walling demonstrated the shortcomings of a majority Anglo-German-Irish police department whose recruitment was often predicated on political patronage, stature, and an ability to brawl. In 1886, he believed there were between six thousand and seven thousand residents of the city who were born in China or were of Chinese descent, likely a more accurate figure than the US census, which did not show the Chinese population of New York City surpassing six thousand until 1900.[3] "There is probably no American who does not regard the Chinese as beings dissimilar to and dissonant with himself; as a caste shut out by its fantastic personality from his sympathies and associations."[4] Despite the racialized depictions of the Irish and Germans during the mid-nineteenth century, they were not deemed nearly as enigmatic to the police as the Chinese living in the section of the Five Points that would become Chinatown. Echoing earlier depictions of the Chinese as unassimilable, Walling wrote: "Of all foreign colonies in New York, the Chinese is the most picturesque. Emigrants from European countries merge themselves in the American population, acquire the English tongue . . . but the Chinaman is a unique and isolated figure."[5]

Evoking sensational scenes of opium dens and underground gambling rings that titillated the late nineteenth-century reader, Walling depicted a Chinese culture completely illegible to Americans and especially American police. Language, writing, gambling, behavior, and even religion are all depicted as being so "fantastic and bewildering" that no American could fathom their meaning, except those "degraded" men and women opium smokers accepted into Chinese circles.[6] With promotions as an incentive, police who focused on honing their skills for fighting and graft were often ill-equipped or disinterested in learning to understand their Chinese American neighbors.

One of the greatest imagined moral threats posed by Chinese New Yorkers was the proximity between white women and the enigmatic Chinese man. "In

Pell Street and vicinity," continued Walling, "there are three houses of prostitution whose sole patrons are Chinamen. The inmates are Irish, American, German, and Italian females who have fallen from one stage of degradation to another until they are more brute than human."[7] In developing a knowledge of the city, police often understood vice districts, and especially sex work, to be overlaid on neighborhoods dominated by racial and ethnic minorities. Although prostitution could and would flourish in many parts of the city, it was predominantly the prostitution that occurred within or in proximity to minority enclaves that was targeted for specific policing and moral condemnation. Reformers of various ilk and ideologies, stemming from religious to scientific—or a combination of the two—trafficked in multiple, sometimes conflicting philosophies of opposing prostitution. Depending on their generation and political affiliations, police, reformers, and politicians differed on whether to attribute the existence of Anglo or white immigrant sex workers in these neighborhoods to the deviance, violence, and manipulative nature of Chinese and nonwhite men or to the economic precariousness of working-class women. These "brutish" women risked not just moral corruption, but having their own whiteness called into question by continued and especially voluntary proximity to vice-involved nonwhite and immigrant men.

The sexual accessibility of these women to the racial and ethnic minorities was perceived as a threat, not just to the salvageable morality of the white women, but also to the moral fabric of the Anglo-supremacist city. Black and Chinese women, and to a somewhat lesser extent working-class Southern and Eastern European women, were not always afforded the same presumption of innocence as native-born white women. Irish and German women existed somewhere in-between, where proximity to Black or Chinese men through respectable channels like missionary or charity work could be forgiven without impugning their character, but prolonged exposure in romantic and leisure settings could raise suspicions.[8]

The late nineteenth-century concern with public decency, morals policing, and paternalistic and coercive policing of women who sold sex was a bit of a departure from public attitudes of a few decades prior. The passage in 1873 of the Comstock Act, which made it illegal to mail or sell "obscene, lewd, or lascivious" materials, signaled an erosion of a more freewheeling "sporting male" culture, in which both dockside dives and stylish bordellos were a tolerated, if not accepted, aspect of the social-sexual world of upper-class male New Yorkers. Under this old regime, women who sold sex often turned to the local government for protection when men instigated violence against them.

Left to decide between policing prostitution or defending the business of selling sex, administrators, watchmen, and magistrates, as historian Timothy Gilfoyle has shown, often defended the property rights of the women against their male aggressors. Toward the end of the nineteenth century, attempts on the part of reformers to defend the supposed moral purity of upper-class white women from seduction, the sexuality of nonwhite men, and venereal disease often led to increased sexual regulation of women, a supercharged criminal justice system that penalized working-class women, and the criminalization of immigrant and Black men.[9]

The lack of cultural knowledge and the racial identity of investigators, including police, often created challenges for patrolling those neighborhoods. Reportedly, all an American needed to do to see an "evil expression on a human creature's face" was enter a Chinese gambling den and watch as its inhabitants "worked themselves into an agony of nervousness." The problems that arose when non-Chinese-speaking police patrolled Chinese neighborhoods continued for decades, as there were no Chinese-speaking NYPD officers until 1904. Recreational slummers, private vice investigators, and the police department alike relied on informants or guides whenever they hoped to penetrate a world of Chinese vice often amplified by fantastical stories in the press and Orientalist imaginings.[10]

Black New Yorkers were also subject to complex calculations of difference. Walling's exaggerated characterization of African Americans put them closer to Chinese immigrants in terms of perceived criminality and barbarism, but more familiar and understandable to Anglo-Irish officers, and therefore more easily policed. As will be discussed later, assumptions about the innate ability of Anglo-Irish officers to police Black neighborhoods, while cultural barriers necessitated the inclusion of European immigrant officers, meant that Black activists had to struggle for years to achieve the police integration that other racial groups were granted because of their language skills and ethnic knowledge.

Nowhere was police preoccupation with supposed Black criminality more apparent, according to Walling, than in their terror over "Black-and-Tan" saloons and dance halls that facilitated interracial socializing and sexual contact. "It would be difficult to say where the Black-and-Tan got its name. It is a resort of black men as well as white, but the girls are all white! This mixture of races is all the more revolting; and the scenes which go on here in this underground dive are as bad as imagination can picture them." In *Recollections*, Walling frames the Black-and-Tan as free from the mysteries that plagued patrolmen tasked with policing Chinese spaces. Even the bodies of Black leisure seekers seem more familiar to him than the unreadable figures of Chinatown. "It takes a good deal to satisfy the best of these dull-sensed negroes. They dance until the perspiration rolls in streams down their faces, and then they drink until they are stupid. The other male visitors besides negroes—sailors, young clerks, countrymen—indulge in sensuality *almost* as vigorously." Walling's racism and assumptions about Black deviance tinged what he saw, and he did not assume there was anything "bewildering" or confounding about it, the way he did in Chinatown.

White American-born investigators hoping to infiltrate vice districts and their varying types of saloons, dance halls, and gambling dens often entered with a set of assumptions about the types of people and crimes they would be surveilling. Even in Black-and-Tans, which were thought to be less perplexing than immigrant enclaves, the events they witnessed through middle-class eyes often confirmed their assumptions. Or, in situations where the prostitution or homosexuality they sought to find were not plainly visible, investigators tried to create the conditions for it by soliciting people. White observers of Black leisure saw the deviance they wanted or suspected they would see in the bars and gathering spots in multiracial neighborhoods. The frequency of everyday interactions between Black and white New Yorkers also meant that spaces like the Black-and-Tan were more susceptible to police infiltration than leisure spots frequented primarily by only one ethnic group.[11]

While on the street, European-descended people often escaped the assumption that Chinese and Black New Yorkers were subjected to, that they had a proclivity for crime. This assumption of innocence on the street did not always extend to the popular texts of the time, which articulated the idea that wholesome white masculinity could be mitigated by genetics or the environment. Politicians and scientists of the era were quite concerned with the existence of criminals whose criminality was not immediately apparent on their faces or bodies. "It is a preconceived and not always well-founded notion," wrote one New York City police chief in the late nineteenth century, "the vast majority of persons that men who war upon society must of necessity bear the brand of their evil doings on their brows. This is not so."[12] Despite this academic discourse about hidden criminality, to possess a body that allowed one the presumption of innocence was a luxury only sometimes afforded to immigrants and their immediate descendants, but police almost universally denied this presumption to Black urbanites.

The conjoined construction of manliness and whiteness dictated that white men, and especially Anglo white men, could inhabit the right balance of civilized and polished but still manly. Immigrant and Black men, on the other hand, were often depicted as a swinging pendulum. They could be seen as too feminine due to a lack of stoicism or a supposed inability to provide for and support a family—while also having the capacity to swing into uncivilized and hypermasculine violence and sexual depravity. And yet, the daily evidence of crime committed by white men, including native-born white men, could reiterated the notion that anyone could commit crimes. For Walling, the omnipresence and unpredictability of criminal behavior complicated scholarly notions that criminality could be read on the body.[13]

Even before some social theorists and scientists read Charles Darwin's 1859 *Origin of Species* as a treatise on racial difference and evolutionary development, writers looking to justify race-based chattel slavery, colonialism, and criminalization had developed well-articulated scientific models of inferiority that could be read onto the bodies of African-descended peoples. Historians have written extensively about how racial science from the 1850s onward attempted not only to show the difference between white and Black bodies, but also to demonstrate that the bodies of African-descended people were "suited, even designed, for specific roles—namely, servitude or civilization." By the 1880s, however, the influential field of criminal anthropology, which speculated that people carried around phenotypical and physiological manifestations of their inner character and criminality, was just taking root in Europe and had only a few followers in the United States until its popularity boomed in the mid-1890s.[14]

Just because Walling was unwilling to read crime onto Irish New Yorkers, as many of his contemporaries did, does not mean that the criminalizing scientific gaze could not be turned on people of European descent. Walling's fascination with the incongruity of respectable appearance and criminality may have been a reaction to the well-circulated notion of *degeneration*, the concept that Western civilization had produced a generation of overcivilized urbanites, with weak brains, bodies, and morals. "Over and over again," Walling observed, "instances have come to my notice where young men, and women, too, who have been well bred, and whose natural traits are far from vicious, have drifted (and I can find no better word in the English language) into crime purely and simply through want." Historian Daniel Pick has argued that there was no predominant definition of degeneration, but there was instead an ideological production of scientific discourse to address Europe's falling birth rates, rising rates of property crime, and the "social problem" of economic inequality. One such theory of degeneration was that "the city, progress, civilization, and modernity were paradoxically, the very agents of decline" within modern society. Walling's notion of degeneracy tied crime to white bodies through the circumstances of modern life, rather than the naturalist discourses used to link crime and Blackness.[15]

Anti-Irish Sentiment in the Campaign Against Police Corruption

For good government reformers during the 1880s and 1890s, however, the biggest crisis was not Black-and-Tans or Chinese gambling, or even the moral degeneration of the upper strata of society. Moral crusaders in the emerging Progressive Era were more concerned with the perceived level of corruption that infected every level of the NYPD, from the lowliest patrolman to the inspectors and commissioners. Like investigators' assumptions about Black leisure-seekers in the Tenderloin or the supposedly elusive gamblers of Chinatown, Anglo and Irish police had their own racialized identities, which were also susceptible to embodied moral failings.

Police corruption, reformers asserted, not only manifested itself in the entrenched system of quid pro quo management that allowed citizens to pay for appointments and police to pay for promotions. It also encouraged patrolmen to extort protection money from business owners and facilitated the bribery of officers in exchange for laxity in enforcing certain laws. Chief among the neglected statutes were those concerning alcohol, including closing times for saloons and blue laws that prohibited the sale of alcohol on Sunday. Dr. Howard Crosby, one of the founders of the Society for the Prevention of Crime, wrote that of all the causes of crime in New York City, the five largest were: "the unrestricted sale of distilled liquors"; legal loopholes that hindered any attempts to prohibit the sale of alcohol; the apathy of the public for the "sad condition" of the city; the influence of partisan politics and spoils system on the governance of the city, and finally, the "unnatural" ability of police to "not see" crime.[16]

The famed reformer Rev. Charles Parkhurst would later echo Crosby's concern about the force. "The Department which, in my rustic innocence, I had supposed existed for the purpose of repressing crime," Parkhurst explained after a few years in New York, "had for its principal object to protect and foster crime and make capital out of it."[17]

Parkhurst arrived in New York City from Western Massachusetts in 1880 to take the pulpit of the large Madison Square Presbyterian Church with little explicit intention of preaching against the moral failings of the city's inhabitants. His transition from optimistic rural preacher to jaded urbanite happened slowly over the first few years of his tenure at the Madison Square Church, but by 1890, in his own description, he, "commenced to push out quietly in the two directions of gambling evil and the social evil, and the first obstruction against which I ran was the Police!"

The campaign Parkhurst launched against the New York City Police Department between 1892 and its election-day "victory" against Tammany on November 6, 1894, would, one scholar argued, launch the Progressive Era and usher in a new period of municipal reform. This was a war Parkhurst fought on multiple fronts. With the assistance of private detectives employed by the moralistic Society for the Prevention of Crime, Parkhurst often went in disguise into establishments in order to drum up press and to send signed affidavits to the state that he had seen the illegal sale of alcohol or gambling. He repeatedly reported to the state that police were willfully neglecting their duties to shut down certain establishments.

In one instance, while strolling in the shadow of police headquarters, Parkhurst and a private detective encountered what he guessed were "no less than fifty women" walking the streets as sex workers. The detective recalled Parkhurst remarking, "I suppose that none of the police officers in yonder building know what is happening on this street," at which both men laughed. Allowing segregated red-light districts to proliferate made it possible for police to harvest bribes, create more male-dominated leisure spaces, and supposedly maintain the innocence of respectable white women by designating spaces where "ruined" women could ply their trade without risking the morals of the wider city. The new generation of Progressive reformers disagreed. As historian Anne Gray Fischer characterizes their beliefs, "The corruption of white womanhood that took place in red-light districts—which not incidentally, was directly connected to the political corruption that sustained them—threatened to degrade the basic functions of democratic society." The philosophy of social hygiene preached by the reformers dictated that the white women could be saved, in part through the repression of female sexuality.[18]

Parkhurst was also able to use his legitimacy and audience to critique Tammany. In two highly publicized sermons, on February 14, 1892, and March 13, 1892, the first of which was often referred to as the "First Gun of the Campaign," the minister railed against police corruption. "Unless all signs are misleading," he preached, "your average policeman or your average police captain is not going to disturb a criminal, if the criminal has means, if he can help it."[19]

Parkhurst's 1890 realization that in many districts police enabled rather than suppressed crime was by no means the beginning of anti-Tammany activism. As early as the 1870s, reformers' attempts to clean up the city had met with lackluster results. Police, specifically those notorious enough to have been given a public persona by the press, were repeatedly acquitted for brutality, graft, and neglect of duty by boards of police commissioners appointed by Tammany mayors. No one exemplified the legal escape act better than Scotch-descended Alexander "Clubber" Williams, also referred to as "The Master of the Club" and the "Czar of the Tenderloin," who evidence suggests emerged from over a dozen trials for graft and brutality unscathed.[20]

Williams was a man of almost legendary proportions; the press drenched every aspect of his life in the mythos of prizefighting and Victorian manliness. Upon his death in 1917, the *New York Times* recounted his appointment to the force: "According to the story told, when young Williams determined that he wanted to become a policeman he went to Metropolitan Police Headquarters to ask Commissioner John W. Bergen for a position." When Bergen questioned Williams, supposedly telling him, "You may be a convict from Sing Sing, for all I know," Williams shook his fist in the police commissioner's face and stormed out. Bergen was reportedly so impressed that he sent a policeman to retrieve Williams and appointed him on the spot. Similar to the spontaneous appointment of Leonard Walling during the 1863 Draft Riots described earlier, Williams's career also seemed from its beginning to be predicated on a fighting spirit and deftness with a club.[21]

At his first deployment, on the corner of Broadway and Houston Street, Williams earned his reputation and his nickname, "Clubber," by seeking out and battling the most combative neighborhood toughs. After his 1872 promotion to captain of the Gas House District, Williams used his "rough-and-ready methods" to break up the notorious Gas House Gang. However, his most infamous moment came when he was transferred to the notorious vice district surrounding the police station on West Thirteenth Street. In an area teeming with brothels, gambling halls, and saloons, the opportunity for personal enrichment through extortion and bribes proved enticing. There was good reason for the neighborhood's reputation. On just one block of West Twenty-Ninth Street, the New York district attorney's office believed that there were "disorderly houses" at 106, 108, 110, 112, 114, 115, 116, 118, 120, and 122. When a newspaper reporter asked how Williams liked working in the neighborhood, his response was supposedly, "I like it fine. I have had chuck for a long time and now I am going to eat tenderloin." His excitement at upgrading from cheap to expensive cuts of meat gave the district its new moniker. For decades following the apocryphal story, the neighborhood was referred to as the Tenderloin, with Williams's persona intertwined with the district's reputation for sex, vice, and bribe-hoarding police. It also did not help the case for Irish respectability that during the years following the migration of Irish, and later Germans, to New York City, the young prostitutes admitted to the city's House of Refuge went from 33 percent with parents born abroad in 1829, to 79 percent in 1849, a trend that no doubt shaded expectations about immigrants and first-generation women in the city.[22]

Despite Williams's Scottish heritage, his synonymity with graft and unnecessary violence meant that he and other Protestant police were implicated in anticorruption critiques that were couched in anti-Catholic and anti-Irish rhetoric. In his "First Gun" sermon of February 14, 1892, Parkhurst attempted to elevate Protestants to a higher moral standing, comparing the current campaign against Tammany to the Protestant Reformation against the Catholic Church:

> But you ask me perhaps, what is the use of all this asseveration and vituperation; what is the good of protesting? What is the good of protesting? Do you know what the word Protestant means? A man who protests? And did not the men who protested in the sixteenth century do a good deal? Didn't they start a volcano beneath the crust of the whole European civilization? . . . Why, the truth will frighten even a policeman, if you will lodge it where David did when he fired at Goliath."[23]

The press covering the sermon and its Tammany backlash capitalized on Parkhurst's equation of police corruption with Catholicism, presumably Irish Catholicism. In one newspaper article clipped in Parkhurst's 1894 book *Our Fight with Tammany*, Tammany is sarcastically lampooned for its "delicate moral sense," "exquisite religious tact," and "fervor for the gospel of mediaeval theology."[24]

Parkhurst received support for his cause from the Woman's Christian Temperance Union (WCTU), the large majority Anglo-Protestant international organization that leveraged notions of women's innate moral superiority to advocate against alcohol, saloons, prostitution, and men's sexual and economic exploitation of women and children, often fueled by vice. Although repeatedly advertised as a nondenominational organization, its president and founder, Frances Willard, often bemoaned how hard it was to turn Catholic clergy to the temperance cause. Closing her convention address in Cleveland in 1894, Willard remarked, "It is the eighth wonder of the world for an archbishop of the Catholic Church to sit meekly by while a woman gives a bible reading." Both on the street and in the pulpit, Protestant reformers depicted the Catholic Church and its adherents as an opponent of progress.[25]

Anti-Irish critiques of Tammany Hall did not go unnoticed by the Democratic municipal machine, nor did the hypocrisy of Republican attempts to court Irish votes. "It is very early in the next Presidential campaign," read one humorous jab in the *Tammany Times*, "for the Republicans to fish for the Irish vote, but we notice they are already being called 'Celtic-Americans' in one of the Republican organs. It was formerly customary to refer to these estimable persons as 'flannel-mouthed Micks.'" By 1892 and the start of Parkhurst's campaign against police corruption and brutality, deep associations spanning decades made it nearly impossible to critique one side or the other without implicitly or explicitly maligning constituent religious and racialized national groups.[26]

The Irish detective and memoirist Arthur Carey also attempted to counter the stereotypes that Irishness was the cause of police corruption and brutality. Instead, he flipped the narrative on its head. Yes, Irish people were innately well-disposed for policing, but not in the way that others had accused them of. "Here in America the opportunity opened up to them, starting with police duty. They were well equipped by nature too, for the job," not because the Irish were so good at fighting, but because, "they were possessed of that smile which often takes the string out of tight, temper-trying situations." Ultimately, Carey claimed, the same qualities that *made* generations of Irish New Yorkers Irish also made them good police. The invention of policing as an Irish American tradition, only decades-old but already deeply entrenched in the New York City landscape, ran counter to the nineteenth-century nativist popular culture that began putting more value on long-standing American lineage. The entwining of Irishness with civic participation by way of policing undermined the popular and emerging notion that patriotism could be measured by one's blood relation to passengers on the *Mayflower* or participation in the American Revolutionary War. Undertaking the project of urban governance and state-sanctioned violence gave the Irish a counternarrative: They may be unrefined at the moment, but immigrant newcomers and those for whom whiteness was perpetually inaccessible made them acceptable by comparison.[27]

In addition to having fought in the Civil War and served on police forces, Irish Americans were at an advantage in attaching themselves to ideal Americanness, even when compared to contemporaneous German immigrants, by virtue of their shared language with Anglo-born Americans. "The German-Americans consider that unfair," a representative of a conference of German American societies told the US House of Representatives Select Committee on Immigration and Naturalization in March 1890, that any proposal to make proficiency with the English language a requirement for naturalization would place other immigrants "at a disadvantage as compared to Irish immigration." The new immigrants coming from other regions of Europe just "can not assimilate," an anti-immigration labor leader testified, "it would take them as long to assimilate as the Chinese." If the gauge for acceptance into American life was the speed of assimilation, many believed that newcomers from Southern and Eastern Europe, when compared to the already English-speaking Irish, were as incompatible with American life as Chinese immigrants, who had been barred in most instances from immigration eight years earlier by the 1882 Chinese Exclusion Act.[28]

Policing Women

Building on the animalistic depictions of Irish rioters earlier in the century, the late nineteenth-century debate about what good and bad policing looked like focused on innate and embodied characteristics of police. When reformers racialized critiques of bad policing by discursively conflating corruption and foreignness, they argued that by replacing bad (foreign) bodies with good (Anglo-Protestant) bodies, the police force would naturally become more moral and effective. These embodied characteristics extended across gender. The WCTU, in advocating for the moral superiority of women, declared that the problem of police corruption could be solved by a female police force. "The futility of expecting that a police force composed of men will array itself adequately against the pleasures of other men is demonstrated in all our cities. What we need," Willard argued in her 1894 presidential address, "is a police force in which strong, trusty, and true women are represented— matronly women whose character has been thoroughly proved in difficult situations, and who are vouched for by a committee of women of the highest character and conduct." In much the same way that abolishing the consumption of alcohol would improve the moral standing of the nation and protect women from abusive men, women police would "effectively close the saloons and houses of ill-fame." Indeed, "the streets of cities will never be really safe for women until other women help to patrol them."[29] At the time of the speech, it had only been three years since the introduction of police matrons responsible for women jailed in New York City. It would be another eighteen years before the city's police department appointed its first female detective.

By the 1920s, it was common for women employed by both the police department and private vice squads as undercover operatives who could investigate abortion providers and women seeking sexual and romantic company with other women.[30]

Frances Willard and other female reformers operated under the assumption that women out in public, especially white women, would be less subject to the whims of aggressive male police officers. Given Willard's criticism of Catholicism as being backward-looking when it came to the treatment of women, it would not be wholly wrong to think that she, like Parkhurst and other reformers, understood corruption in the police department as being at least somewhat synonymous with Irishness. Black and immigrant women especially moved around the city at the mercy of police who often doled out violence and arrest on a whim—motivated by racial assumptions of deviance and wrongdoing. A lack of English language skills or knowledge about how the justice system operated made some women particularly vulnerable to unfounded arrest or conviction.[31]

Surviving criminal court transcripts from the early years of the twentieth century give a rare glimpse into the firsthand accounts of working-class or lower-middle-class New Yorkers and their encounters with police. In many of these court cases, immigrant or Black defendants were forced to defend themselves from criminal accusations based on racialized assumptions about the predisposition to criminality and vice.[32]

The case of Dora Miadowicz is a particularly clear example of how vulnerable immigrant women were to the whims and assumptions of police on the beat. Chronically ill and susceptible to internal bleeding after complications from childbirth, Dora Miadowicz got off the train at Grand Central terminal on a cold evening in 1910 in order to do some shopping. She intended to re-check herself into the hospital the next day and hoped to buy her six-year-old daughter a pair of slippers to cheer her up in her absence. At 8 p.m. she encountered Thomas Hickson, an officer in plainclothes who was likely of Anglo-American descent. Miadowicz told the court that as he approached they smiled at one another. He stopped to ask her why she was smiling and she dismissively responded with the same question and kept walking. He pursued her and placed her under arrest.[33]

She told the judge that she had responded: "What for?"

He said "Never mind, you will find out later, you have no right to speak to a man or answer him when he speaks to you."

I says to him "I want you to understand I am a married woman and I have a husband and child waiting for me at home."

He said to me "Shut up, tell it to the Judge."

I says, "I will."

He says "He won't believe you anyhow."

Hickson brought Dora Miadowicz before the night court and, as he had predicted, the judge did not believe her and found her guilty of soliciting for the purposes of prostitution. The conviction was eventually overturned, but it took Miadowicz bringing in her doctor, an American-born white man, to testify on her behalf. At the retrial, the arresting officer was unsurprisingly absent.[34]

At the appeal hearing, the physician, Frederick J. Barrett, testified to a second judge that Miadowicz was in no physical condition to offer sex for money. "It seemed extremely unlikely that a woman in her physical condition would even think of soliciting, if she at other times were so inclined to do so even. Her sense of outrage was apparently so great that we talked it over, and we thought under the circumstances that an injustice or mistake must have been done." When asked if she was capable of committing an act of sexual intercourse the doctor replied, "I do not think it is absolutely impossible, but I do not think it is at all probable. She would have to pull out her plugs and dressings, and that sort of thing." The judge overturned her conviction and issued an apology. Stories like that of Dora Miadowicz gave more fuel to the arguments made by reform groups that the current mode of hypermasculine policing was ill-equipped to safely look out for innocent white women in the city.[35]

The archives of early twentieth-century policing are filled with stories of police arresting people with the justification that their physical presence in public indicated criminal behavior. Black men and women were often the victims of arrests as police read their presence on public streets as a signifier of moral failing, laziness, or potential criminality. Mrs. James Lockett, for instance, was arrested on the street because she "looked suspicious," and when a robbery occurred on the block where asphalt layer Robert Jefferson lived, his regular presence on the street playing banjo or shooting craps became a central detail in the prosecution's case.[36]

Some white women, particularly those connected to the Tammany-dominated force through kinship or marriage, countered arguments about innate corruption by asserting that both moral and corrupt police were created by their environments and experiences rather than at birth. They argued that any set of men thrust into similar circumstances could fall victim to temptation. Andrea Kornmann, writing under the pseudonym "Policeman's Wife," published the volume "Our Police" in 1887 with proceeds going to the Police Pension Fund. "Policemen differ from poets," she wrote, "they are not born, but those necessary attributes and qualifications of a true policeman are only acquired by months and years of patient, faithful, and earnest attention." And yet, when addressing critiques of police brutality, she argued explicitly that officers cannot be gentle people, and gentle people cannot be officers. Quoting the *Star*, a paper sympathetic to the police department, she wrote, "Some too critical police think the police should be a body of men of saintly forbearance... this is absurd. Courage and audacity are as necessary on the force as in the army, and a meek officer is totally out of place. A little roughness, though mistakenly applied occasionally, is yet excusable when the dangerous duties and excellent general capacity of the police are considered." Commissioner Walling agreed that police of all races were not fated for corruption, but rather could be taught the etiquette of respectable policing. "I have sometimes fancied," he wrote, "that it might not be *wholly impossible* to attempt to endow policemen with those elegancies and courtesies of life which make refined social intercourse so pleasant and improving." He continued that politeness is never more important than physical prowess.[37]

Both the WCTU and the "Policeman's Wife" attempted, as scholar Laura Wexler has articulated, to make the civic and the municipal seem "domestic." These domestic representations, of the morally superior WCTU mother-officer and the policeman's wife, turned the masculine, public, and often violent labor of policing into effective propaganda. Seeing police as fathers and husbands helped to legitimize their supposed paternal firm-but-necessary control of the city in a way that readers could respond to. It also helped to consolidate whiteness around police officers of many ethnicities by uniting them under a shared banner of productive masculinity and patriarchal responsibility. Simultaneously, the WCTU asked Americans whether they would rather have an abusive, corrupt father or a benevolent mother preside over punishment in cities. Both claims conjured the daily negotiations of power in American homes and were intended to resonate with readers and listeners.[38]

The Lexow Commission

After two years of campaigning to reform the NYPD, Parkhurst, the WCTU, the Society for the Prevention of Crime, and other Anglo-Protestant organizations and outspoken activists, got their wish. On January 29, 1894,

Clarence Lexow, a member of the New York State Senate announced an investigation into the corruption of the New York City Police Department. It called for an exploration of the charges that "grave abuses exist in said department; that in said city the laws for the suppression of crime and municipal ordinances and regulations duly enacted for the peace, security, and police of said city are not strictly enforced by said Department." Among the other charges falling within the investigation's parameters were partiality and favoritism between patrolmen and citizens, patrolmen paying for promotions or lucrative postings, the extortion of legal businesses and citizens, blackmail, and gambling, as well as enough brutality to "engender bitterness and hatred in the minds of multitudes." Lexow's was one of a number of state-level panels, including the Mazet and Curran commissions, to investigate corruption in the New York City municipal government and police department from 1894 to 1900.[39]

The investigation began on March 9, 1894, and lasted until January 1895. It heard the testimony of dozens of city residents who had been victims of police extortion and brutality, reformers, and police ranging from low-level patrolmen all the way up to Alexander "Clubber" Williams, by then serving as the inspector of the police department, the highest-ranking position on the force that did not require a political appointment. Williams's testimony would without a doubt confirm to the state Senate and well-to-do New Yorkers that the police department under Tammany was guilty of graft and brutality in all their enumerated forms.

When questioners speculated that Williams had refused to shut down eighty-three "houses of ill-fame" in his precinct because the owners had bribed him, Williams countered that he neglected his duty not for money, but because the houses were "fashionable."[40] Later, despite Williams's swearing that he had "never touched a dollar" outside of his police salary, investigators were curious as to how he could afford multiple properties, including a house in the fashionable suburb of Cos Cob, Connecticut, and a yacht that often employed up to eight crew members for races. His answer: Stocks and six to eight lots in Japan, a country he had become familiar with during his time as a young ship carpenter. The opposing attorney retorted, "The consul of Japan informs me that at the time it was impossible for a foreigner to hold a title there." For reformers in the audience, Williams's brazen and antagonistic attitude, exemplified on the witness stand as well as on the street, must have seemed like an appropriate final gesture for a style of policing they were determined to leave in the nineteenth century.[41]

Even more damning was the cooperative testimony of Captain Maximillian Schmittberger, a German immigrant and Williams's right-hand man during his lucrative deployment in the Tenderloin. Schmittberger, in his position under Williams and afterward as captain of the Broadway and Steamboat squads, earned a reputation almost as infamous as that of Williams. His decision to appear multiple times before the committee as a star witness earned him the scorn of Tammany, and most likely allowed him to continue in the department after the Republican victory in the mayoral election of 1894. Among the suspicions Schmittberger confirmed for the committee was the claim that patrolmen and sergeants regularly paid superiors for promotions. In 1887, he testified, he was offered a promotion in exchange for $6,000, an offer he allegedly declined. This system worked both ways. Schmittberger also confessed to paying an assemblyman $10,000 to prevent a rival from being promoted to captain. Schmittberger's place as both a police captain and as a Bavarian-born immigrant served to strengthen arguments relating immigrants to corruption. His role as a key witness in the investigation, however, pointed toward future redemption. If vice-ridden Schmittberger, a pillar of the old police department, could become a productive and honest member of civic society, there might be hope in the future for a police force in which many ethnicities could be consolidated under the banner of whiteness against less assimilable communities.[42]

While he acted as a cooperating witness, Schmittberger's wrongdoings were also aired. In the course of examination, Augustin F. Forget, an employee of the French Line Steamship Company who worked frequently on the West Side docks, disclosed bribes adding up to $500 that Schmittberger demanded during his tenure as captain of the Steamboat squad. As part of the well-entrenched extortion system, Schmittberger and other police officers demanded fees from businesses to provide special protection.[43] Schmittberger, in league with other precinct captains around the city known as "policy kings," also facilitated the thriving "policy" business. In this endeavor, up to six hundred locations around the city ran illegal lotteries that depended on numbers being drawn as far away as Kentucky before being telegraphed back to New York in code. According to one testimony, it was impossible to open a policy shop in the city without "sanction" of the local police, who usually charged bribes of up to fifteen dollars per shop.[44]

The ultimate findings of the investigation were devastating to the credibility of Tammany rule, and mostly unsurprising to working-class residents of the city. In their conclusions, the committee of state senators confirmed what many had learned the hard way, "that the police formed a separate and highly privileged class, armed with the authority and the machinery for oppression and punishment, but practically free themselves from the operation of criminal law."[45] That May, just four months after the conclusion of the Lexow Committee, Alexander "Clubber" Williams, the man who "never walked away from a fight," retired from the police force with a pension of $1,750 a year.[46] Three days after Williams's announcement, Thomas Byrnes, the chief of police and famed detective, stepped down.[47]

As perhaps the highest-ranking Irish immigrant in the city, Byrnes became known as an innovator in the field of investigations and was regarded as a bit of a celebrity because he popularized modern investigatory tactics. In 1886 he published *Professional Criminals of America*, a book version of a "Rogues' Gallery," the primary tool for identifying repeat offenders at the time. Until the publication of this landmark tome, cooperation between police departments was particularly cumbersome. If a detective in Cincinnati believed an arrested man had also committed crimes in New York, he had to describe the man in a letter, or visit New York's Rogues' Gallery, customarily a large wall or cabinet filled with photographs of arrested offenders. Byrnes's book contained images, pseudonyms, as well as personal and criminal histories of hundreds of criminals from around the United States so that police and civilians in other cities could use it to cross-reference suspicious persons. His innovations in detective work and to policing more broadly made the trauma of losing the American Sherlock Holmes all the more jarring for New York's police. It was also made clear what type of Irish American upward mobility could occur in a city dominated by Anglo-New Yorkers. Whiteness and the mobility that came with it were accessible, but only for those who played by the rules.[48]

Theodore Roosevelt and the Racial Hierarchy of Good Policing

The election of 1894, bookended by the shocking revelations and daily headlines from the Lexow Committee investigation, all but assured that a reform Republican would take the mayor's mansion for the first time since 1874. "There has been elected to the Mayoralty," wrote Parkhurst after the election, "a man with a clean record, and one who did not purchase his election by mortgaging his administration either to any party or to any individual aspirants."[49] Elected on an explicitly anti-Tammany ticket, Col. William Strong, a longtime businessman and acting president of Central National Bank, quickly began filling his government with anti-Tammany Democrats and Republicans dedicated to reform.[50] With so much attention on the police department, however, Strong found it hard to find well-suited appointees to the Police Board of Commissioners. Only three days after being sworn in, and in a flurry of continuing Lexow Committee headlines, rumors began swirling around New York City that prominent reformer and the United States Civil Service Commissioner Theodore Roosevelt would be appointed to the board. "Supremely Absurd," Mayor Strong told the *New York Times* on January 4, 1895, when asked about a Roosevelt appointment.[51] As the spring wore on and the "purge" of officials hindering reform continued, Strong could rarely keep police commissioners for more than a few weeks.[52] Finally, on April 1, 1895, the press announced that he had sent a letter to Washington, DC, asking the thirty-seven-year-old Roosevelt to accept the post of New York City police commissioner.

Roosevelt was no stranger to the city's politics. A wealthy New York City native descended from residents of the original Dutch colony, the Republican Roosevelt served three terms in the state legislature before launching a failed mayoral campaign in 1886. From 1889 until accepting Strong's offer on April 24, 1895, Roosevelt served as the US Civil Service Commissioner, where he attempted to curtail the use of federal government jobs as spoils of patronage. This position, in conjunction with his Good Government reputation in New York State, made him an ideal candidate to carry out the new mayoral administration's reformist agenda.[53]

As a police commissioner, Roosevelt was renowned and reviled for his zealous preoccupation with police professionalism and his unapologetic insistence on the enforcement of blue laws that restricted the sale and consumption of alcohol on Sundays. On a number of occasions, Roosevelt made headlines by walking home from social clubs late at night and sneaking up on sleeping patrolmen or those who were distracted on the job.[54] Police were so frightened that he might be lurking around the corner that some political cartoons of the era depicted patrolmen too frightened to walk down Roosevelt Street near the foot of the Brooklyn Bridge.[55] Juxtaposed with the department under Tammany's selective enforcement of alcohol-related laws, Roosevelt's methods seemed fanatical. In one instance, the press joked that the "man-hunting" Roosevelt's latest "drag net" had arrested an iceman who sold five cents worth of ice to a small girl.[56]

Concerns were also raised that stricter policing of leisure spaces like saloons and beer halls would jeopardize the strides being made by a new generation of women asserting a more active presence in the homosocial masculine world of city nightlife. One political cartoon depicted Roosevelt's overzealous policing of blue laws burning the "New Woman" at the stake.[57] There was also no shortage in the Tammany-sympathetic press of scathing characterizations of Roosevelt as an opportunist and press hound. "Police Commissioner Roosevelt Lectured at Princeton Last Night on 'An Object Lesson in Municipal Reform,'" one Tammany blurb read. "He was the object."[58] Despite the mounting changes Roosevelt made in enforcement procedures, the department's evolution was hindered by the many holdovers from the Tammany era it employed from top to bottom.

While crafting a directive for the NYPD that drastically differed from that of the department under Tammany, Roosevelt still could not escape the political and racial tensions that were deeply embedded in the huge organization he had inherited. Less than a year after assuming the position, Roosevelt was still fielding reformist concerns about the overwhelming Irish-Catholic and Democratic makeup of the rank-and-file police. After one local attorney suggested that the only way to reform the police force was to remove all the "drunken Roman Catholics," Roosevelt was able to assert his belief in meritocracy and civil service. "If you know anything whatever about the Police," he responded, "you would know that some of the best men in the Department, and some of the worst men also, are to be found in the ranks of every creed. Anything more wicked as well as more silly than the proposal you apparently endorse to discriminate against men because they happen to be Roman Catholics would be difficult to imagine." Roosevelt attempted to move beyond the narrower and more biased version of reform sought by Parkhurst and other Good Government Protestants. Roosevelt advocated for a multiethnic meritocracy united under a banner of white masculinity and an aspirational Americanness, in which good policing could be practiced by white men regardless of ethnicity—although some groups would have to work harder than others to achieve it.[59]

Despite Roosevelt's policies, the Lexow Committee's findings, and the brief overthrow of Tammany had inspired an even deeper feeling of resentment among the Protestant upper classes toward the disproportionately Irish police department. During his tenure as commissioner, Roosevelt was forced to defend Irish officers on a number of occasions after English travelers visiting New York claimed Irish officers had failed to protect or had harassed them because of deep-seated Irish animosities toward the English. In one instance, the Duke of Marlborough was arrested for driving too quickly and claimed the arrest had been motivated by prejudice. After troublemakers pelted a well-known English tennis player with snowballs, Roosevelt had to explain to the British consul general that there was no evidence to support her claim of racially motivated police neglect.[60] In these instances, Roosevelt was able to act on his deeply held belief that all white men, regardless of background, should be allowed to prove their mettle on the police force.

Roosevelt's understanding of how race and manliness interacted often complicated his investment in a white man's ability to self-fashion and made clear the stark limits to which men were so able. In a Rooseveltian meritocracy, proximity to whiteness determined how much time and work would be required for a man to refashion himself into the ideal masculine archetype: the American man. Gail Bederman has described how his beliefs, informed by the conquest of the West and the violent domination of American Indians, meant that "American men must struggle to retain their racial innate masculine strength, which had originally been forged in battle with the savage Indians on the frontier; otherwise the race would backslide into over civilized decadence."[61]

For Roosevelt, American men, as the epitome of toughness and masculinity, were required to engage in controlled "savagery" through war and conquest in order to keep their racial edge. While nonwhite nations were the grindstone on which white men could hone their masculinity, colonized subjects were denied access to the same process of masculine self-making. Immigrant and immigrant-descended patrolmen, fighting side-by-side with American-born police, proved to be the perfect test of Roosevelt's gendered racial theory. In a city that was also flourishing with Black boxers and prize-fighters, the exclusion of African Americans from the police force denied them access to jobs where violence was legitimate and respectable. For the time being, their pugilism was relegated to the world of "disreputable leisure rather [than] respectable labor."[62]

Like Tammany commissioners before him, Roosevelt believed the primary test of a policeman's ability was his aptitude for fighting, but unlike his predecessors, Roosevelt articulated this view with scientific and ethnographic discourse. By the time of his tenure with the NYPD, the police force's population was almost as diverse as the city it patrolled, yet within that racial diversity was an embodied hierarchy of ability. "I cannot on any philosophical ground explain why the average Irishman certainly makes a better policeman in an emergency than the average German" wrote Roosevelt in an 1896 letter, "but it certainly does seem to take a generation to make the German, in point of fighting capacity, come to the Irish or native American."[63] Although Roosevelt harbored some fear that although the native American stock, especially in

New England, faced bodily degeneration and declining birth rates, they still made up the most consistently skilled racial class of fighters.[64]

"They are, on average, men of superior intelligence to any other class," wrote Roosevelt of native-born Anglo-American police.[65] Close behind them, the Irish tapped into Roosevelt's admiration for ferocity among less developed races. Full of "courage, daring, and alert resolution," Roosevelt proclaimed that no one who had studied the US Civil War could deny the innate ability of the Irish to fight. That most Irish immigrants arrived on US shores already able to speak English was also a major factor in their flourishing in the police department.

Unlike the Irish, Roosevelt argued, Germans were hesitant in times of crisis, but their racial similarities to native Anglo-American police ensured that within a single generation the reluctance to fight would fade. After all, Roosevelt's path to self-made manhood was not always an easy one. "After he has once been knocked down by a gang of toughs and soundly thrashed, or has had some similar mishap befall him, all his troubles are at an end. When he again gets on duty, he is a made man." Despite their perceived racial similarities, even German officers were often considered in conjunction with foreign officers, such as Jews and Italians, because of the language barrier. Like their ability to fight, their language was also a hurdle German officers could overcome by removing themselves from culturally homogenous enclaves like Kleindeutschland. The faster a German officer could become "American," the more quickly his skills as a police officer would improve.[66]

Below these earlier groups of immigrants on Roosevelt's hierarchy of police skill were the newcomers, groups perceived as having more severe racial differences than the similar Anglo-German-Irish police. Jews were, he wrote, "of weak physique, and not yet . . . far enough away from their centuries of oppression and degradation to make good policemen." Likewise, the only Greek officer "horrified some of his fellow officers, notably those of Irish birth" for his bluntness in pointing out his comrades' faults.[67] While ethnic diversity within station houses rarely led to conflict, concern that Greeks would jeopardize harmony in the ranks suggests the emergence in the late nineteenth century of a proto-"blue line," a camaraderie among police officers that above all else required unconditional backing and silence. This bond, formed by shared identity, social positioning, and a commitment to helping fellow officers avoid reprimand, emerged slowly as Irish officers routinely chose to back other police over their kin during times of urban disorder and rioting. This meant officers had mixed feelings as both Byrnes and Clubber Williams were brought down, in part by the testimony of other officers, because that testimony could easily be understood as a violation of multiethnic police solidarity. Roosevelt's metric of police homogeneity and Americanization among immigrant officers was in many ways bolstered and enforced by this sense of shared responsibility, identity, and camaraderie.

By the end of Roosevelt's tenure as president of the Board of Police Commissioners in 1897, the procedures for becoming a police officer looked quite different than they had in 1894. The department made physical and mental exams more competitive and rigorous. In keeping with Roosevelt's hierarchy of racial skill, these enhanced tests seemed intended to prevent immigrant police from weakening the force. The reformed civil service examinations had their intended effect by facilitating the appointment of a large number of Anglo-American officers. "The uplifting of the force was very noticeable, both physically and mentally," Roosevelt wrote. "One noticeable feature of the work was that we greatly raised the proportion of native born, until, of the last hundred appointed, ninety-four per cent were Americans by birth."[68]

The new reforms created a self-affirming loop. Because good policing was defined by the operations of Anglo-Irish police, the exams tested for skills perceived to be unique to native English speakers. Therefore, between 1895 and the first few years of the twentieth century, the department appointed disproportionately more Anglo-Irish men to the force. In favoring these groups, defined for half a century as being the best fighters, Roosevelt had no doubt that he was leaving the majority Anglo-Irish police department more capable of policing New York than it had been three years earlier.

Under Roosevelt, scientific discourse, Progressive fascination with categorization and management, and early eugenic thought became crucial tools for governing a multiracial police department. This scholarship dictated that the bodies of Germans were more comparable and familiar to Anglo-Americans than Italian, Jewish, or Greek bodies. That dictated who was deemed most effective at navigating and subordinating the Anglo-Irish-dominated city.

By the late 1890s, scientists in the United States were contributing to the more sophisticated taxonomy of European races being developed around the Atlantic world. Chief among these thinkers was William Z. Ripley, a professor of sociology at the Massachusetts Institute of Technology and a lecturer at Columbia University. In addition to original research, his 1899 foundational text *The Races of Europe* synthesized and distilled decades of scientific scholarship for an English-reading audience, with a bibliography of works in close to a dozen languages from the fields of physical geography; historical, cultural, and racial anthropology; sociology; ethnology; and evolutionary biology.[69] This towering text provided compelling evidence that at least a substantial portion of the scientific community, using the legitimizing discourse of data collection and experimentation, confirmed and supported Roosevelt's racial hierarchy of policing ability.

"Race," wrote Ripley, "is responsible only for those peculiarities, mental or bodily, which are transmitted with constancy along the lines of direct physical descent from father to son." Although Ripley was a firm believer in the environment's ability to shape the mind and body of an individual, hereditary racial attributes could account for embodied characteristics traced through generations without regard for geography.[70] Data collected in armies across the continent of Europe and in the United States suggested to Ripley that stature, chief among Roosevelt's markers of fighting ability, was a ready example of concrete racial difference. Anglo, German, and Irish men were much larger than other immigrant men. Anglo men, he argued, were even known to heal from wounds faster than men from other European races.

Specifically pondering racial division as applied to immigrants' work in the United States, Ripley wrote that "workers in iron, porters, firemen, policemen, are taller as a class than the average, because they are of necessity recruited from the more robust portion of the population." Here, Ripley reinforced the justification for Roosevelt's appointment of more Anglo-Irish police. These new immigrants, Jews, Italians, and other Eastern and Southern European racialized nationalities, were smaller in stature, weaker in constitution, and thus more fit for work like "tailors, shoemakers, and weavers." Historian Daniel Bender has written convincingly of the toll that squalid living conditions and backbreaking labor in the garment industry took on immigrant bodies, ultimately reinforcing notions about small-statured and weak immigrants, especially Jews.[71]

Not only was size a decisive factor in distinguishing between earlier generations of immigrants, the Germans and Irish, and those who came after, but height also seemed to be a product of immigrating to America in the first place. These "natural immigrants," as Ripley called them, came out of a spirit of adventure not "because they were over persuaded by steamship agents . . . or because of the desire of their home governments to be rid of them—in those days investigation revealed that on the average the immigrants were physically taller than the people from whom they sprang."[72] In the eyes of police officials, differences in stature also served as markers of a mental and physical ability to police properly. During his testimony before the Lexow Committee,

Max Schmittberger was asked about the growing diversity of people on the police force. "Can you give us an idea," asked the questioner, "whether or not the class of men appointed upon the police force during the past 10 years, from 1884 to 1894, is an improvement upon the class of men appointed to the force from 1874 to 1884?" Schmittberger's response was "No." The new generation of officers, now coming more consistently from New York's Jews, Italians, and other Southern and Eastern European immigrants, were not as "strong, and able, and intelligent," as the older generation.[73]

Although never explicitly stated as a motive for Roosevelt's civil service reforms, bias against new immigrants manifested at all levels of the department from recruitment to promotion. Under these new reforms, a commanding officer needed to answer eleven multipart questions about the candidate's work habits and personal characteristics when he applied for a promotion within the department. Answering questions like "What is his character as to Fidelity? Promptitude? Coolness? Judgment?" and "What are his habits as to the use of liquor?" required a commanding officer to have a close personal knowledge of his underlings and answers could easily be skewed by ethnic stereotypes about temper, passion, and alcohol consumption. Men were marked on a scale from "not good" to "excellent," which could lead to further complications. In a 1901 report from the municipal civil service commission to the mayor's office, members worried that, "It is evident that 23 men were marked as 'Excellent' because the police board wished to promote them" and that these promotions often followed the lines of political party. This new system allowed the ranks of captains and inspectors to be almost entirely inhabited by old-stock immigrants, whose biases then affected the makeup of the department.[74]

It is also important to note that during this period of professionalization in the years of Roosevelt's tenure with the NYPD, the department exploded in size. The department remained fairly consistent in size throughout the 1890s, with 3,825 employees in 1895, a vast majority of whom (3,310) were uniformed patrolmen. This was an actually slight decrease from its size of 3,859 employees the previous year. But by 1904, the size of the department had nearly doubled, with a force of 8,269 employees, 6,776 of whom were uniformed patrolmen. Arrests grew proportionately with the number of officers patrolling the streets. Citywide arrests went from 74,315 in 1885 to 112,997 in 1895, to a staggering 175,880 in 1904, and continued to grow until hitting a peak, 244,822 arrests in the year 1908—at which point the NYPD employed 10,064 people, including 8,439 patrolmen.[75]

Although science seemed to be on his side, Roosevelt's reforms in recruiting did not anticipate that the nature of good policing itself would change. His assumption that enshrining a native English-speaking majority on the force would ensure a competent police department was ultimately wrong. In designing a police force that predominantly accommodated native English speakers and encouraged immigrant and immigrant-descended police to throw off their foreignness as quickly as possible, Roosevelt created a department designed to fight and contain the citizens, but not to understand them. In the years that followed Roosevelt's departure to become assistant secretary of the navy, NYPD officers and commissioners struggled to learn new ways of policing that accounted for growing cultural and language divides. In 1897, a linguistically diverse population was seen as a hindrance to creating a cohesive department with uniform abilities, but by 1904, it was clearly a necessity for controlling an increasingly heterogeneous New York.

COLONIAL
METHODS

3

Francis Vinton Greene's
Journey from Empire
to Policing the Empire City

In 1899, General Francis Vinton Greene, future NYPD commissioner and a recently returned commander of five thousand men in the Philippines and Cuba, addressed the Church Club of Providence, Rhode Island, as part of his new foray into Republican politics. Speaking to the crowded hall, he stressed the importance of the Catholic Church in pacifying and uplifting the resistant Filipinos. "I also believe," he said, "that in governing these distant and foreign races we shall evolve a system different from any which has hitherto existed, and more beneficent to the native." This rule would supposedly be distinct from the more draconian colonial practices of the Dutch, French, Spanish, and British in its focus on incentives and coercion. He hoped to instill within the diverse peoples of the Philippines the values of liberal democratic citizenship and civic and religious obligation. "Order must of course first be restored, and this can only be done by the strong arm of the military power," he added, "but as soon as order is established, civilization and education to understanding of what civilization, freedom and liberty mean must follow." If the proponents of a United States model of imperialism vocally advocated for civic, religious, and economic uplift, it was always done with an implicit and explicit threat of military violence.[1]

During the years of occupation, from 1898 until Filipino independence after the Second World War, the US military drew on age-old tactics, omnipresent in French and British colonies, of recruiting and socially uplifting indigenous informants and soldiers in an attempt to render foreign subjects more vulnerable to control.[2] As the US military attempted to harness Filipino collaborators' familiarity with their own country, military governors also prescribed civic reforms that aimed to remake Filipino society in a way that was more comprehensible to US soldiers. The legacies of these "new" strategies of pacification were far-reaching both in the distant locales of the US Empire and at home. When officers, soldiers, and bureaucrats returned to the urban centers of the United States in the midst of a massive wave of immigration, they found police departments struggling with problems almost identical to those they had faced while attempting to pacify the diverse, multilingual, and densely populated archipelago. New York, like the Philippines, had to be remade and its people made more legible before the state could claim total control. "It would have been difficult [otherwise]" continued Greene in 1899, "to have governed a race so alien to us in training, surroundings and habit of thought." This process was part of a larger imperial circuit, in which information traveled from the homeland to the empire and back again—what other scholars have referred to as "imperial feedback."[3]

Not only did tactics and soldiers make their way back from the empire as part "imperial feedback," but so did distinctly colonial ways of understanding race. Early militarization of the police included more than just introducing larger weaponry, khaki uniforms, or counterinsurgency tactics in domestic urban policing. It also meant reframing the police-policed dynamics. Well within the boundaries of the United States, interactions between the state and racial others, including subjects from the Philippines and other colonies, similarly came to reflect a "colonizer" and "colonized" relationship. There were those in US cities, like Europeanized urban Filipinos, who politicians and bureaucrats believed would eventually be compatible with the American way of life. These people, predominantly white European immigrants, could be coerced and conditioned into becoming useful and productive citizens. But there were others, like the Muslim populations in the southern islands of the Philippine archipelago or African Americans residing on US soil, whom authorities dismissed as unassimilable and thus subject, almost exclusively, to pacification by force. The continuity of violence and the circuit of racial governance is one reason why racial comparison and metaphors abounded among US soldiers and politicians who compared Filipino subjects to Native

Americans, African Americans, and even a larger multiethnic and global cohort of anti-imperialist revolutionaries, anarchists, and radicals.[4]

The US Empire remade race in the metropole to resemble colonial relations, complete with a sense of unfamiliarity, illegibility, and the overwhelming pull of the state to exert control over all populations within its boundaries, no matter their perceived difference.[5] For the next decade, police administrators, in New York and across the country, increasingly saw their cities' residents as existing on a spectrum of racial and cultural difference, and as a result, enacted policies that mirrored colonial methods of law enforcement. Even groups like Germans, who had been in New York for decades and thrived inside the police department, suddenly triggered a seemingly newfound insecurity among police commissioners over their inability to communicate with English-speaking police. According to the colonial imperative to surveil and to subordinate, speaking German in front of a police officer who spoke only English now posed a potential threat to the prevailing order. As more and more of the city seemed foreign to American-born New York officers, more and more of it seemed uncontrollable, and the tactics for subordinating multilingual New York came from abroad. For the better part of three decades after 1898, experience in the US colonies—whether with military, colonial governance, businesses, or a mixture of the three—became a prerequisite for knowing how to police a modern multiracial global city. The need for police to navigate racial and ethnic difference left a lasting imprint on the shape and functions of the American police department—but in their attempts to understand and police New Yorkers they deemed foreign or different, police also rhetorically, legally, and politically shaped the contours of race in America.[6]

Immigration to the United States from Southern and Eastern Europe hit its all-time high in the years between 1900 and 1915, with more than forty million individuals settling in industrial centers across the United States.[7] During this period the previous model of good policing, which relied heavily on the embodied traits of native English-speaking Anglo-Irish officers, began to show cracks. Beginning under Francis Vinton Greene's one-year tenure as police commissioner between January 1, 1903, and January 1, 1904, the police force commanded by the army general fresh from the Philippines and Cuba began to rely more heavily on a style of policing that required inside knowledge.

Greene's tenure at the police department, as well as that of his successor, William McAdoo, represent a brief turning point in the history of policing New York City, marking a shift away from valuing a policeman's ability to embody Theodore Roosevelt's notions of American or Americanized manliness toward a reliance on immigrant officers for the skills imparted by their foreignness. Although the eventual importation of European models of policing would overturn any regime that relied on skills brought into the job, be it fighting or linguistics, in favor of skills that could be classroom taught, the years that the NYPD actively deployed immigrant officers illustrates how policing became an engine of race-making in New York just as it was in overseas colonies.

Francis Vinton Greene

The man who initiated much of this transformation epitomized the Anglo-American heritage celebrated by many white native-born Americans at the turn of the last century. Francis Vinton Greene was born in Providence, Rhode Island on July 27, 1850, and grew to be one of the many forgotten architects and intellectual contributors to the project of modern policing, colonial governance, and the places where they overlap. His father, George Sears Greene, from a wealthy family with roots in Rhode Island and New England dating back to the colonial period, was a second cousin of the Revolutionary War general Nathanael Greene as well as a civil engineer and West Point graduate. In 1861, at the age of 61, George Greene was recommissioned as an officer in the US Army, eventually rising to the rank of brigadier general and playing a crucial role in two of the bloodiest battles of the Civil War: Antietam and Gettysburg. Having been born into a military dynasty, Francis Greene was sent to West Point, where he graduated in 1870.

Greene spent his first ten years out of West Point in various military posts and working as a civil engineer assisting in the expansion of US imperial ambitions. In 1874, as tensions rose between the invading army and the Lakota Sioux in the Montana, Dakota, and Wyoming territories, the army sent Greene to the Pacific Northwest with a detachment to mark and map the border between the United States and Canada. In 1877, after almost four years of mapping the boundaries of the expanding nation, the army sent Greene to Saint Petersburg to serve as an emissary of the US Army to the Russian imperial military. There he found himself a foreign observer on the frontlines of the Russo-Turkish War (1877–78) as two armies, one led by plumed aristocratic officers and the other, in his words, "500 years behind in the race of civilization," clashed at the eastern edge of the Ottoman Empire.[8]

Greene's letters from the front to Gen. William Tecumseh Sherman and Maj. Gen. Emory Upton relayed detailed descriptions of military tactics and munitions with a sense of urgency—he believed that the lessons he gleaned from the modern Russian army might be helpful to his home nation in future conflicts. As he observed the latest in European warfare, however, news from home in the form of letters and newspapers made the type of open-field fighting he witnessed, or that his pen pals had seen in the Civil War, seem further and further removed from the actuality of violence at home. "The riots have quieted down," wrote Major General Upton from Fort Monroe, Virginia, on August 18, 1877, "but four of our five companies are still in Pennsylvania and Maryland."[9] Only a month earlier, one hundred thousand workers in multiple states went on strike for higher wages and were confronted by federal soldiers in what was later dubbed the Great Railroad Strike of 1877.[10] Likewise Sherman, writing after a trip out West, told Greene that "Indians are now frozen up and quiet but as soon as the grass grows we must expect trouble."[11] For Greene, the specter of a "great" war, like the type he witnessed in Russia, coming to America seemed to be disappearing. Upton concurred with Greene that "the proposition that 'bushwhacking,' and Indian fighting with one or two companies do not qualify an officer for the position as general." He worried that in the next generation's war there would be no officer in the army with experience "in action which will not merit the title of skirmish."[12]

Following his time in Russia, where he frequently suffered from bad health, Greene returned home to practice civil engineering in Washington, DC, and New York City. There he published two books on his time in Russia, *The Russian Army and Its Campaigns in Turkey* (1879) and *Sketches of Army Life in Russia* (1880), both of which were hailed as necessary information should the United States find itself at war again.[13] In 1891, after the death of his friend and longtime pen pal William Tecumseh Sherman, Greene went through their old letters in the hopes of compiling an edited and complete volume of Sherman's papers, a project that faltered later that year.[14] In those letters Sherman conveyed valuable advice that followed Greene to the Philippines, Cuba, and back to New York: Use every war as a learning opportunity for the next.[15] "You had the chance to see the actual combats, now let us have the picture of it fresh and accurate enough to profit by its lessons," wrote Sherman in one letter. By the time trouble began between Spain and the United States in the run-up to the 1898 Spanish-American War, Greene was an authority on military tactics, an accomplished author, and a professor of artillery at West Point.[16]

Upton and Greene's prediction that future battles would be little more than skirmishes in comparison to the open-field battles of old seemed to be validated by the "splendid little war" of 1898.[17] During the war, Greene played a central role in the decisive capture of Manila in the Philippines, one of the central theatres of conflict with Spain. His ship arrived in Manila Bay on July 17, 1898. Leading five regiments of infantry, two batteries of field artillery, and fighting in proximity to a detachment of Filipino soldiers eager to win their independence from Spain, he commanded men up the beaches toward the fortified city of Manila.[18] For almost two weeks, the five thousand men under Greene's command camped in a large thicket and fired upon the Spanish defenses, eventually allowing US troops to take the city, seize control of the municipal government, and solidify their refusal to recognize the emerging independent Filipino republic.[19]

On December 10, 1898, after less than eight months of combat and relatively light casualties on the US side, representatives of Spain and the United States met in Paris to end the war and transfer power over imperial possessions in the Caribbean and Pacific. The people who formerly lived under the Spanish yoke would not see self-determination for some time. With the war with Spain ending and a new round of fighting just beginning, this time against advocates for Filipino independence, Greene and the other commanders of the US Army had new problems to solve: counterinsurgency and colonial governance.

Eleven days after Spain's surrender, on December 21, 1898, President William McKinley circulated instructions on how the Philippine archipelago should be governed,

> It should be the earnest and paramount aim of the military administration to win the confidence, respect, and affection of the inhabitants of the Philippines by assuring them in every possible way that full measure of individual rights and liberties which is the heritage of free peoples, and by proving to them that the mission of the United States is one of benevolent assimilation.[20]

As the mechanics of modern liberal governance solidified in settler-colonial and extractive colonial powers in North America and Europe in the nineteenth century, countries often used individual liberties as an incentive to preserve order and to ensure peaceful streets, citizens' willingness to respect the rule of law, and to maintain the legitimacy of their rule. This often meant differentiating between those deserving recipients of liberties, and those racialized colonial subjects deemed unruly and therefore unworthy of the benefits of liberalism.[21] The benevolence within the "benevolent assimilation" model rested upon the ability of the US Army to offer the illusion of liberal citizenship, including individual liberties, while readying an occupying force eager to pacify by violence.

As Greene and US Army commanders understood it, Filipino subjects' ability to receive, comprehend, or utilize this benevolence was intertwined with race and racial characteristics. Subjects of colonial rule in the Philippines existed on a racialized spectrum of compatibility with, and worthiness of, American-controlled democracy as the US Army forced Europeanized northern Filipinos into municipal governments and subjected Muslim and non-Christian southerners to brute force. Between 1898 and 1902, Greene and the rest of the US military government advocated for the Americanization of the diverse Philippine archipelago through education and civic restructuring in what was presented as an act of benevolent uplift, but was also understood as an attempt to render Filipino society more acquiescent to control by US troops.[22]

As soon as the fighting ended in Manila in the late summer of 1898, Greene threw himself into the problem of governing the foreign archipelago. Greene spent his weeks in Manila going into bookshops in the oldest part of the city and collecting "every book he could find bearing upon the history of the Philippines," including studies of Spanish rule, administration, and religion. Even after President McKinley called Greene back to Washington in mid-September 1898, his study continued.[23]

Greene had spent no more than a grand total of eight weeks on the archipelago before traveling home. On the journey back to the United States, he traveled clandestinely with a representative of Emilio Aguinaldo, the de facto political and military leader of a large faction of predominantly working-class Filipinos and the declared president. By the time the pair arrived in Washington, his reading and the weeks of conversation helped Greene to formulate ideas about colonial administration. To the likely objection of his travel companion, the report Greene presented to President McKinley did not recommend self-determination for the Philippines.[24]

Despite its rushed preparation, the report, Greene's shallow knowledge of Filipino society, and his proposals for a future administration there must have impressed the president because on October 11, 1898, he received an order to report to Jacksonville, Florida. His presence was needed in Cuba.[25]

Legibility and Coercive Governance in the Occupied Philippines

It was Greene's contention that the creation and strengthening of benevolent institutions such as schools, hospitals, and municipal governments would prove useful in pacifying residents as well as establishing more familiar social and geographical structures in the territory. The Philippines were plagued, as the US Army saw it, by a lack of structures that were recognizable to American soldiers. "Pueblos" often extended for hundreds of square miles. Barrios, the subdivisions of the pueblos, were recognized by US soldiers as "wards" within an urban neighborhood. However, unlike the clear boundaries between the densely packed wards of New York City, barrios were often located very far apart within the pueblo.[26]

Two general orders given by the army within two years after Greene's report reflected these concerns. GO 43 was issued on August 5, 1899, and GO 40 on March 29, 1900. "For the first time," GO 40 read, "the Philippine people are to exercise the right of suffrage in the election of municipal officers," a right that the US colonial governor had the authority to restrict for the purpose of "rewarding as well as encouraging the people in their just and natural aspirations to become educated, and worthy to enjoy all the benefits of civilization."[27] The development of local governments offered solutions to a number of problems with governance that US military command sought to address. First, it provided the people with an illusion of self-rule, a bribe of liberty in exchange for loyalty and legitimacy. Second, it remade Filipino society in a way that reflected municipal life and local power structures at home in the United States, creating a landscape that US troops and bureaucrats could traverse and survey with more ease.

The civic restructuring of the Philippines came couched in the rhetoric of improvement and undergirded by a threat of violence. But that improvement was also its own form of violence, coercion, and control. On a gauge that measured improvement as Americanization, and Americanization as susceptibility to state power, benevolent state-building served to deepen the power disparity between the military and colonized Filipino subjects. In a report written in Manila and dated August 30, 1898, Greene advocated for what would eventually become GO 43 and GO 40. The "natives might settle down again," he wrote, should they be "conceded" a "simple form of self government in the interior . . . under strict supervision and inspection."[28] By 1900, the military had discovered the utility of these municipal governments. Not only did the orders provide concessions to pacify the seekers of self-rule, they also restructured society in a way that was more susceptible to surveillance. Writing about the success of GO 40, Maj. Gen. Arthur MacArthur wrote that the new structure was, "a conservative system, which, it is thought, gave the necessary impulse and initiative to municipal life and at the same time permitted the necessary inspection by and subordination to, the military authorities."[29] By making citizens accountable to municipal governments, and municipal governments accountable to the military regime, the US Army believed it could create a kind of civic panopticon—a society structured so that residents could be watched by the United States, just as the inmates in Jeremy Bentham's proposed prison could be surveilled from a single watchtower.[30]

Civic and benevolent institutions became one avenue through which the United States could exert control over Filipino subjects in a way that seemed overtly "uncontaminated with business or politics."[31] Proposing "the establishment of schools, of hospitals, of asylums, of missions supported by private funds and managed by men who confine themselves to their legitimate business of spreading the Gospel will be a revelation of a new idea to the natives," Greene hoped that lessons on the values of passivity and assimilation would be regarded with less suspicion if they were disseminated through neutral third parties. In addition to churches, public health institutions like hospitals and asylums similarly promoted understandings of health and healthfulness in keeping with the mission of US domination. Greene felt confident that this process had the potential to make natives *part of the machinery for maintaining order.* In addition to police forces and US-sanctioned violence, the military government in the Philippines hoped the introduction of moralizing and evangelizing public services on the islands would prove effective at developing self-disciplining subjects.[32]

Colonial Policing in the Philippines and Cuba

Shortly after the Treaty of Paris of 1898 and until the army's partial withdrawal in 1902, military and civilian leaders became increasingly aware of the inability of American soldiers to learn Filipino languages, earn the trust of locals, or infiltrate insurgent groups. "Whilst the American soldier is unsurpassed in war," read the report of the Taft Commission to the President of the United States, "he does not make the best policeman, especially among a people whose language and customs are new and strange to him." By 1901, when the secretary of war penned his report, one of the major problems in both municipal law enforcement and counterinsurgency appears to have been the inability of American troops to effectively police Filipino subjects. The secretary proposed a solution: "We therefore earnestly urge the organization of ten regiments of native troops of infantry and cavalry."[33]

Colonial powers recruited natives for the purposes of law enforcement and anti-insurgency for different reasons in different contexts. In some instances, colonialists recruited from within specific ethnic groups in order to create factional divides or to tap into preexisting power structures and animosities. In the British Empire, recruiting native police and soldiers was often seen as an economic matter—an unwillingness on the part of the colonial regime to pay Englishmen to relocate to police the colonies.[34] For this reason, native police were often depicted as wholly unreliable forces with dubious loyalties.[35] Despite the unreliability of indigenous troops and police in various regions of the British Empire, one benefit they offered was their ability to gain access to places, gatherings, and groups that were unreachable or indiscernible to colonizers. Under Spanish rule, local recruits often served the colonial government, but in a role more closely resembling a militia member than a police officer. Reminiscent of the US Army's use of native police on American Indian reservations a decade or two earlier, in the guerrilla war between US troops and Filipino insurgents after 1898, soldiers and police who could speak native languages and retain the trust of community members became invaluable to the colonial government.[36]

In a 1901 report from Manila, Major General MacArthur wrote that the single "greatest obstacle to successful operations here, as elsewhere upon the islands, was the inability of Americans to get reliable information."[37] Distrust of US troops and language barriers as well as the threat of retribution from insurgent community members all hindered the ability of US troops to gather valuable intelligence on the ground. In the one year between 1900 and 1901, however, MacArthur claimed that the implementation of native police had shown incredible results, including being "instrumental in the arrest of numerous insurgents and insurgent aiders and sympathizers in and about the city of Manila."[38]

Especially after General Order 87 officially armed native police after June 18, 1900, the ability of police departments to recruit native officers increased. Perhaps this rise in interest was a way for men to find US-sanctioned reasons to carry a firearm while engaging in an insurgency. Regardless, the ease with which the military could recruit native police was often determined by the community's previous exposure to US governance and the incentives it offered in exchange for subordination. "The co-operation of the inhabitants was obtained, and it became possible to find men among the natives who, as policemen, would be loyal to the government." They were, in the words of one American politician, essential because their "knowledge of the country, language, and the ways of the people make them especially valuable in hunting down ladrones." Natives not only found work as officers but also, as in European empires, as clerks because American bureaucrats would be inefficient, "on account of the expense in salaries, natives being willing to work much cheaper."[39]

Although plenty of people in the military hierarchy were skeptical of the loyalty of native police, that view relied heavily on the ethnicity of the recruits. The perceived capacity for self-rule, assimilation, and loyalty varied radically depending on the inhabitants, racial makeup, and dominant religion of a particular island. "The question as to the best methods of dealing with the non-Christian tribes is one of no little complexity." Both the "Pagan" and "Mohammedan" tribes, which made up a substantial part of the archipelago's population, were often subjected to the most extreme and blatant military force. "These Moros will have to be eventually soundly thrashed," wrote General Leonard Wood in 1906, even as northern Filipinos were given the freedom to elect municipal representatives.[40] Racial scientists and military officers alike saw in the Moro peoples of the southern Philippines a racial and religious proxy for Indigenous North Americans. Not only did many soldiers in the Philippines have lived experience in the violent colonialization of western North America, they also brought with them the same racial logics and pacifying tactics. Even political thinkers, looking to craft policies to subordinate specifically non-Christian populations, revisited and redeployed rules and regulations that had supposedly subordinated the "wild tribes" of the North American West.[41]

Despite having served in the 1898 war, Black soldiers were denied entrance into the recently reorganized police force of Manila. Since the colonization of the American West, African Americans had been called upon to serve as foot soldiers of empire—but to some Black observers back home, denying them the ability to participate in the ongoing project of racial governance and subordination further denied their entrance into national belonging. "That no Afro-American," read one op-ed in the *New York Age*, "occupies any place of honor and responsibility in the government of the Philippines is a standing mark of shame and disgrace to those who would lead the race politically." Although the police departments of many cities in the United States had hired Black officers for decades, New York City, like occupied Manila, continued to deny that post to African American applicants.[42]

Besides the local municipal police, the United States military organized the Philippine constabulary, a centralized nationwide police force responsible for maintaining order in each territory. Based on colonial policing in British colonies, the structure of the constabulary made it a descendant of European-style policing like the French gendarmerie, which answered to national, rather than local, authorities and was deployed to every corner of the nation.[43] One American observer recalled the necessity of filling the Philippine constabulary with Filipinos of different ethnicities and from different regions of the archipelago, presumably as a way of making sure no particular group would prove able to avoid policing and surveillance. "The scouts number fifty companies in all, of which a considerable number are composed of Macabebes, while others consist of Ilocanos, Bicols, Cagayans and Visayans. By far the larger proportion of these scouts are of the Macabebe and Ilocano origin." He continues that "few of these groups . . . are sent away from home and into Visayan or other districts."[44] The replicable and multiethnic constabulary became a primary tool of maintaining the colonial order in the Philippines, as well as in Puerto Rico, the Panama Canal Zone, and later, the United States.[45]

In addition to American distrust of native soldiers and police as secret insurrectionists, men and women on the peninsula also grew to distrust the Philippine constabulary after its members developed a reputation for committing abuses. This both undermined the ability of native troops to effectively gain community trust and gather intelligence and further mobilized dissent against US rule on the archipelago.[46]

In November 1898, as the US Army was using Greene's reports to crystallize its restructuring of Filipino society by Americanizing it and supplanting native and Spanish hierarchies of power, Greene was sailing from Tampa Bay to Havana. In port, Greene received a letter from Secretary of War Russell A. Alger, declaring, "The President directs that you, in addition to your duties of laying out a camp for your Division, for the time being at least, take upon yourself the preliminary work of organizing a police force for the City of Havana."[47] The initial necessity for a Cuban police force came, according to Alger, not from an inability to communicate with or infiltrate the Cuban people, but because American soldiers stationed in Havana were dying at a faster pace from yellow fever than those stationed outside the city. Having police who are "immune to yellow fever," not only prevented US causalities, it also ensured a more consistent police presence in the city. Upon initial justification, it was these men's bodies, rather than their cultural and linguistic knowledge, that made them useful to the colonial project.[48]

In Havana, Greene went about organizing and reforming the municipal government, sanitation and street cleaning crews, and the police. Although well versed in military governance, having seen it both in the western territories as a young man and in the Philippines, Greene until this point had had little experience with law enforcement and day-to-day policing. Luckily, the army provided him with help in the form of a New Yorker with plenty of policing experience. "The organization of the police force ... is proceeding rapidly," wrote Greene in a report, "and it is believed that the force will be organized, uniformed, equipped and ready for service by the first of January," thanks to "expert advisor" John McCullagh, the recently retired superintendent of the NYPD and Theodore Roosevelt's successor.[49]

McCullagh performed the lion's share of the planning, ultimately presenting Greene with the organization of the new Havana Police Department. The layout may have seemed familiar to Greene, as it was reportedly almost identical to the structure of McCullagh's former employer, the NYPD.[50] The new department was broken into precincts that consisted of detectives, sergeants, and patrolmen. In addition to the new structure, long dark blue jackets like those worn by NYPD patrolmen and ill-suited to the tropical climate, police clubs, and revolvers replaced the rifles and military-style uniforms of the Spanish-controlled Havana police.[51]

McCullagh's presence in Cuba, as well as the proposed organization of the Havana Police Department, made visible the New York City Police Department's footprint on the American Empire. McCullagh was not the only former member of the NYPD to make its presence known in the empire. On the beaches of Manila, not far from where Greene's battalions were situated, Alexander S. Williams, son of the infamous NYPD officer Alexander "Clubber" Williams. was injured during an exchange of fire. In 1902, the *New York Times* reported that the old "Czar of the Tenderloin," retired since his brush with the Lexow Committee, was traveling to San Francisco to retrieve his convalescing son.[52] One man from the police steamer patrol, Edward M. Powers, resigned from the police force for good in 1898 when Mayor Van Wyck refused to give him back pay for the months he missed while serving in the US Navy during the war. Although it is hard to determine how many of the more than 125,000 US soldiers who served in the Philippines between 1898 and 1908 came from the ranks of the NYPD, newspapers indicate that many did.[53]

In December 1898, President McKinley offered Greene the position of military governor of Havana after only about a month of work there, an offer that Greene quickly declined. He was anxious to return home to take care of his long-neglected finances and family affairs, and on December 30, 1898, Major General Greene was honorably discharged from the US Army.[54]

"Colonial Feedback" and Returning Soldiers

Greene was one of a generation of men whose entrance into the field coincided with the rise of colonial tactics in the expanding professionalization of law enforcement. According to sociologist Julian Go, of 114 police departments across the United States between 1890 and 1915, at least 40 percent had a police chief with military experience. This certainly became standard practice within the NYPD and the forces of other large cities. August Vollmer, an infantry soldier and son of German immigrants from California, served on the beaches of Manila alongside Greene and his men. On his return to the San Francisco Bay area after the war, Vollmer ran for the position of marshal in Berkeley, California. Within a few years, he became one of the leading police intellectuals behind the expanding role of police departments across the country. Referred to often as the "father of American policing," Vollmer was credited for introducing things he had seen in military combat onto the streets of American cities, including patrol vehicles and other innovations that would eventually eclipse beat cops and call boxes. According to one reporter, Vollmer, "put into effect some of the methods he used in chasing river pirates on the Pasig [River] and bushwhackers in the steaming wild jungles."[55]

In addition to his many scientific and technological innovations in policing, Vollmer went on to champion the creation and expansion of the state police system in the United States. State police departments in the United States are an explicit importation of the centralized constabulary model from European countries, their colonies, and the US Empire. In arguing for the extension of the state police system in 1935, when only a handful of states had such a system, Vollmer cited what he believed were the most successful uses of the centralized constabulary. "In the island-state of Ceylon, south of India is to be found another highly efficient state of police organization. On this island, which has been under British rule for more than a century, England presents a striking example of the use of a unified force to police a large area."[56] Searching for other examples, Vollmer found one in the United States' own empire. "These state police systems of foreign countries," he wrote, "have been taken as a pattern by the United States for the policing of American island possessions, where foreign populations are numerous and where America has found, as has England, that the simple way to police such areas is by the use of one police force for the entire territory."[57] As a colonial innovation believed to be particularly well suited for policing "foreign populations," different forms of the centralized constabulary proliferated in the United States in the years following the creation of the Philippine Constabulary in 1901.

The earliest of those new constabularies was the Pennsylvania State Police. Created in 1905, the centralized and state-based rather than municipally controlled group was immediately put into action against the multiethnic labor unions striking the state's coal and steel industries. Many of the earliest state police departments were formed in states where the growing labor movement was most vocal and active like New York, New Jersey, Oregon, and Michigan.[58]

The organization of the state police force, sneeringly referred to as "the American Cossacks" by strikers and labor organizers in Pennsylvania, was not the only thing about the unit that bore the mark of the US Empire. While voicing their concerns that the military appearance of the state police made strikers feel like colonial subjects, one representative of the American Federation of Labor observed, "Most of these men in the State Constabulary have served for two or three years in the regular army" serving in the Philippines or the Caribbean.[59] The warlike manner with which the state had fought against the laborers convinced them they were fundamentally seen as a population denied their rights as American citizens. By standing in opposition to the colonial constabulary, workers expressed a concern that they were being othered in much the same way as Filipino subjects. Staring down an occupying force of government troops took on new meaning in the years following the occupation of the Philippines, unlike similar strikebreaking work undertaken by private organizations like the Pinkertons.[60]

Anti-imperialist Filipinos understood the same parallels as those Pennsylvania strikers. One circulated propaganda letter found on the island declared that "now is the time to strike a decisive blow of Filipino independence," because in addition to fighting on the archipelago, the United States "in is in the midst of a bloody civil war. The coal miners in Pennsylvania have risen against the government and at Chicago a great battle was fought in which 1600 regular soldiers were killed." Aguinaldo himself told people that Americans had, "robbed the Indians of their lands and homes and had followed them into the forest and hunted them down like wild beasts. They had now come to rob the Filipino in the same way." The history and contemporary US repression of racialized and working-class communities became a valuable tool for recruiting anti-imperialists in the Philippines and the world to their cause.[61]

Centralized police systems were not the only state experiment tested in the colonies and brought back to the metropole. The US military government also concerned itself with health and sanitation in a way that necessitated as much exertion of state power and force as preventing crime. Lieutenant Colonel Hoff in Puerto Rico referred to his manner of preventing disease on the island as distilling itself "down to its simplest form, 'policing.'" In the American colonies, public health advocates who had tried years earlier to develop mandatory vaccination programs in the United States suddenly found themselves with military-backed support. As early as January 27, 1899, the American governor of Puerto Rico, Guy Henry, issued General Order 7, which mandated smallpox vaccinations on the island. Similar programs were created in the Philippines in the following years but constant fighting prevented them from being as successful. In the urban center of Manila, however, over two hundred thousand people were inoculated against smallpox and the city's public health program became a model of how mandatory vaccination could work in the United States. Like many other aspects of civic life, the US military's vaccination programs traveled home from their colonial laboratories to become "a lesson for the world."[62]

The empire also became a place where the United States could continue projects of policing sexuality and enacting gendered subordination, sometimes violently. For a short time sex work in and around military bases in the US Empire—although criticized by reformers as state-sanctioned vice—was heavily surveilled as a way to control venereal disease and subject to police and military intervention. In this way white men could indulge their desires and exercise their claims on the bodies of colonial subjects with women whose innocence was not in need of guarding like that of the white women back home. This policy angered stoics like Theodore Roosevelt and the WCTU for potentially threatening the vitality of American soldiers and having the "potential to encourage miscegenation abroad and contagion at home." These fears eventually traveled the imperial circuit home to result in panic, and resulting policing, over relationships between white women and Filipino men who had traveled to the United States.[63]

Contact between the American state, American soldiers, and the diverse peoples of the Philippines had also remade race and racialization in the United States in ways that affected how the state understood incoming immigrants. To imagine themselves as inheritors of empire-building, American imperialists racialized themselves as a unified "Anglo-Saxon" race, just as they cast Filipinos as a racially fragmented and tribalized people.[64] The Filipinos' racial division supposedly made them incapable of a unified culture and therefore incapable of producing a unified project of nation-building. In New York and other cities across the United States, immigrants settling in insular enclaves were producing the exact same fragmentation imperialists saw as incompatible with liberal state-building. To paraphrase historian Paul Kramer, "ethnological homogeneity," and the liberal states that homogeneity was said to produce, became an evolutionary factor that separated societies seen as savage from those forms recognized as civilized and political.[65] At home, the ideal of the American melting pot required dissolving the heterogeneous population into a unified national body. Settlement houses, English lessons, and coerced Americanization under the watchful eyes of the police all aspired to create self-disciplined and English-speaking Americans whose foreignness could not disrupt the operations of the state.[66]

In the Philippines, guerrilla warfare contributed to US troops' attempts to paint Filipino soldiers as uncivilized and racial inferiors; in the United States, the tactics and weapons of immigrant criminals echoed that racial othering within the same colonial framework.[67] American soldiers often remarked on the "formidable" nature of the large bladed weapons carried by tough-fighting Moro Filipino insurgents, many of which made it back to the United States as plunder. Of these weapons, many were thick-bladed farming tools similar to machetes that US troops took as evidence of the amateurishness and underhandedness of the insurgents.[68] At home, the same colonial discourses of race-making that impacted how the military understood the Moro were put to work racializing immigrant groups, some of whom had been living in New York in large numbers for decades. Of the newly arrived ethnic groups in New York and the United States bullied and stereotyped by the Anglo press, Italians were subjected to some of the worst rhetoric about their supposed brutality. In the period between the 1880s and 1910s, the image of the Italian criminal was inextricable from the image of the stiletto, a thin and very sharp knife developed centuries earlier in Italy. Because the knives were easily concealable, they were interpreted as weapons of cowards and sneaks and often associated with being stabbed in the back. Newspapers in New York carried almost daily graphic descriptions of knife fights between two stiletto-wielding Italian men, or attacks on unsuspecting victims.[69] "The stiletto should be banished," wrote one New York City resident in a note to the *Evening World*. "It has no business in America."[70]

The foreignness of the weapon itself, the surreptitious tactics it evoked, as well as the image of its swarthy foreign wielder, contributed to the understanding of immigrants as less civilized and racially inferior to the

Anglo-Saxon race—and echoed those rhetorical strategies employed against insurgent Filipinos.[71] In both instances, tactics and weaponry as markers of behavior remade race and racial hierarchies in relation to colonial warfare, combat, and an Americanized brand of violence.

Greene's journey from the empire to the police department began in the period after 1899. Upon his return to the United States, Greene traveled the East Coast giving speeches about the situation in the Philippines and recounting his involvement in the siege of Manila during the summer of 1898. In 1900, Greene, now starting a new life in politics, served on the New York Republican County Committee and campaigned across the city for President McKinley and his running mate, Greene's old friend Theodore Roosevelt. The duo's successful national campaign, and McKinley's September 1901 assassination, led to a sweep of Republican victories, including the November 1901 New York City mayor's race. Republican Seth Low, a former mayor of independent Brooklyn and recently retired president of Columbia University, appointed the party loyalist Greene to the top post at the police department one year into his tenure. Greene's predecessor, John Partridge, announced his resignation in early December 1902, citing illness and fatigue.[72] Members of the press suspected that Partridge's timely resignation and Greene's appointment were the product of Greene's close personal friendships with Republican governor Benjamin Odell and President Roosevelt.[73]

As a veteran of the American Empire and a pioneer in the coercive pacification of foreign subjects, Greene soon began to see continuities with his time in the Philippines and Cuba. "I have some clearly defined ideas as to what I shall try to accomplish," wrote Greene to President Roosevelt days after his impending appointment became public knowledge. He wasted no time in attempting to implement those ideas.[74]

Within weeks of being sworn in, Greene dismissed Inspector Nicholas Brooks, the head of the detective bureau. Brooks and his detectives, Greene told the press, had failed to secure evidence, or in some instances gain admittance, to gambling locales around the city. "Owing to their inability to gain admittance to these premises," wrote Greene in a statement, "and their lack of success in forming the acquaintance of persons who might be of assistance to them in this work, their detail was discontinued." He continued that his detectives were fundamentally unqualified to undertake this kind of undercover work because of their "general appearance and lack of knowledge of the ways of the gambling fraternity."[75] Once again, a lack of knowledge and a policeman's inability to blend in with native populations was obstructing Greene's ability to exert control over spaces.

Greene's time abroad in non-English-speaking countries exposed him to lessons that former commissioner Theodore Roosevelt never had to learn: There were some policing problems that Anglo-Irish brawn could not solve. If detectives were having trouble infiltrating gambling dens on the West Side, then it only made sense to send in a gambler. In February 1903, weeks before Brooks's dismissal, Greene wrote to a friend in Indianapolis in search of more viable working-class detectives, men who would be less recognizable to city residents as NYPD coppers. "I also have in my employ a young Irish-American named Frank McCabe," wrote Hugh McGowan to Greene. "He is very youthful in appearance and would never be suspected by any one of being a detective, and yet he has been of the most valuable service to me in ferreting out stealings."[76] This tactic proved useful, not just in gaining access to working-class areas or in infiltrating gambling dens that catered to tourists capable of sniffing out an undercover native New Yorker, but also for penetrating New York's many racial, linguistic, and cultural barriers. Greene spent his year as police commissioner increasingly reliant on Italian detectives to solve crimes in the city's growing Italian enclaves.[77]

"Have We Not a Czar?": The Colonial Subject at Home

Even if New Yorkers were unaware of the arrival of ideas and personnel from the outskirts of the American Empire in their own neighborhoods, some Americans found the treatment of Filipino subjects abroad all too familiar. Critiquing what many in the Black press referred to as "bayonet-imposed civilization," Black anti-imperialists were quick to make comparisons to the mechanisms of racial state-building at home and abroad.[78] "Maybe the Filipinos have caught wind of the way the Indians and negroes have been Christianized and civilized," read one column in the Salt Lake City *Broad Ax*, "and that is the reason they are loathe to surrender their form of government."[79] Despite the technical citizenship guaranteed to Black Americans during Reconstruction under the Fourteenth Amendment to the Constitution, the relationship between colonial subjects and people of African descent living in the United States seemed identical to many.

Facing a state with a growing capacity to racially catalog citizens; mounting Jim Crow laws and formal segregation; as well as federal, state, and local disciplinary systems that not only denied protection to nonwhites but often actively collaborated in legal and extralegal violence, many saw themselves as colonial subjects living inside the United States. As one Black writer noted in the *Illinois Record*, the question of colonization "has agitated the mind of ten million American Negroes, who look with fear and suspicion upon the motives of those most anxious to extend the strong arm of protection around a people not unlike the Negroes of this country, who are even yet denied the liberties of American citizenship." The daily labor done by police to protect white Americans was expected by virtue of their unquestioned citizenship— and was contradictory to how the same police acted in predominantly Black neighborhoods.[80]

In the summer of 1900, headlines about anti-imperialist groups organizing to defeat McKinley in the upcoming presidential election mingled with stories of catastrophic anti-Black violence on the streets of New York. While political groups decried the "perfect orgy of looting and wanton destruction" that occurred in the Philippines, James Weldon Johnson, the famous writer who became the executive secretary of the National Association for the Advancement of Colored People (NAACP) in 1920, later referred to the state and state-sanctioned racist violence that rocked the Black neighborhoods of Manhattan in August 1900 as a "brutish orgy, which if not incited by the police, was, to say the least, abetted by them."[81]

At around 2 a.m. on August 13, 1900, Arthur Harris, a Black man out to dinner with his common-law wife, Mary Enoch, stabbed and killed Robert J. Thorpe, an undercover police officer, on the corner of West Forty-First Street and Eighth Avenue. Thorpe had seen Enoch standing on the sidewalk while her husband ducked into a store to buy a cigar, and believed her to be a prostitute soliciting clients. It has been well documented that Black and other nonwhite women out in public in New York often suffered the consequences of the common stereotyping that depicted them as sexually deviant and criminal. These women, even those who conformed to middle-class notions of dress and respectability, were often denied the presumption of innocence afforded to white urbanites. They were therefore routinely arrested, assaulted, or hassled by police in the belief that their very presence on the street was synonymous with moral deficiency, indecency, and disorder. When Harris saw Thorpe, a white man in plainclothes who did not clearly present himself as a police officer, assaulting his wife, he stepped in to defend her.[82]

The incident, and Thorpe's death, resulted in multiple nights of chaos and violence as police and other Anglo-Irish residents in the multiracial neighborhood of the Tenderloin unleashed a torrent of brutality against Black people on the street. Dutch-born police officer Cornelius Willemse, a long-time veteran of the NYPD, described the riot as "the fiercest mass battle I have ever known."[83] Although African Americans were the target of violence perpetrated by civilians and the police, African Americans were arrested for attempting to flee or defend themselves. A reporter for the *New York Times* observed that "every car passing up or down Eighth Avenue between the hours of 8 and 11 was stopped by the crowd." Every Black passenger found in a vehicle was dragged out and "beaten until he was able to break away" from the white mob looking to get revenge for the police officer's death. The *Times* reporter was particularly struck by the NYPD's lack of interest in reining in the chaos. "The police contented themselves with trying to protect the negroes," wrote the reporter, "and it was remarked by witnesses of the riot that they made little or no attempt to arrest any of their assailants."[84] But most eyewitness accounts from African Americans disputed the notion the police were doing any protecting of Black targets of the rioters. In addition to neglecting to protect African Americas, police reportedly failed to arrest white assailants and even participated in the violence against Black New Yorkers. The chief of police himself eventually admitted that his officers had been too rough with innocent bystanders.[85]

On August 15, Chief William Devery was compelled to address the charges of brutality in a public statement. "I will watch this thing closely this morning and if any man in a police uniform does anything more than enforce the law he will be dismissed instantly. This has been an unfortunate outbreak, but it won't happen again." The statement shocked the members of the press, who saw it as an admission of guilt. "This would seem to indicate," wrote a reporter for the *Associated Press*, "that Chief Devery believes that police, having Thorpe's death in mind, were a little too zealous against the blacks."[86] Coming from Chief Devery and the white press, this seemed like an unexpected acknowledgment that police in the Tenderloin did not protect African Americans from criminals, as they would have done for white people, or act as the agents of a system that sought to reform, rather than punish, criminal behavior. Instead, police represented a purely punitive force that was allowed to exercise state violence on Black residents as long it did not become "a little too zealous."

On September 3, a group of Black and white lawyers, physicians, businessmen, community leaders, and clergy gathered at St. Mark's Church on West Fifty-Third Street and Eighth Avenue, just a few blocks from the epicenter of the previous month's violence, to organize the Citizens' Protective League.[87]

In addition to publishing *The Story of the Riot*, a pamphlet containing the firsthand testimony of victims of racial violence, the group's efforts culminated in a mass meeting that took place in Carnegie Hall the following week. With over 3,500 people in attendance, and speeches from notable members of the League, the group collected donations of over $1,000 and disclosed plans to see that justice was done and that police and civilians who had spent the better part of a week traumatizing and assaulting Black residents of the Tenderloin were punished.[88]

Imperialism also took front stage at the event. "This talk I hear about imperialism strikes me as humorous," one speaker remarked. "Some of our countrymen seem to have more concern for the brown men on the other side of the world than they have for the negro at home. Does not imperialism flourish in New York? Have we not a Czar?"[89] Although conjuring a Russian czar as the ultimate imperial boogeyman, the speaker differentiated African Americans from other colonial subjects, namely Filipinos—"brown men on the other side of the world"—as being more deserving of immediate action to cast off the colonialist yoke.

In addition to accountability for the police and an acknowledgment of their behavior, many prominent speakers involved in the movement against police brutality settled on a new goal: Black officers in the New York City Police Department. It would take over a decade after the riot of 1900 for the NYPD to appoint its first Black officer. Meanwhile, the conversations on the street and behind the closed doors of the commissioner's office were very different. Overseas, US attempts to subordinate the multiethnic Philippine archipelago seemed to necessitate the use of native informants even while African Americans were denied entrance into the colonial police forces—or New York's. Linguistic and cultural differences between police and residents apparent on the streets of predominantly immigrant neighborhoods necessitated that the department diversify. A generation earlier, police administrators regarded the Irish with suspicion because of their presumed racial characteristics. Now, finding officers who could make foreign subjects understandable to the state became an increasing necessity. Their foreignness was their value and not a liability—and the supposed familiarity of African Americans allowed police administrators to resist integration for many more years.

THE RISE OF ETHNIC POLICING

4

Warren Charles,
Cornelius Willemse,
and the German Squad

One of the biggest challenges for the NYPD, especially in the years following
the turn of the twentieth century, was policing the newcomer immigrants
settling throughout Downtown Manhattan. These communities became sites
where the NYPD eagerly attempted to recruit informants, and eventually, officers as a way to make up for the existing department's lack of language skills
or cultural knowledge. With the exception of the formalized ethnic squads,
created and deployed as specific forces to police immigrant neighborhoods
in the opening years of the twentieth century it is unclear if there was ever a
specific written directive to diversify the department. No memoranda survive
directing recruitment priorities or altering civil service exams to make them
more accessible to multilingual officers. However, it is clear from the writings of police administrators as well as the number of high-profile immigrant
officers regularly reported on in the press, that during those years the NYPD
dedicated considerable resources to developing a model for policing immigrant neighborhoods.

White politicians, police, and social scientists alike agreed that, while immigrant crime and the subordination of immigrant neighborhoods was an administrative challenge—it was a challenge that could, at least theoretically, be solved. They deemed that white immigrant crime, especially attributed by police to large and growing Italian and Jewish neighborhoods, was not inevitable, and to a somewhat lesser extent, neither was the crime that existed in the Chinese community. Police believed both issues could be solved and crime could be eradicated by a coercive combination of Americanization, pacification, surveillance, and proactive policing. To this end, the police department dedicated a large amount of resources in the year between 1903 and 1910 to infiltrating, surveilling, and forcibly policing immigrant neighborhoods. Francis Vinton Greene's successor as police commissioner, former Assistant Secretary of the Navy William McAdoo, saw immediately upon taking the post that the "closeness of the living quarters, the narrowness of the streets, and the mixture of races," made the densely packed and diverse immigrant neighborhoods, "the most complex and difficult police problem of any similar place on Earth."[1] He firmly believed that this "problem" could be solved by assimilation and more thoughtful policing. He wrote that if an intelligent foreigner or a curious rural American wanted to see "how under American laws and customs we assimilate and make over the raw foreigner, or even the semi-barbarous alien" they need only venture down to the Lower East Side to see how "the educational process goes on steadily, and the police as a general rule are tolerant and show intelligence in handling these masses." There is ample evidence that police were not always as thoughtful and helpful in their dealings with immigrants. After all, McAdoo's assertion that the "police must study these people, their habits, customs, ideas and somewhat of their history" did make a substantial impact on how police deployed detectives into some neighborhoods—but was not at all incompatible with a style of policing that involved heavy use of the club and arbitrary arrests.[2]

The Sexual Crime Panic in Black and White

In addition to the vice, political radicalism, labor organizing, theft, and the occasional murder that police believed thrived in immigrant communities—the issue that most concerned respectable upper-class white society and the politicians that represented them were the fears over what they called "white slavery." Over the first two decades of the twentieth century, fears of white slavery and immigrant men's contribution to the social, moral, and personal harms associated with it drove both federal immigration reform as well as ground-level policing of immigrant communities.[3]

The panic concerned the fear that immigrant and non-white men were seducing, forcing, or otherwise coercing women with the illusion of love or perhaps substance addiction, into a form of sexual slavery. The "white" in "white slavery," referred specifically to the assumed victimhood of white women, and differentiated this act from chattel slavery of people of African descent in earlier centuries, as well as explicitly contrasted white women from Black and sometimes Asian women who reformers rarely painted as victims but rather willing participants in systems of sexual exploitation or depravity. Like the policing and regulation of sex work in the reaches of the American empire, who anti-white- slavery crusaders thought was worth saving reiterated the innocence and redemptive qualities of white womanhood and the supposed entitlement of men to the bodies of Black and non-white immigrant women. Saloons and other establishments where people may be doing drugs, especially cocaine, that catered to only people of a single race or ethnicity, and which served only men, were far more likely to avoid police attention than other more diverse drinking spots. Because drugs and alcohol were often understood by police as mind-altering substances that loosened inhibitions and served as a key tool in the seduction and sexual disgrace of white women by Black and immigrant men, the substances and the spaces where they were consumed were subject to particular consideration from authorities.[4]

The specific threat of racially different and sexually deviant men was enforced and disseminated in a handful of popular accounts that typified the white slavery panic. George Kibbe Turner's *The Daughters of the Poor* focused specifically on the role Jewish men played as "cadets," men who procured innocent and unsuspecting women to serve as prostitutes by entrapping them with violence, coercion, or seduction.[5] One police official claimed "cadets" were equally made up of Irish, Italian, and Jewish extraction, although each was "a graduate of the street gang."[6] By connecting petty street crime and children's gangs in immigrant neighborhoods as a gateway to the looming menace white slavery posed to white womanhood, police intellectuals validated the notion that stricter and more brutal control over immigrant neighborhoods would also curtail society's most noxious moral ills. In part, proponents and amplifiers of the myth of white slavery were building off xenophobic fears of immigrant sexual deviance based on their existence in quasi-homosocial spaces. In many immigrant communities, men immigrated, lived, and worked around other men who came to the United States in advance of their families in order to build a life, find a job, or send money home for survival or the cost of a ticket. These largely homosocial immigrant spaces gave rise to xenophobic fears about foreign-born men as being sexually promiscuous, bad providers, or harboring same-sex desires.[7]

Despite the staggering scale of violence unleashed on Black New Yorkers by both police and white urbanites during the Riot of 1900—which was itself triggered by police presumptions of Black women's sexual deviance—and similar moments of upheaval, McAdoo and the broader police establishment's thoughtful consideration of crime and communities did not extend to the Tenderloin, San Juan Hill, or other Black neighborhoods. Even as politicians scrambled to find solutions to what they believed to be a widespread problem of immigrant men's exploitation of white women—police still portrayed Black men as the more existential threat to public safety. "The Negro loafer is a more dangerous character than the white cadet," wrote Police Commissioner McAdoo, "as he is subject to violent fits of jealousy, and, when filled up with the raw alcohol which is dispensed in the neighborhood, murder comes naturally and easy to him." Even as police scrambled to find immigrant police officers capable of understanding immigrant neighborhoods, he still considered places where Black and white New Yorkers could mingle, "far more dangerous for a certain class of young white women than Chinatown."[8]

While McAdoo believed that part of the solution to sexual exploitation of white women in immigrant communities was, "working in conjunction with the Commissioner of Immigration, Hon. Robert Watchhorn who earnestly requested such co-operation in endeavoring to depart these criminals," his prescription for similar instance in the Black community were much more brutal—after all, Black New Yorkers could not be deported. In the case of Hattie Warren—a white woman allegedly held against her will after passing out, possibly by drugging, after drinking at a Black-owned bar—McAdoo wrote, "A negro beast holding a white woman—even a depraved one—in captivity, arouses the fierce spirit of lynch law." Simply put, the New York City police commissioner thought that in this instance, the lynching of the suspect, presumably by a white crowd, and possibly with police assistance, was an appropriate punishment. While police puzzled over how to better infiltrate or assimilate European immigrants to make them more compatible with American life and less susceptible to criminality—in Black neighborhoods, death and violence were the only prescription.[9]

It is important to note that, in New York City at the time, there were no laws officially barring the sharing of social, recreational, and commercial spaces between white and Black people as there were in the American South at this time. Starting with an 1873 state civil rights law, and buttressed by a number of subsequent laws, public accommodations and amusements had to provide equal service to people regardless of race. But that did not stop police from enforcing a kind of de facto segregation. "Morals policing" became the new method by which police could allow white men to continue to seek leisure and vice in Black neighborhoods, use discretionary power to restrict bodily autonomy and public access to Black women, and enforce a prohibition on the interaction between Black men and white women. This justified both the omnipresence of police in Black neighborhoods where they sanctioned some vice, profited from graft, and protected white male clients— all while neglecting the policing needs of the Black community in favor of arrests and brutality for trespassing on enforced the racial, gender, and sexual dominance of white men in public.[10]

Despite Black business owners personally beseeching the NYPD commissioner and asserting their right to serve customers of any race, the harassment continued. McAdoo claimed he harbored no racial hatred but still made the eradication of places where interracial socialization was a top priority. "The mixed-race resort," he wrote, "is an unmitigated and disgusting evil, and the technical arguments as to the legal rights of a licensed resort should not prevent the police in the placing it under constant surveillance and in enforcing the law with the greatest vigor." So many of the daily acts of policing, like the iceberg, happen below the waterline of officially documented priorities. Some scholars have called this the "informal world" of policing. There was no official law against interracial socialization just as there were no laws against so many of the small acts of everyday living that police repressed in an attempt to assert their priorities to uphold racial hierarchies in the city.[11]

The Need for Police Translators

When American-born police arrested immigrants, criminal trials were often fraught with miscommunication, overreliance on translators, and attempts on the part of police to wrap up speedy convictions by taking advantage of the defendant's lack of English-language skills or knowledge of the US legal system. For instance, in 1910 when police arrested Francesco Sansone for the murder of a friend and fellow Italian immigrant, arresting officer Francis McGee told the court of Sansone's confession. The officer recalled the defendant saying, "Me no afraid, I shoot the son-of-a-bitch, he all the time make trouble for me and I can no longer stomach him." But when Sansone himself took the stand, aided by an Italian translator, he claimed he could speak no English at all—let alone speak in colloquialisms like "son-of-a-bitch" or "no longer stomach him." It is possible that immigrants on the stand had the ability and willingness to retreat into feigned ignorance and accentuate their foreignness in order to subvert police narratives and avoid conviction. It is also true that police could have very likely invented English-language confessions like the one attributed to Sansone to speed up trials and ensure timely convictions.[12]

Whether police or immigrants took advantage of their foreignness as a way to obscure the truth, one thing was certain: the language barrier in New York was becoming an increasing hurdle for the carceral and judicial systems. The rising need for translators in courtrooms, as well as on the streets, also had an impact on the administration of justice. Even in instances where foreign-born or first-generation translators were called in to analyze the testimony of the accused and witnesses, their interpretations and cultural knowledge were often held as suspect or unintelligible to an all-American, all-male jury. In the 1911 trial of a Chinese-born man, Leon Jung, for running a gambling ring, the prosecution called Quan Yick Nam, a California-born and bilingual interpreter and regular police informant to translate papers found in Jung's Chinatown office.

In hopes that a piece of paper taken into evidence included a list of people who had placed bets, Quan Yick Nam corrected the cross-examiner. "Chow Lee" he said, maintained the naming convention of a firm or company, rather than an individual. "Objection," cried an attorney. He maintained that the naming convention "John Smith," similar to "Chow Lee," would clearly be an individual's name and contested the translator's interpretation as speculation. The courtroom often became a site where different types of knowledge about culture and language came into conflict.[13]

Judges in these two cases both seemed acutely aware of the impact that both the need for translators, as well as prevailing prejudices and stereotypes about immigrants in the city, might have on juries deciding the cases. In Sansone's case, the judge warned about the complications that might arise when English-speaking police interface with translators, "I think it is only fair to the witness and the defendant to say," said the judge, "that the statements concerning which this witness is now being examined are supposed to have been made some time since the charge here, by this witness, in Italian to an officer. That officer then translated the alleged statement made by this man into English, and it was typewritten, and now another Italian interpreter is taking that statement out of that translation and putting the questions to this man. I say that to you so that you may have a fair notion of the value, as evidence, of a contradictory statement proved from that sort of transaction." It was very easy for contradictions in stories that seemed pertinent to the case and meaningful for assessing guilt to arise from the retelling of the story multiple times in multiple languages.[14]

In Leon Jung's case, Judge Thomas C. O'Sullivan warned the jury that they had to, in pursuit of justice, leave behind their larger feelings about Chinese people and their immigration to the United States. "You gentlemen are to look into this case as I know you will, absolutely divested of any prejudice toward the defendant in this case or towards his people. You are not on account of certain suggestions that we cannot reach the Chinese by our law as it exists to endeavor to apply the law to this defendant simply for that purpose, because they are as much entitled to the protection of our law as any people living under it." Both on the street and in courtrooms—for reasons of justice and effective pacification—a new model of policing and adjudication had to consolidate quickly to effectively manage the diversifying city.

A New Model of Ethnic Policing

Applicants to the police department who had been passed over during the Roosevelt era, whether because of perceived disrespectability, mediocre English-language skills, or political ties to the Tammany machine, could now get a second chance at appointment if they had language ability and cultural knowledge useful to the department. One such officer was Cornelius Willemse, a middle-class Dutch immigrant who arrived in New York City in 1888. After immigrating, the twenty-four-year-old Willemse became a bouncer, and later a bartender and "lunchman," at the Tiger Café at 12 Center Street, a popular hangout for Tammany politicians and strongmen.[15] His association with saloon culture and the Tammany machine earned him a rejection from the force as it existed under Theodore Roosevelt, but by 1899 and the insurgent Democratic reign of Mayor Robert A. Van Wyck, Willemse was able to find a place with the NYPD in the Twenty-Eighth Precinct on West Sixty-Eighth Street—and eventually onto the short-lived German Squad.[16]

Not long after joining the force, Willemse realized that what differentiated him from other police, and therefore made him eligible for promotion, was not his ability to brawl, a holdover from his days as a bouncer, but his language skills. Only a few years earlier, Roosevelt had explained that the sooner an

4.1 An NYPD detective in Chinatown, 1909. Bain Collection, Library of Congress.

immigrant could Americanize, the sooner he would become a better police officer. In Willemse's case, his utility to the police force came because of his un-Americanized traits. "When superiors learned that I could speak German, French, Holland Dutch, and Flemish and could take a fling at Italian, they kept calling on me as an interpreter when foreigners were brought to the station house." As a result, Willemse was always assigned the beat closest to the station house so he could rush back should the need for translation arise.[17] He learned firsthand that interpreting and translating were becoming an increasingly necessary and vital part of policing as New York City's demographics continued to shift, both for solving crimes and maintaining relations with the community they were meant to patrol. "A very necessary adjunct to a busy precinct," he wrote in a later memoir, "for occasionally a foreigner comes in with valuable information and if there is no one available to translate his message but the bootblack or some other person not connected with the department, the informant's usefulness is lost."[18] It was hard enough for police to find members of an immigrant community willing to come forward and inform detectives, but if an exclusively English-speaking precinct was forced to rely on civilian interpreters, there was certainly plenty of room for subversion and accidental miscommunications.

For the gifted linguist, New York's diverse neighborhoods presented endless opportunities to learn new languages. Already conversant, if not fluent, in Dutch, Flemish, French, German, and English, Willemse also picked up Yiddish through proximity to Eastern European Jews living in Brooklyn and Manhattan's Lower East Side. "I improved my Yiddish vocabulary by eating a lot of kosher food and it wasn't long before I was taken for a *Jehude* or a 'good goy.' I was proud of that, for it stood me in good stead many times."[19] His reputation as a good "goy," or a non-Jewish person, helped him to investigate crimes that involved collaboration with Yiddish witnesses or victims, but the language skills also became a useful tool for detection. In one instance, Willemse questioned a married couple accused of committing a crime on behalf of a gang. "Do you speak Jewish?" the suspect asked him. Not wanting to let on that he did, Willemse posed as a French speaker thinking, "A Frenchman wouldn't know Yiddish or German." Assuming he would not be understood, the suspect started speaking rapidly to his wife in Yiddish. Willemse, translated the Yiddish outburst as, "The game's up. After I'm taken to the station house, hurry downtown and see the gang. Tell them what's happened. Have them arrange bail for me." He then arrested the surprised man.[20] As Willemse told the story, had the detective investigating not spoken Yiddish, the crime might have gone unsolved. NYPD administrators worried that versions of this scenario played out every day and in every corner of the city. If criminals could lean into their foreignness in order to avoid detection and arrest, that meant that large swaths of the city patrolled by monolingual police were essentially lawless.

Willemse's career was indicative of the style of policing coming into vogue under Commissioners Greene and McAdoo, not only because he could speak his native language—but also because he embodied a generic "foreignness" that made him more useful in *any* immigrant neighborhood, and not just his own. His childhood exposure to Dutch, German, and French meant he could be incredibly useful in those communities in the same way police administrators imagined other immigrants could be useful in their own communities. But he also had a knack for picking up new languages. This aided a reputation that foreignness was in itself an innate skill independent of a person's specific cultural and linguistic identity.

By the 1910s and 1920s, police commissioners would eventually steer the department away from ethnic policing and the police-as-translator model of policing and rely heavily on classroom training American-born officers on how to speak and engage with the civilians they encountered every day. In the years that followed, it would take relationships with universities, large police department libraries, and other policing-based higher institutions of learning before the NYPD expected its American-born officers to pick up the skills that Willemse seemed to have accumulated naturally.

Willemse was far from the only police-as-translator to walk the streets during the first years of the twentieth century. Warren Charles, the son of a Chinese businessman and a white novelist from Chicago, helped the NYPD "clean up Chinatown" and "braved hatchetmen" before his eventual 1904 appointment to the NYPD.[21] After receiving his badge, Charles took a post in East New York in Brooklyn, and married a "little blonde American wife," a fact rehashed often in the press.[22] In 1909, the immigrant-crime-obsessed police commissioner Theodore Bingham, with much fanfare, offered Charles a spot in the Chinatown precinct. "The police commissioner asked me recently if I would care to serve in Chinatown," Charles recounted to the press, "I told him I certainly would not. I had visions right there of camera men, reporters."

Warren rejected the post citing his biggest fear: the spectacle and novelty of a Chinese-descended police officer, in uniform, patrolling Chinatown. "There, ladies and gentlemen," he imagined tour guides saying through a megaphone, "you observe the only Chinese policeman on the New York police force. He is working in Chinatown among his own people."[23] Although Charles was the only Chinese American in his Brooklyn precinct, close proximity to Chinatown, and the perception that he belonged there, felt to him like a greater marker of racial difference than being the solitary Chinese-descended person in his neighborhood. But by defying the project of race-based policing, Charles was also hindering the NYPD's informal project of recruiting officers capable of extending state control into immigrant communities. The problem of effectively policing Chinese neighborhoods was not unique to New York, as cities across the country struggled to develop effective tactics. In one instance, the San Francisco Police Department found an unusual short-term solution to the problem of Chinese gambling. In 1896, the department struck an arrangement with a group of "regularly organized" Chinese police sent to San Francisco by their government in order to report regularly to the consul general on the behavior of Chinese residents. Although "the blue-coated guardians of the police do not regard their Chinese brethren with a great deal of favor," they were issued credentials by the police department as a testament to their usefulness.[24]

Across the city, officers like Cornelius Willemse and Warren Charles were making the jump from translator or informant to patrolman and detective. Along with their new position came increased social mobility and steady salary, along with notoriety and novelty. Some, like Willemse, who went on to write two memoirs about his time as an officer, embraced their unique position on the police force. Others, like Charles, appreciated what the job had to offer while simultaneously rejecting the pioneer status of early ethnic police, both in that moment and in future generations.

In 1904, the same year as the appointment of Warren Charles, the increasingly routine deployment of sending immigrant officers would get its first semiformalized unit: the NYPD German Squad.

The *General Slocum* Disaster and the NYPD German Squad

It was around 8 a.m. in the morning on June 15, 1904, when the thirteen-year-old paddlewheel steamer *General Slocum* pulled up to the Third Street recreation pier. The ship was entirely made of wood and by law was allowed to carry 2,500 passengers. That day, it was commissioned to take 1,358 excursionists to a picnic on Long Island as part of the St. Mark's Lutheran Evangelical Church's yearly Sunday school outing. A majority German church, the building as well as many of its congregants resided in the old Kleindeutschland, which had been steadily losing German-speaking residents since its heyday in the mid-nineteenth century.[25]

Piloting north on the East River, Captain Van Schaick managed to make it as far as the Bronx, a distance of about eight miles, when the cries of "fire" rose from the deck. To this day, it is unclear as to what started the fire. The federal investigation, carried out by the Department of Commerce and Labor shortly after the tragedy, speculated that the fire began in the ship's storage area where either a discarded match or an open lamp ignited the canvas, charcoal, oil, or other flammables stored in the room. Within six minutes of the fire being noticed by the captain, he beached the bow on North Brother Island, located between the shoreline of the Bronx and the larger Rikers Island.[26]

At around 10:15 a.m., James Collins, a policeman at the Alexander Avenue station in the Bronx was detailed to the wharf on 134th Street when he saw the *General Slocum* traveling north on the river, "a solid mass of flames," and quickly ran it in to the station.[27] Despite the speedy rescue attempts on the part of police, firemen, nearby boat captains, and civilians, the combination of the fire, faulty life preservers, and the panic aboard the boat resulted in a devastating loss of life. The final tally, according to the Department of Commerce and Labor's findings, was that 955 of the 1,358 passengers could be confirmed dead, only 893 of whom were ever identified. Due to the nature of the trip, a majority of those killed were children who had attended St. Mark's Sunday school.[28]

Although prolonged exposure to the fire and water had made some of the bodies unidentifiable, the language barrier presented another troubling hindrance to the police's project of recovering and identifying the deceased, missing, and wounded. Talking to survivors and victims' families, and handling the grieving throngs that gathered outside the church and at the neighborhood morgue, required police with some knowledge of the German language. Cornelius Willemse was one of those multilingual officers, released from usual duty to assist with the disaster's aftermath. "There were 1,003 bodies in the morgue," as he described it later, "and I was sent there as a German-speaking officer under Max Schmittberger, the Inspector, who was German and had charge of the detail with several men who spoke German." It became quickly and abundantly clear to Willemse why it was so necessary to assemble a squad of German-speaking officers. "It is surprising to know that a great many of the old German settlers on the East Side," he recalled, "could not speak a word of English, and interpreters were essential in helping them when they came to identify their dead."[29]

Germans in New York were racially similar to Anglo-New Yorkers, especially in comparison to recent immigrants from Asia and Southern and Eastern Europe, but the language barrier remained a present reminder of their foreignness. This thoughtful attempt at crisis management was, in many ways, a commitment to the belonging of Germans in a way that other ethnic-based squads were not. The state rallied its ethnic and linguistic resources into providing state care and governance to German-speaking New Yorkers that other communities had yet to see.

Max Schmittberger, the veteran inspector who had survived the purges of the Lexow Committee by cooperating with investigators, was an unusual, but not an altogether unpredictable choice to head up this post-*Slocum* "German Squad." In the years following his appearance before the Lexow Committee, Schmittberger had climbed the ranks all the way to inspector by attempting to disavow his former reputation as heir to Alexander "Clubber" Williams. In 1903, the newly appointed police commissioner Greene had reached out to President Theodore Roosevelt with concern about Schmittberger's potential promotion to inspector. Roosevelt returned his correspondence on personal letterhead from the Oval Office saying, "Under me Schmittberger behaved admirably. I started in with a violent prejudice against him because of his statements when he was states evidence: but he certainly turned to be one of the most efficient members of the force." With some trepidation, the president concluded, "If he has done good work since. . . . I am inclined to say that he has earned his promotion."[30] Having been at the NYPD's highest rank for a little over a year earlier at the time of the *Slocum* disaster, Schmittberger was newly useful, not just as an inspector and an administrator, but also as a German.

In the week or so following the disaster, Schmittberger assembled a collection of "100 policemen who speak German" from a number of precincts across the city. Although not all of the one hundred German-speaking policemen made the Roll of Honor, in the NYPD's end-of- year report for 1905, of the 214 people cited for "Heroic conduct at the 'Slocum' Disaster," or "Meritorious service in connection with the 'Slocum' Disaster," thirty-seven have recognizably German surnames.[31] These men canvassed German-speaking neighborhoods, knocking on doors to ask residents if anyone in the house had been injured or killed. Although Schmittberger was quick to admit its possible inaccuracies, the German Squad's attempt to create a master list would be the most complete accounting of the tragedy during the following months.[32] The organization of the squad, like the detective bureau of the NYPD, was centralized, with officers from every corner of the city, now dispatched to wherever headquarters sent them. What made the German Squad more akin to the Philippine constabulary than the detective bureau, however, was its organization through shared ethnicity. Germans had served on the NYPD for decades, but with the *Slocum* disaster and a new influx of German and Yiddish speakers among immigrants settling in New York City, German patrolmen were suddenly necessary for their linguistic ability and cultural familiarity in the same ways Filipino officers were more effective than American-born police officers. In both instances, understandings of race, illegibility, and extending the government's reach became driving factors in recruiting and deploying certain kinds of officers.

As city demographics changed between 1895 and 1904, it became increasingly urgent that the NYPD develop a method to police immigrant neighborhoods. The department that Roosevelt left in 1897 was one designed to value the presumed skills of native English-speaking or thoroughly Americanized immigrant officers. By 1904, the skills inherent to Rooseveltian policing— the ability to brawl and the forceful exertion of crowd control, chief among them—were still important, but were no longer the sole identifiers of effective policing. As the quick and necessary mustering of the German Squad after the *Slocum* disaster demonstrates, NYPD administrators were increasingly aware of the shortcomings inherent in maintaining a majority monolingual Anglo-Irish police force. German-speaking officers were not the only immigrant group organized into necessary squads in 1904. That same year, the NYPD also organized its much longer-serving ethnic squad: the Italian Squad. Called upon by police administrators, politicians, and an alarmist press, the initial collection of seven Italian-speaking officers was tasked with easing heightened fears about Italian crime.

POLICING THE "ITALIAN PROBLEM"

5

Criminality, Racial Difference,
and the NYPD Italian Squad,
1903–1909

At around 5:30 in the morning of April 14, 1903, Mrs. Frances Connors of 169 Avenue D was walking to a bakeshop when she spotted a large barrel placed peculiarly on the corner of Avenue D and East Eleventh Street. She noticed part of an overcoat hanging over the side; looking inside, she saw a corpse with its throat cut. Although the victim, an Italian immigrant from Buffalo, NY, named Maduenia Bendetto, would not be positively identified for another five days, clues in the barrel immediately pointed police toward the conclusion that the culprit was Italian. A woman's handkerchief and a note in Italian reading, "Come at once," led investigators to believe the victim had been lured into an ambush.

Even in the absence of these clues, for New Yorkers living in 1903 the nature of the crime itself would have seemed familiar and characteristically Italian. "The fact that the body had not been hidden away or disposed of in the river or through some other means would indicate that the killing was the result of a plan by some secret society such as the mafia," reported the

Evening World. Two days later, the NYPD had twelve Italian men in custody, all of whom had already been under suspicion as the possible leaders of a counterfeiting ring in New York. Although police believed all or most of the men arrested on suspicion were at the Stanton Street butcher shop where the murder allegedly took place, the scant evidence collected over the next year could ultimately be used to convict only one person of the crime. Police found Tommaso Petto, one of the arrested men, in possession of a pawn ticket for a very distinctive pocket watch that the victim's stepson had described to detectives. The trial culminated in two convictions for perjury, but only one for the murder. Much to the public's dismay and frustration, the rest of the "swarthy dozen" or the "barrel murder gang" were released.[1]

During the decades leading up to the turn of the twentieth century, Southern and Eastern Europeans arriving in the United States expected to find more comfort and opportunity than in the failing economies and job shortages they left overseas. Instead, they found the United States in the throes of economic and political strife. American middle and upper classes, supported by a growing availability of white-collar jobs and the rise of global industry, increasingly regarded the newcomers, many fresh from labor and radical movements in Europe, as bomb-throwing anarchist assassins and foreign knife-wielding purveyors of vice. In the age of the immigrant radical, even American-born radicals were made to seem more foreign, and therefore unsympathetic, by employers and the press. Amid the widening economic disparity of the era, American-born radical and labor movements fused with immigrant activism and made employers fearful, defensive, and xenophobic. Upper-class fears of economic disruption and antiforeign sentiment warped American-born New Yorkers' perceptions of the large communities of immigrants.[2] The 1903 Barrel Murder marked a turning point in how NYPD administrators perceived the supposed threat of Italians in society and their own inability to surveil, understand, and police immigrants in the city. In 1903 and 1904, the New York daily press, politicians, social scientists, and police all made urgent efforts—or demands—that the police department find some way to address the distinctly foreign, and therefore elusive, Italian crime problem.[3]

This chapter explores how police officials grappled with the challenge of effectively asserting control over a foreign population living in large numbers in New York City. In an attempt to address this problem, police engaged with transatlantic racial science and early criminology, colonial counterin-surgent tactics like "native policing," as well as federal immigration law and the growth of a deportation bureaucracy. The large number of foreign-born New Yorkers was a perpetual reminder to police that New York did not exist in a vacuum. In an age where people, goods, capital, and ideas were constantly crossing the ocean, local problems often required national or international solutions. The arrival of European, and specifically Italian, criminal anthropology and racial science gave social scientists and police administrators in New York an intellectual foundation for their policing of Italian immigrants. The work of thinkers like Cesar Lombroso, the late nineteenth-century inventor of criminal anthropology, persuaded police intellectuals that the racial and cultural divide between Anglo-Irish New Yorkers and Italian immigrants warranted the recruitment of officers who could metaphorically and literally speak their language. This scientific dis-course legitimized and even necessitated the use of "native policing" as a way to bridge a divide that policing itself made wider, and make Italians more knowable to the state.

While the implementation of colonial tactics like native policing was the go-to strategy for contending with Italian crime in the first decade of the twentieth century, the lasting legacy of the NYPD's encounter with immi-grants was its willingness to utilize federal immigration law as a tool of local law enforcement. The 1903 Immigration Act, passed the same year as the Barrel Murder, provided a federal mechanism by which local police could address immigrant crime. The act, expanded in 1907, prohibited criminals, anarchists, and those considered sexually deviant from entering the United States and allowed the government the to deport anyone who violated these conditions. The 1910 Mann Act, or the "White Slavery" Act, criminalized the transportation of women for "immoral purposes" across state lines and was disproportionately used to police immigrant men and men of color and legally punish interracial couples with imprisonment or deportation. It has also been commonly hailed as one of the first major interventions of federal law into local law enforcement. In New York, the tactic of deporting im-migrants with documented proof that they had committed crimes in their home nation long outlived any targeted counterinsurgent policing measures aimed at Italians. Federal immigration enforcement mechanisms remain to this day a common method of addressing perceived criminality within im-migrant communities.[4]

5.1 Italians and police officers around a suspended bank, likely in Little Italy, 1909. Bain Collection, Library of Congress.

Race, Criminality, and State Power in Italy and the United States

As the most recognizable and omnipresent agents of the municipality, the police, Commissioner McAdoo understood, embodied all the functions of the US state for immigrant New Yorkers. If police officers in immigrant communities were corrupt or brutal, immigrants would assume that the larger operations of government were corrupt as well. Likewise, through their power to arrest and fine, as well as their monopoly on legitimate violence, police were conditioning immigrants on how to behave in public in the United States. McAdoo believed that a newly arrived immigrant's internalized behaviors, learned under threat of arrest or a baton to the head, were doing "far more important work, so far as the future citizens are concerned, than probably any other officials in this land."[5] McAdoo and later police officials asserted that hassling immigrants over what would later be called "quality of life" crimes such as loitering, littering, public intoxication, and other activities that most often went unpunished in their homelands, might turn them into self-disciplined Americans.

Police understood their interactions with immigrants, in tandem with civic engagement, settlement houses, and English-language and literacy classes, as helping to build hyphenated identities.[6] Susceptibility to US state power in the form of policing played an important role in turning Italians into Italian Americans and forged a relationship between immigrants and the state that underpinned the legal transition from alien subject to citizen.[7] Under Italian-born detective Joseph Petrosino's guidance, the duration of the Italian Squad, which had its heyday between late 1904 and 1909, was marked by experimentation by the NYPD to assure that no New Yorker was beyond the reach of the state and immune from this coercive process.

For immigrants, particularly those traveling from remote parts of Southern Italy and Sicily where Petrosino was born, their first few days in New York City often meant learning for the first time how to operate in a society where the punitive power of the state was exerted consistently. Many historians have discussed how interactions between working-class Sicilians, Southern Italians, and the fledgling Italian state were often characterized by the periodic brutal suppression of mass action and disorder, rather than the well-dispersed disciplinary power exerted by major metropolitan police departments like those of New York, London, or Paris.[8]

In the southern reaches of the country, Italian women, specifically the population of "widows in white" whose husbands were part of the mass migration of male Italian laborers to North and South America, often relied on the expanding purview of the liberal state even while they protested against it. The frequency with which Italian women utilized bureaucratic structures to register their children or search for a lost husband in the United States suggests that those Italian women who migrated along with Italian men in the period between the 1880s and 1920s may have had more experience to draw on when interacting with agents of the US state.[9] However, citing racial, cultural, and linguistic differences, the agents of the United States often had a harder time understanding Italian communities than immigrants had maneuvering through municipal bureaucracies.

By the late nineteenth century, Sicilians and Southern Italians, while still in Italy, were already categorized by social scientists as a different, and fundamentally inferior race, especially when compared to residents in the north of the country. For social scientists, stereotype, complexion, stature, economics, politics, and crime statistics, fused to confirm an innate and biological inferiority and natural criminality in Southern Italians. To no one was this distinction more pronounced than Cesare Lombroso, the controversial and well-educated Northern Italian physician who popularized the field of criminal anthropology in the 1880s and 1890s. Over the course of his work, and particularly in his two most popular texts, *The Female Offender* (1890) and *Crime: Its Causes and Remedies* (1895), Lombroso came up with a theory of biological determinism that the criminality of so-called "born criminals" was innate and embodied in certain physiological characteristics. Lombroso set out to prove a correlation between physical characteristics and specific criminal behaviors including assault, murder, theft, and political offenses like a dedication to anarchism by analyzing the facial and bodily features of thousands of male and female prisoners.[10]

While "born criminals" could exist anywhere, Lombroso believed that "criminaloids," people who engaged in criminal behavior without a biological predisposition to evil, could be made by dozens of factors including, climate, religion, poverty, and physical and mental health. Race, Lombroso wrote, also played a major factor in the relative moral weakness of criminaloids. For example, the Irish, he asserted, were a people racially predisposed to committing theft. Likewise, in addition to a supposed proclivity for political radicalism, the residents of the Southern Italian islands of Sardinia and Sicily seemed more likely to commit violent assault when compared to Italian citizens of different racial backgrounds.[11] European Jews, on the other hand, seemed predisposed to insanity, "in which they have an unfortunate leadership," but Lombroso admitted that "remarkably" they showed a lower degree of criminality than non-Jewish Europeans.[12] Southern Italians and people of African descent, however, still received the lion's share of demonization as being the most uncivilized, violent, and morally bankrupt of the criminaloids.[13]

For a generation of race scholars like Lombroso, Southern Italians and the hundreds of thousands of immigrants traveling across the Atlantic represented a distinct race different and inferior from taller, fairer Northern Italians. In a paradoxical argument that suggests a move toward the understanding of a racial binary, scientists attempted to argue that the region's proximity to Africa, and Italians' geographical proximity to Africans, had created a people wholly un-European. "Imagine the black hair and eyes," wrote William Ripley, "with a stature scarcely above five feet, and a very un-European appearance is present."[14] Ultimately, the proximity, both in complexion and geography, to Africa and Africans, allowed scientists interested in race to posit Southern

Italian inferiority. Their imagined similarities also made it twice as necessary for Southern Italians in the United States to find ways to reaffirm their differences from Black citizens in order to maintain the privileges of whiteness.

Italians and the Color Line

In addition to navigating civic life inside the United States, settling in New York meant recent immigrants were forced to encounter the US color line. From their disembarking onto US soil, Italians were "white on arrival," even if they were considered *racially* inferior to the Germans, Irish, and Anglo-Americans who dominated urban centers. US naturalization papers, as numerous historians have pointed out, recorded the color of Italian immigrants as "white," their complexion as "dark," and their race as "Italian."[15] Their precarious whiteness, which afforded Italians a certain amount of political and economic mobility, autonomy, and privilege denied to Black and Chinese New Yorkers, gave recent Italian immigrants the choice of embracing or rejecting the hardening color line in New York, a position Italians often used to reaffirm their own anti-Blackness in a way that benefited them socially, economically, and in their racial standing.[16] In turn however, the slow and begrudging acceptance of immigrants like Italians into the ranks of whiteness as they continually asserted their difference from African Americans, hardened a racial binary that consisted primarily of Black and white.[17] By the mid-twentieth century, "ethnicity" became the new marker to distinguish among different kinds of European-descended people under a regime of consolidated whiteness. During the era of the NYPD's Italian Squad, ethnicity and race operated in an overlapping fashion; Italians were simultaneously non-Anglo and fundamentally white.

Despite having access to the fundamental privileges of whiteness, immigrants leaving Italy in hope of finding more political freedom and economic opportunity in the United States found a public and scientific community already saturated with anti-Italian prejudice and feelings of racial superiority. After the arrival of the first wave of Italian immigrants in the late 1870s and early 1880s, the American press pointed to the everyday behavior and politics of Italian newcomers as proof of their racial difference from Anglo-Americans and earlier generations of immigrants, particularly the Irish.[18] To quote historian Matthew Frye Jacobson, "It was not just that Italians did not look white to certain social arbiters, but that they did not act white."[19] Writing for *Popular Science*, attorney Appleton Morgan found the lifestyle of

Italian immigrants incompatible with life in the United States. In his article, "What Shall We Do With the 'Dago?,'" Morgan advocated that imprisonment, which he warned would be nothing more than "warmer clothing and better beds" for most classes of Southern Italians, would not be enough to overcome their supposed predilection for crime.

Not only did he assert that Italians had no use for, or even grasp the concept of, a house, but Morgan also recalled one group of Italian laborers in proximity to a small circus who consumed scraps left from the feeding of lions and tigers. As a testament to their habits, Morgan recounted that the Italian railroad workers "collected the bones" left by the circus animals, "and boiled them for their soup! What terrors have jails and prisons for such human beings? What have they to lose by pilfering, assaulting, robbing, or murdering?"[20] By depicting US prisons as an improvement upon the lifestyle of Italian immigrants, Morgan and other writers helped lay rhetorical groundwork for an eventual panic about the ungovernability of immigrants, and the complete inability of police to control immigrant, and specifically Italian, crime.[21] If prisons and policing as they existed would not work to curb what many believed was a rise in Italian crime, then the NYPD would be forced to develop something that would achieve the necessary results. They had just the man to try.

Joseph Petrosino

Although already well known as one of the ablest investigators in the NYPD's detective bureau and one of the only detectives who could speak Italian, Detective Sergeant Joseph Petrosino became a national celebrity thanks to the Barrel Murder case. Shortly after the body was found, Petrosino was dispatched to Buffalo to interview the victim's stepson. This led to the acquisition of the case's only crucial piece of evidence, the detailed description of Bendetto's pocket watch, which was used to convict Petto.

Born Giuseppe Petrosino in Padula, Italy, in 1860, the detective immigrated to the United States with his family in 1874. As a teenager, Petrosino worked as a shoeshine boy and slowly gained a reputation as being useful to police. After serving as an informant within his own immigrant community, Petrosino became an official member of the NYPD in 1883. By 1901, so few police spoke Italian that his presence on the force was more necessary than ever. "Detective Petrosino is a detective of much merit," recalled the *Brooklyn Daily Eagle*. "He has handled difficult cases and especially among the Italian colony. He is a linguist and a man of great ability."[22] Petrosino's status as a "linguist" conjured his image as a translator able to cross the borders between English-speaking New York and the foreign colony of Italian speakers growing in southern Manhattan.

Renowned for his linguistic ability, rather than an inherent pugilism, the 5-foot-3-inch Petrosino represented a profound shift in the bodily representation of good policing in New York City.[23] Like other immigrant men, Petrosino was portrayed by newspapers with the same racial discourse that marked other Italian men as overly emotional, a trait said to result in impulsive violence, the shirking of the manly duties of breadwinning, or both.[24] "Far from being of the conventional bull dog type," the *Tribune* recalled in 1909, "Petrosini was of the artistic temperament.... [H]e was sensitive and emotional."[25] This temperament was not the stoic and calculating masculinity expected of American men during the Progressive Era, but that was to Petrosino's benefit. American-born police were perceived as having little to no aptitude when it came to patrolling Italian neighborhoods and the old adage "it takes a thief to catch a thief" supposedly rang true for Italians as well. The insurmountable language and cultural barriers in tightly packed immigrant neighborhoods increasingly required a new kind of police force, one less focused on the brawn of its individual officers and capable of more than pacification by force.

Crafting "Italian" Crime

The criminality supposedly visible on the bodies of Southern Italians constantly reasserted itself in Italians' imagined proximity to two often intertwined phenomena: radical anarchism and transatlantic organized crime. Deep associations between Southern Italian men and women and anarchism have often seemed to historical observers proof of a rejection of the type of hierarchical governance found in Western democracies. Between the 1870s and the 1901 assassination of US president William McKinley by self-proclaimed anarchist Leon Czolgosz, anarchists attempted or succeeded in assassinating almost a dozen heads of state around the world, as well as a number of industrialists, local politicians, and police officials.[26] In many of these instances, Italian nationals were the assassins. While anarchism seemed to be a growing phenomenon in almost every industrialized nation, many believed that Southern Italian anarchists in particular believed in the "propaganda of the deed," meaning spectacular violent acts committed in the name of anarchism.[27]

"What is peculiar to Italy is the diffusion of the anarchist spirit on the one hand, and, on the other, the readiness of that spirit to vent itself in attempts upon the lives of elevated persons, be they sovereigns, princes, or political men," wrote one professor of political economy at the University of Naples in 1898.[28] The tendency of Southern Italians to drift toward anarchism, he argued, was caused by the same economic conditions that spurred the mass migration of laborers from Italy in the same period. The peculiar susceptibility of Southern Italian anarchists to regicide, on the other hand, was "a historic tradition" in Italy, which "has never been interrupted."[29] From the viewpoint of thinkers in the United States, the newness and weakness of the Italian state only exacerbated the problem of violent anarchism, as it was unable to enforce anti-anarchist laws in ways that did not create martyrs or a global Italian anarchist diaspora.[30] The criminal anthropologist project of mapping the physiognomy of anarchists came to the overwhelming conclusion that even though the facial characteristics of anarchists could be compared with other less radical political notables of the era, anarchists still presented an embodied *difference* from normal political actors. Viewing them through a criminal justice lens did not just identify dissimilarities, it actively contributed to making and perpetuating of dissimilarities. As large numbers of Italians sailed into US ports, they arrived alongside a vast literature that inscribed both their bodies and ideas with foreignness and racial difference.[31]

In addition to anarchism, organized crime was a major concern for citizens and law enforcement. Many believed the so-called Black Hand, a large and well-organized fraternal organization, pulled the strings behind any and all crimes in New York City's Italian neighborhoods. Diplomatic incidents in which immigrants arrested in New York were found to have criminal convictions in Italy, a violation of the 1903 Immigration Act, occurred often and built resentment among officials in the United States and the Italian government. This illegal immigration led to a public misconception that the Black Hand was a flourishing transatlantic organization thanks to the Italian state's neglectful, if not malicious, tendency to allow convicted criminals passage to America.[32] Once in the United States, police intellectuals believed these criminals would lean into their foreignness in order to avoid the detection of English-speaking police, understood to be ignorant of their practices and languages.[33] Lack of awareness of Italian customs and language, factional and regional differences, and general xenophobia led English-language New York City daily newspapers across the political spectrum to embellish their favorite boogeyman: the Black Hand.

Later in the decade, recent immigrants hoping to rehabilitate the image of Italians in New York attempted to counteract the Black Hand myth by asserting that the Mafia brought over from Sicily and the Camorra from Naples were distinct and loosely organized groups—counter to the police view that all of the violence was connected and orchestrated. Although their leaders were sometimes in contact, "they are no more organized, however, than are the many thousands of lawbreakers of other nationalities in America," one Italian writer insisted in 1908.[34] Middle-class and aspirational members of Italian neighborhoods tried in many ways, including encouraging police infiltration of their neighborhoods, to demonstrate that criminal enterprises were far from monolithic or hegemonic within the community.

English-speaking police finding bodies in the streets failed to distinguish among loosely organized fraternities like the Mafia and the Camorra and the Black Hand, the Frankenstein's monster of all Italian crime invented by the US press. Even before the infamous 1903 Barrel Murder that sent the public into a panic about Italian crime, there was the 1902 "Sack Murder," in which a murdered man, Giuseppe Catania, was found in a burlap sack in Brooklyn.[35] Because of their strange and horrific characteristics, and the shocking inability of the police to make headway on the investigations, both murders made headlines across the country.

Violent acts that were read by an American public as political in nature, particularly assassinations motivated by anarchism, extralegal feud killings known as *vendetti*, or a combination of the two were of particular concern to writers, politicians, and law enforcement. Attorney Appleton Morgan wrote an article in *Popular Science*, inspired, he said, by the "recent murder of David C. Hennessey, chief of police of the city of New Orleans," which appeared to have directed "public attention to a class of immigrants which has recently sought the hospitable ports of the United States."[36] On October 15, 1890, David Hennessey was gunned down in the street as he was walking home after a meal at an oyster saloon. When fellow officers arrived on the scene and asked who had done it, Hennessey reportedly whispered the racial slur "Dagos."[37] The sensationalized story served, Morgan noted, as a rallying cry for those who saw Italian violence as simultaneously politically motivated and also senseless and random. This atmosphere of anti-Italian sentiment led to the lynching of eleven Italian in men in New Orleans the following year.[38]

After almost two decades of debate about limiting Southern and Eastern European immigration to the United States, the horrific nature of the 1890 slaying of Hennessey in New Orleans, Maduenia Bendetto's Barrel Murder, and the Catania Sack Murder in New York, as well as the inability of the police to speedily wrap up all three investigations, convinced many in the public that special precautions needed to be taken to limit Italian crime. Four months after Bendetto's body was found, the headline "Italian Crime and Police Incompetence" blared across page one of the *New York Tribune*. "The city is confronted with an Italian problem with which at the present time it seems unable to cope," the story read.[39] As people understood it, the problem resulted from the NYPD's inability to speak Italian or understand the culture of recent immigrants. "The Italian problem is peculiarly hard for the American to solve, because its roots go far deeper than American soil. The crimes of the Italian quarter have a character more in keeping with feudal times than the present age."[40] Italians were, the *Tribune* proclaimed, a misplaced generation ill-equipped and disinterested in participating in modern liberal democracy.

Police intellectuals believed Italians had inherited a sense of lawlessness stemming not only from the invisibility of the Italian government in the villages and cities of Southern Italy but also from a historic tradition of violent vigilantism. Combined, these problems were too foreign and rooted in the past for the American policeman to comprehend, let alone effectively prevent. As the NYPD's end of year report for 1905 phrased it, "We are trying to handle medieval criminals, men in whose blood runs the spirit of the vendetta, by modern Anglo-Saxon procedure."[41] This official document, written and published by the department, framed the difficulty as a conflict between races, with sophisticated Anglo-Saxon policing on one side, and the uncivilized and brutish Italians on the other. The chasm between the two seemed so vast that any attempt to control one with the methods of the other seemed futile. The Italians' unfitness for democracy and their lack of a capacity for liberty meant that police must use any means necessary to either make them fit or subordinate them through force.

Downplaying a population's "capacity for liberty" operated as a discursive tool in many colonies around the globe, including the Philippines, and marked a group as subjects for experimentation and for the more violent aspects of the state's coercive policies. Italians were not colonial subjects, but they were racially and culturally different enough to trigger the colonial gaze that emphasized legibility and subordination. In this instance, the "coloniality" inherent in the relationship between the Anglo-dominated state and newly arrived European immigrants relied on the contingent process of "both differentiation and connection"—the idea that Italians were different but *could be made less different* set them apart from groups like African Americans, Asian immigrants, or actual colonial subjects like Filipinos who were different and could not be made any less different. This process resulted in a multiyear campaign by the NYPD to understand and mitigate that racial difference by incorporating Italians into the policing process.[42]

For Italians, popular media depicting them as predisposed to violence and criminality presented hurdles on the street and in institutions of the criminal justice system. Juries made up entirely of native-born white men carried with them into the courtroom the same racial biases and assumptions that police harbored. The surviving court transcript of the 1910 trial of Leonardo Broncado offers a rare glimpse into jury selection by providing a firsthand look at how individual sentiment shaped justice for foreign-born New Yorkers. In addition to asking if the potential jurors harbored prejudice against foreigners and Italians in particular, many were also asked if they were aware of the large-scale Italian migration to the United States. One juror, William Rothwell, said he did, indeed, harbor prejudice against foreigners. "Well, I have not got the right feeling for the Italians as I would for our own race here." When asked if foreigners or more likely to commit crimes, he replied, "Yes, sir; I think foreigners is more hot blooded, and more apt to murder men then our own race here." Even if the "spirit of the vendetta," as the *New York Tribune* called it, did not actually exist in the men, women, and children who made up the Italian diaspora in New York, many American-born New Yorkers certainly behaved as if it was a settled scientific fact.[43]

Assumptions that Italians were criminals, or at least uncivilized and incompatible with American life, hurt victims of crime as well as those accused of it. When Violet Perano, a thirteen-year-old Italian immigrant girl, accused the local cobbler, Francesco Purpura, of raping her in his studio apartment and storefront, the defense attorney used her family's status as recently arrived immigrants to cast doubt on the crime. The attorney for Purpura questioned whether her birth certificate from Italy might actually reveal that she was over eighteen, perhaps as a way of suggesting the unreliability of Italians' testimony and Italian government documents, and therefore arguing that Perano was not a child in need of special protections by the state. The attorney even challenged Violet Perano's father to see if he was capable of doing the simple subtraction necessary to calculate her age. Buried in the cross-examination of Violet and her father were also prejudiced assumptions of neglectful parenthood and hypersexualized and promiscuous girls consistent with prejudices of the time. The jury convicted Francesco Purpura on May 26, 1909. The case, handled by Officers Miceli and Digilio, was to another success chalked up to the NYPD's Italian Squad.[44]

The Italian Squad

The arrest and successful prosecution of Purpura, an Italian man, while attempting to safeguard a young innocent Italian woman was emblematic of the ways Italians in the city were both foreign and criminal but also capable of redemption and respectability through civic participation. The state's impulse to protect Perano's innocence even while the defense attempted to besmirch it, shows that Italian women were beginning to receive the moral protections from police that Black and Chinese women were often denied. It also took a specific type of police officer to bridge the gap between Anglo New York and Italian immigrant communities for the purpose of extending morals policing into supposedly insular communities.

In spring 1904, a year before the Purpura case, the only man who seemed capable of bridging that chasm and organizing other officers to do the same was Joseph Petrosino. Serving for years as Manhattan's only Italian detective, he was tasked with investigating crimes affecting the hundreds of thousands of Italians living on the island. In the months leading up to the Barrel Murder, Petrosino's cultural knowledge and language abilities became increasingly useful and were increasingly called upon by Commissioner Greene. In early 1903, Petrosino made so many high-profile arrests in Black Hand cases that, by April, a worried Greene revoked weapons permits for 322 Italians in the city. That same year, Greene asked for Petrosino by name when a box of dynamite was discovered on the Cunard pier. Although no concrete evidence suggested that the box was of Italian origin, a warning letter signed "Pietro Demartini" was enough to warrant Petrosino's involvement. *The Sun* reported that, "Because of the Italian name signed to Gen. Greene's letter and the fact that the men who brought the box to the pier were Italians, Detective Sergeant Petrosino was sent to the Italian quarters of the city to see what he could learn."[45] When a woman named Carmella Nappe was the sole witness to a crime committed by Raffaelle Cascone, Petrosino was sent to Bridgeport, Connecticut, to retrieve her. Whether the assignment was in the Bronx, the Bowery, or even Connecticut, if it involved Italians Petrosino was expected to handle it. By virtue of his ethnic background, by 1904 Petrosino was one of the most valuable and busy detectives in the NYPD.[46]

Already famous and easily recognizable in Manhattan's Italian enclave, Petrosino was called on by Police Commissioner McAdoo to organize an "Italian Squad." McAdoo became police commissioner in 1904 a few years after his four-year stint as undersecretary of the navy between 1893 and 1897. Although he served before the 1898 war, McAdoo spent his tenure touring the Caribbean, evaluating the navy's positioning, and socializing with British colonial administrators. McAdoo put Petrosino's small new squad in "plain clothes" and sent them out to patrol and investigate in Italian neighborhoods. "The very existence of this secret service," McAdoo believed, "had a deterring effect on the professional criminals."[47] The initial group consisted of Italian-speaking police, half of whom had served only one year, signaling a recent and rapid rise in the appointment of Italian officers. They were Rocco Cavone, Ralph Micelli, Joseph Digero, Morris Bonnoil, Peter Dondero, Michael Mealli, Paul Simonetti, and John Archiopoli.[48] The department's grouping of patrolmen and detectives who lived in Queens, Brooklyn, and as far north as Harlem demonstrates the extent to which commanders attempted to consolidate cultural and linguistic knowledge from across the city under a single organizational umbrella. The group formed a centralized squad of racial others, not unlike the Philippine constabulary or other forms of colonial policing Greene had witnessed in the empire or McAdoo would have seen in the British-occupied Caribbean. Likewise, the fact that only one of the original members of the Italian Squad had been appointed before 1898 demonstrates the expeditious attempts on the part of the administration to ethnically diversify the force as immigration increased in the years following Roosevelt's tenure at the NYPD.

By the year's end report of 1905, the NYPD had upped its number of Italian speakers on the squad from around nine to forty, now making the ratio of Italian police to Italian New Yorkers one to ten thousand. This also included regular support from Petrosino's Brooklyn counterpoint, Detective Sergeant Antonio Vachris, and his own squad of Italian detectives. Although the ratio was improving in favor of the NYPD, a major limitation was that only four of those forty spoke Sicilian. This may or may not have yielded results in the form of arrests. In 1904, the year Petrosino formed the Italian Squad, the NYPD recorded 13,156 arrests of people who had been born in Italy—accounting for roughly 7.5 percent of all arrests in the city that year. By the end of 1905, police had arrested 19,186 men and women born in Italy, totaling roughly 9.6 percent of the entire force's arrests for that year. For reference, by 1908 the NYPD estimated that there were around 145,433 Italians living in the city, just over 4 percent of the city's population of just under 3.5 million people.[49]

There are almost no remaining files or documents from inside the Italian Squad (like the larger NYPD), but the press and public's ongoing fascination with immigrant crime can help trace its trajectory of rise and decline, from six detectives to a major division before becoming defunct by 1910. As early as April 1905, just a few months after the squad's creation, local newspapers began chronicling its hard-fought successes and its failures. That spring, members of the squad successfully tracked Luigi De Palo to an address in Providence, Rhode Island. De Palo was in hiding after slashing Detective Archiopoli's face during an incident on the street in an Italian neighborhood in Brooklyn two years earlier.[50] From its headquarters, reported to be located on Lafayette Street in 1904 and then in a room above a saloon on Centre Street in 1906, the squad attempted to track down accused blackmailers, counterfeiters, kidnappers, and murders from Brooklyn to the Bronx and beyond.[51]

As in the De Palo case, the NYPD's Italian Squad often had to rely on connections in Italian communities and police departments across the country to track down criminals fleeing prosecution and arrest in New York. Around the country, other municipalities and police departments were experimenting with similar methods of extending control into seemingly unpoliceable Italian enclaves. Across the country, local newspapers reported on the deeds of Petrosino in New York as if he were a local officer. Italian police hired in other cities were often compared to Petrosino and the work he was doing in New York. The New York model became, at least until 1910, the preeminent model for policing Italian immigrants in the United States. Often called the "Petrosino of Chicago," Detective Gabriel Longabardi oversaw the prosecution of crime in the city's growing Italian enclaves.[52] Peter Angelo, a special policeman and Italian court translator turned full-time officer often resorted to "one of his famous disguises" to infiltrate saloons and brothels in Pittsburgh.[53] Amid mass Italian immigration, the New Orleans Police Department promoted John D'Antonio from clerk to patrolman after he had been called upon to serve as an interpreter.[54] As early as 1902, even the Pinkerton Detective Agency, notorious for the infiltration of labor organizations and heavy-handed strikebreaking tactics, employed Frank Dimaio out of Philadelphia to assist with investigations requiring knowledge of Italian.[55] Despite this developing network of cooperation among cities, major flaws in the system of Italian policing persisted. The inadequacies of identification technology often allowed suspects to use false names, disguises, and general uncooperativeness to avoid recognition. Likewise, a suspect's ability to flee back to Italy and disappear beneath the unwatchful eye of the Italian state proved a frustrating and ultimately insurmountable problem for Italian detectives in the United States.

After January 1, 1906, the incoming police commissioner, Brig. Gen. Theodore Bingham, would prove a major, although temporary, boon to the Italian Squad's mission of policing immigrant neighborhoods. The deeply xenophobic Bingham had served in the army in many capacities, including as a mapmaker in the Arizona Territory in the 1880s, and as a military attaché to the US embassies in Berlin and Rome. Although he had never been in combat, Bingham was known as a strict disciplinarian and ruthless in his enforcement of standards.[56] Bingham, the department, and the press all understood that the fight he planned to wage against the phantasm of immigrant crime in the city was nothing short of actual warfare—not the type that occurred on the open fields of Europe, but the type of counterinsurgency happening in the empire. "As his title implies," read one paper, "General Bingham is a solider. Though no longer in the United States Army, he is commander of a corps of about 9,000 men, the police force of the greatest city on the continent. He cannot mobilize this force in its entirety and go out after the Black Hand to crush it, because the Black Hand never fights openly." Bringing a renewed martial spirit to the force, Bingham went after the populations he believed to be the primary cause of disorder in the city: immigrants.[57]

"In New York 90 per centum of all malefactors arraigned in the courts are of foreign birth," wrote Bingham in 1908, "and the New York Police, moreover, are compelled to deal not only with the predatory criminals of all nations, including our own, but with the feuds of the Sicilian Mafia, the Neapolitan Camorra, the American Hunchakists, the Chinese tongs, and with other internecine quarrels of the scum of the earth."[58] Bingham, much to the ire of Jewish community members in New York, went on later that year to erroneously claim that up to 50 percent of all crime in New York City had been committed by Jews.[59] It makes sense then that Bingham would initially offer up more support and resources to the Italian Squad, especially in light of speculation that the city faced a crime wave.

Bingham was not alone in his fears. The summers of 1907 and 1908 were marked by panic and hysteria over rising crime in New York. "Heat wave?" wrote one fed-up columnist in the *Evening World*, "Pish, tush; have those every summer; twice some summers. Crime wave? Same as above, except more pishes."[60] Although varying interpretations, from extended politician vacations to evolving women's fashion, were offered by the press to elucidate the consecutive summer crime waves, immigrants emerged as the most popular culprit.[61] "I think above all the present crime wave is due to the character of the immigrants we have been receiving in recent years." This sentiment, voiced by one popular New York City preacher, was one that could be heard throughout the city during the consecutive hot summers.[62] "The unprotected taxpayers have made their demands for additional police," scolded one citizen. "The scum of Europe has mingled with the dregs of New York . . . against such elements the honest girder of the city's 'apron' desires it better secured."[63] Like the scares after the 1902 Sack Murder and the 1903 Barrel Murder that led to the creation of the Italian Squad, the mounting panic led Bingham and the NYPD's to grow the group to fifty detectives in spring 1907, and establish an offshoot of plainclothes detectives hopefully less recognizable to repeat offenders than celebrity detectives like Petrosino or Vachris.[64]

Theodore Bingham, Deportation, and the Decline of the Italian Squad

Mounting fear of immigrant crime waves after the summer of 1907 collided with growing public concern over "white slavery," or the kidnapping and impressment of European and American white women by foreign and Black men into sexual servitude. Denounced as more nefarious than nineteenth-century chattel slavery because of the inherent sexualized threat that nonwhite and immigrant men posed to the innocence of white women, white slavery became a moral panic that dictated the public agenda for the next three years.[65] In 1907, the year of the Italian Squad's largest expansion, Congress passed increased restrictions on immigration that specifically targeted men and women whose crimes involved "moral turpitude" for deportation alongside anarchists, polygamists, and the physically and mentally disabled.[66] The White-Slave Traffic Act of 1910, also known as the Mann Act, followed three years later, a federal prohibition on transporting women across state lines for "immoral purposes." As a blanket response to the white-slave panic, these acts, including their immigration components and the Mann Act's disproportionate use against immigrants and men of color, indicate a public understanding that the larger problem in need of addressing was the sexual threat immigrant and Black men posed to white womanhood. It followed on the heels of a growing body of nationwide legislation that cracked down specifically on what was claimed to be the dangerous sexuality of foreign-born men.

For Theodore Bingham, immigrants were solely to blame for white slavery, as well as the vast majority of crime in New York. In part because of his publicized distrust of anyone foreign born, Bingham likely also believed that immigrant police could not be part of the solution to foreign-born crime. Bingham's potently anti-immigrant sentiments began to leach into his assessment of the men in his department. Just as Irish police a generation earlier met both upward racial mobility and deep suspicion stemming from negative associations with Irishness and foreignness, the widely circulated cautionary tales about immigrant men left Italian officers in a precarious position. Although their badges allowed members of the Italian Squad access to social and racial mobility, they could not fully escape the taint of white slavery, organized crime, and the bodily degeneracy being projected onto Italian subjects. Depictions of Italians as lacking intelligence and bodily health certainly impacted Commissioner Bingham's views of the department he inherited.

Summoning rhetoric that demonstrates continuity with the Roosevelt era of the NYPD, when Anglo-Irish brawn was the accepted indicator of a capable patrolman, Bingham was quoted as greeting his captains by saying, "You look like manly men. I love manly men."[67] A few weeks later, speaking in his capacity as police commissioner at an event for the Regular Army and Navy Union, Bingham said that a good soldier, "was a good Christian as well as a good citizen."[68] For Bingham, manhood, religion, and citizenship came together to create a good officer who was neither small nor Jewish, and whose citizenship was not made questionable by foreignness. After all, it was Bingham who early in his tenure had characterized Jews as being "not physically fit for hard labor," including the hard labor of policing.[69] Likewise, Bingham's distrust of Italians insinuated a belief that small-statured and "artistic" men like Petrosino and his Italian Squad were unable to get the job done.

Many citizens believed the best way to counteract the summer crime waves of 1907 and 1908 was to double down on the thinking that had created the Italian Squad in the first place. Concerned that the ongoing crime waves resulted from the inability of English-speaking American police to navigate Italian languages and customs, citizens and the press frequently called out for an increase in the number of Italian police. John Freschi, for example, a lawyer interviewed at a meeting of middle-class Italian Americans speaking out against the Black Hand, declared that the only way to curb the exceptional problem of Italian crime was to hire more Italian detectives and make legal penalties more severe.[70]

However, by 1908 and the second summer of panic, Bingham seemed increasingly skeptical that Italian police were a sustainable solution. "The reply is that the Police Commissioner is compelled by law to select his men from lists furnished him by the Civil Service Board, and that Italian names are few on these lists because the young men of that nationality generally prefer business life to public service," Bingham reasoned. However, a lack of interest in public service was not the only reason the commissioner saw little reason to pursue Italian recruits. "There are few of that race," Bingham added, "who would be able to pass the examination for probationary members of the police force."[71] These comments had profound implications for his relationship to the Italian Squad. The squad was not only the largest and most concentrated group of Italians on the force, it was also one of the highest-ranking, with almost all of the associated men serving at the rank of detective or detective sergeant. However, in a comment that seemed aimed at Petrosino's inability to curb the continuing perception of an Italian crime wave, and by extension, the ability of Italians to serve as detectives, Bingham wrote, "to tell the honest truth, there is at present no great detective in the employ of New York city.... Take a policeman out of uniform, putting him into civilian's clothes with a shield on his waistcoat"— meaning they operated in plainclothes as the Italian Squad did—"and telling him that he is a detective, will not make him one."[72]

Despite the April 1907 increase of the squad's numbers, their performance during the summer crime wave allowed Bingham to critique the squad's ineffectiveness into the spring and summer of 1908. Arrests had been steadily increasing for the last few years. The total number of arrests citywide per year skyrocketed from 186,671 in 1906 to 200,772 in 1907 to 244,822 in 1908—but still the commissioner was not satisfied. Chief among his complaints was that the members of the Italian Squad were too well known within their communities and therefore unable to gain access to the "cheap little cafés" where criminal plots were hatched.[73] This was by no means a new problem; as early as 1904, and resulting in part from the creation of the Italian Squad, the recognizability of Petrosino in Manhattan and Vachris in Brooklyn was already creating complications for their detective work. Bingham's proposed solution was to hire new and well-paid detectives to live their entire lives undercover so as to escape any associations with the police department, a prospect that would make the current Italian Squad redundant. Citing their increasing inability to blend in and their failure to "make good" on Black Hand cases, on July 6, 1908, Bingham began the slow process of downgrading and shrinking the Italian Squad by decreasing the salaries of its leaders, and reassigning twenty people to other station houses around the city.[74]

Like immigrant police patrolling their own neighborhoods dating back to the Irish in the mid-nineteenth century, members of the Italian Squad were often foiled by their inability to make witnesses of their "tight-lipped" neighbors. After a meeting of the Italian Chamber of Commerce at which its members were said to have begged Italians to report crimes to police, the *New York Tribune* said that some of the most commonly heard Italian proverbs in the city were "The poor resort to force, fools resort to law," and "Do not speak of what does not concern you."[75] It was often observed that Italian residents refused to answer the simplest questions. A reporter captured one man responding to, "What is your business?" with a grunt, and "Where do you live," with "I've forgotten."[76] One young member of the Italian Squad recorded in his memoir the story of an Italian man on Mulberry Street who witnessed the murder of his own son. When the police questioned him on his stoop, only feet from the body, the father repeatedly maintained that he did not know the identity of the slain man.[77]

There may have been a strong feeling in Italian neighborhoods that Italian detectives who helped the strong arm of the US state extend into their insular enclave were traitors to their kin. Many immigrants of all nationalities turned against their police counterparts amid accusations that immigrant police were complicit with, if not sometimes overtly guilty of using their extralegal power to abuse and extort community members. In many instances, the resentment of a neighbor's cooperation or enlistment with police had community-specific contexts. Commissioner McAdoo recalled that "In Ireland for seven hundred years there has been one name, there has been one character, which excites not only horror but a certain superstitious awe, and that is an 'informer.'"[78] Despite their now half-century-old associations with policing, Irish New Yorkers still reportedly held onto the wrongs informers had done them in English-dominated Ireland. According to McAdoo, many Irish policemen had to justify their arrests of fellow Irish men and women by identifying more with the department than their kin. When asked about reporting fellow officers, one Irish policeman said that he'd be unable to look his children in the face if he ever "turned informer" and denounced another patrolman for taking bribes.[79] For these men, the widening police-civilian divide during the fifty or so years of Irish involvement in the police department had created a police solidarity that exists to this day.[80] Rather than seeing themselves as "turning" on fellow Irish people in the city, they chose to defend and protect their new family: police. The impulse never to incriminate a comrade stayed intact in the period between the 1850s and 1910s, and that impulse to protect shifted over time from ethnic kin to police brethren.

The combination of animosity against Italian police officers, especially among neighborhood criminals, and the local celebrity of the detectives, often proved to be a deadly and dangerous combination. Two men waiting for the "Petrosino of Chicago," Detective Gabriel Longabardi, assaulted him at his well-known address at 116 Bunker Street. Although Longabardi survived the attack, he sustained multiple slashes and a blow to the head.[81] Less than one year later, he withstood another assassination attempt after being ambushed by two men lying in wait for him in an alleyway.[82] Petrosino, whose home addresses was usually well known within the Italian community, also faced domestic disturbances. It was not uncommon for Petrosino to return to his Little Italy apartment to find crude notes and death threats left on his stoop, including drawings of skulls and daggers.[83] Perhaps out of fear of reprisals, the NYPD civil service rosters recorded Petrosino living in at least four different homes between 1902 and 1908.[84]

For years, detectives as far away as Pittsburgh had warned of whisperings that there was an impending plot to assassinate Petrosino, but it was not until spring 1909 that the ultimately successful plan was orchestrated.[85] At the time, the Italian Squad had been shrunk to only twenty-seven members, with Petrosino taking on more responsibilities as part of Bingham's effort to use deportation as a tool to curb immigrant crime in a way that he deemed more effective than the all-but-defunct squad. Petrosino planned a trip to Italy to gather criminal records that could be used to deport recent arrivals to the United States. The mission was undertaken in secret, with Petrosino traveling under a false name.

Bingham and Petrosino's joint effort to remove presumed criminals from New York, and the country altogether, is only one chapter in an entwined history of law enforcement and deportation in the United States. For those distrusting immigrants, whether they be criminals, civilians, or police, restrictions like the 1903 and 1907 immigration acts and the United States' fledgling deportation apparatus seemed like a forceful tool in the fight against immigrant crime. High profile and well-publicized episodes like the Haymarket Massacre in 1886, the murder of David Hennessey in 1890, and the ongoing labor unrest that threatened the authority of industrial titans, led many politicians, capitalists, and scholars in the United States to wonder if the threat of immigrant radicals warranted a further tightening of the gatekeeper state.[86] It had been well over two decades since the United States Congress, after a grassroots campaign that combined vicious racist stereotyping with fears of shrinking job availability for white laborers, had passed the Chinese Exclusion Act of 1882.[87] If police decided they wanted to expel someone from the country the evidence could be quite thin. In April 1907, NYPD officers arrested Enrico Alfano, a suspected organized criminal, in connection with a murder investigation in Italy. With a lack of real evidence from Italy, the charges were dropped, but immigration authorities took Alfano to Ellis Island and held him for deportation nonetheless.[88]

The fight for immigration restrictions did not go unopposed. Grassroots organizing and new groups like the East Coast-based Immigration Protective League founded in the 1890s lobbied against restrictions and literacy tests for immigration. In Italian and Jewish communities, especially in those communities propped up by the wealth and political standing of the earlier generation of German-Jewish immigrants, immigration restrictions meant a vote of no confidence from the Anglo-Protestant elite that people of Southern and Eastern European origin could not assimilate properly into American culture. Benevolent associations tried to help to Americanize their communities and overcome the stereotypes that made recent immigrants seem more foreign or dangerous.[89]

Despite ongoing deportations and activists' work to prevent restrictions, in 1908 NYPD commissioner Bingham called on immigration officials to ramp up deportations as a way of curbing crime in New York. "We have records," he said in an interview, "of fifty Italian criminals which would exclude them from this country, or once here, should bring about their deportation. Out of these fifty only six have been deported notwithstanding that the fact that police have been ready to furnish the immigration officials at all times with information." The NYPD's end-of-year report for 1908 discloses that by the time the year ended, police had arrested twenty-four men and delivered them to Ellis Island for deportation.[90]

By 1909, the growing bureaucracy at US borders and ports, the increased capacity for deportations, as well as the immigration restriction acts that allowed deportation on moral, economic, or criminal grounds, made Petrosino's trip to Italy seem like a useful way to gather the evidence needed to eject some troublemakers from the city for good. New York police were not alone in this tactic. Historians have also chronicled how, thousands of miles away on the US-Mexico border, immigration inspectors asked immigrants the question of whether they had been convicted of a crime in a foreign country in hopes of building deportation cases as well.[91]

On March 1, Petrosino, traveling with the cooperation of the US State Department, reached Sicily. It is unclear who initiated the trip, but it was likely the police commissioner, Bingham, who had spent most of 1908 and 1909 arguing for more deportations. Perhaps because of these deportations and his recognizability, traveling under a pseudonym was not enough to protect Petrosino.

Upon his arrival, Petrosino found Southern Italy, Sicily, and US representation in the region in shambles. Three months earlier, on December 28, 1908, an earthquake had devastated the region, leaving most urban centers in ruin. When he received Petrosino, William Henry Bishop, the US consul in Palermo, was overwhelmed. A few weeks earlier, the State Department had temporarily expanded Bishop's responsibilities because Arthur Cheney, the American consul in Messina, and his wife, had been killed when the entire consulate collapsed during the quake.[92] Despite his mounting duties, Bishop found time to give the detective proper introductions to the Italian authorities that could help him on his mission. Armed with a list of New York City residents whom he believed had immigrated to the United States despite extensive criminal records in Sicily, Petrosino spent the next eleven days collecting as many files as he could in hope of building deportation cases back home.

On the evening of March 12, 1909, however, his mission in Palermo was cut short. After dining at the small Café Oreto, Petrosino walked along the Garibaldi Garden on his way back to his hotel, the Hotel de France on Piazza Marina. According to Bishop's report to the assistant secretary of state, Petrosino was confronted during this walk and shot three times. The fatal shot came through his back, just below the right shoulder blade, and punctured both of his lungs, while the other two bullets entered the back of Petrosino's neck and his left temple.[93]

Immediately after the assassination, a media frenzy that trafficked in suspicions and accusations erupted on both sides of the Atlantic. Many believed Commissioner Bingham had inadvertently given Petrosino away to his opportunistic killers. On February 20, the *New York Times* had published Bingham's response to a rumor that Petrosino had taken a long vacation. He had assured the public that the detective was undertaking important work for the department and that "he may be on the ocean, bound for Europe, for all I know."[94] He was not the only one who let word slip of Petrosino's arrival in Europe. On March 6, Consul Bishop had written to a Professor Rallo "confidentially" disclosing Petrosino's presence in Palermo.[95] Bishop had his own theory that Petrosino was found out and targeted because of his own carelessness and hubris. Although he was staying in the Hotel de France under the name "Guglielmo Simone," Petrosino reportedly "drew his money at the bank and received his letters there in his own name . . . the effort to conceal his identity was not really a serious one."[96] Back in New York, Petrosino's old comrade Detective Vachris felt confident that the local police and authorities in Palermo had betrayed him.[97]

It is possible, however, that the frequency with which Italian immigrants traveled back and forth between New York and Italy could have made Petrosino as recognizable on the streets of Palermo as he was in New York. Bishop recounted that one of Petrosino's final journal entries recorded, "Have already met criminals who recognize me from New York."[98] There were at least a few dozen people living in Italy who had been deported from New York because of the detective's efforts. After his assassination, police published a partial list of Italians whose deportation cases had been built by Petrosino. It included fifteen names, and all of them became suspects in his murder.[99]

The information Petrosino collected was incredibly valuable to the NYPD, who were on the hunt for any tangible links between criminal enterprises in Italy and in New York. As the investigation into Petrosino's murder heated up, the evidence he had collected in his final days, now in the possession of Bishop, seemed increasingly vital. The diplomat's new position at the center of an international murder investigation also made him a very visible target for Petrosino's killers. By March 18, US newspapers reported on the increasingly frequent death threats Bishop received from local criminals, claiming he would not be safe in Italy or New York.[100] One month later, he went on an extended leave of absence in an undisclosed location back in the United States.[101]

Although a few arrests were made, as they had been in the aftermath of the 1903 Barrel Murder, a satisfying conclusion to Petrosino's murder has eluded authorities for decades, despite a number of theories presented as recently as 2014.[102] One break in the case seemed to come during the 1910 counterfeiting trial of notorious crime leaders. Giuseppe Morello was one of the twelve men arrested as part of the Barrel Murder Gang, and another was alleged crime boss Ignazio Lupo. The state's key witness was Antonio Comito of Naples, who had immigrated to New York City in 1907. According to his 109-page statement used in the trial, counterfeiters targeted Comito shortly after his arrival in the United States because of his experience as a printer. Forced to live and work in a cabin in upstate New York, Comito was forced to print hundreds of thousands of dollars' worth of fake US and Canadian currency. During his time with the group, Comito claimed to have heard confessions of some of their gang's most notorious deeds, including the 1903 Barrel Murder and the 1909 murder of Petrosino. In his statement one year after the killing, Comito claimed that one man said over dinner sometime in the spring of 1909: "Damn Detective, he guards his hide well. He knows how many lives he has ruined. He is popular because he ruins so many. Now is he popular. Soon he will be dead." Morello reportedly hushed his younger colleague, "Go away and forget what you have heard. The word of success in Palermo will soon come and then we can celebrate. Until then, silence."[103] A few weeks later, when the news from Palermo arrived, the group supposedly celebrated the successful assassination. The convenient connections forged by the confession between the Lupo-Morello gang and two of the most infamous murders in New York City history may have contributed to their hefty sentences. Both were sentenced to imprisonment and hard labor in Atlanta, Georgia, Lupo for thirty years, and Morello for twenty-five.[104] As the future of the Italian Squad seemed increasingly uncertain and underfunded in the wake of Petrosino's death, two high-profile convictions that neatly wrapped up New York's most notorious Italian crimes may have done substantial work to soothe an anxious public.

After a prolonged autopsy, Petrosino's body was returned to the United States aboard the Cunard SS *Slavonia*. The ship arrived on April 9, and Petrosino was buried with full honors and much fanfare on April 12.[105] According to one advertisement clipped by Bishop, a film of the elaborate funeral at St. Patrick's Cathedral and Calvary Cemetery in Queens was shown to the public at Teatro Giuseppe Verdi in Palermo.[106]

The fanfare with which the department buried Petrosino represented not only his utility to the department, his international reputation, and his fame, but also the respectability he had achieved even within the city's most elite, Anglo, and xenophobic circles. In death, Petrosino was not just an Italian, but a model immigrant who could serve as an example for other immigrants from equally humble beginnings. In spending his career differentiating himself from Italians who were seen as more criminal, foreign, and uncooperative with police domination of the city, he marked himself as part of the class of Italians who were eager to embrace whiteness at the expense of his reputation among various sects of the Italian diaspora. Like Irish police before him, he might have been thought a traitor by some of his kin, but he helped to lead the wider community of European immigrants into the mobility and privileges associated with a more consolidated whiteness.

Sometime during the year following Petrosino's death, Bingham's successor, Police Commissioner Rhinelander Waldo, whittled away at and eventually disbanded the Italian Squad with little incident or notice.[107] For a few

5.2 Petrosino's remains arriving at his widow's home in New York after his assassination in Sicily, 1909. Bain Collection, Library of Congress.

months in 1910, the Manhattan Italian Squad was put under the command of Lieutenant Arthur Gloster before he was transferred to another district in November of that year. "The Italian quarters of the city, as well as the Hebrew sections, will be patrolled by detectives of those races," wrote a reporter in the *Tribune*, but those forces would lack the organization and infrastructure of the previous years. The squad's best days were behind it, and with its renowned leader murdered, Waldo might have decided many of those detectives were most useful redeployed to the detective bureau or precincts across the city.[108]

The group's disbanding did not mean, however, that Italian crime was over. Influential and upper-class members of the Italian community in New York continued to lobby for an Italian Squad in the years that followed, and briefly got their wish. Between 1918 and 1922, an Italian Squad was briefly resurrected under the direction of Detective Michael Fiaschetti to investigate the growing rate of Mafia-related crimes, especially in the wake of Prohibition. Born in Rome in 1882, and arriving in the United States with his parents in 1896, Fiaschetti claimed he was "supposed to be a musician," before being swept into the NYPD in 1906, during the time of the first Italian Squad.[109] However, the new squad ran into the same difficulties that plagued the original, including officers' widespread recognizability and an inability to produce witnesses.[110] Finally, in February 1922, Fiaschetti was demoted and the Italian Squad was dissolved for good. With their years of experience with Mafia-made and anarchist bombs, many members of the squad were absorbed by the NYPD Bomb Squad. This marked, somewhat conclusively, the end of the age of the immigrant detective. "Conditions which seemed to require the formation of the nationality organization of detectives some years ago have to a large extent disappeared," reported the *New York Times*. "The present work required different methods and supervision."[111]

The absorption of the Italian Squad by the Bomb Squad in 1922 concluded the period between Petrosino's death in 1909 and the end of World War I, when the police department slowly removed any overt acknowledgment of, or use of, race and racial discourse. During that period, ethnic squads were phased out and replaced by new regimes that standardized and universalized police procedures. When the Italian Squad failed to produce the long-term results the police commissioners desired, new legislative, technocratic, bureaucratic, and race-blind methods of policing emerged.

In 1909, just months after Petrosino's death, Arthur Woods, the thirty-nine-year-old deputy commissioner of the NYPD, argued that the predominant modes of police and detective work, including the Italian Squad "would not get at the root" of Black Hand and immigrant crime. Instead, Woods proposed that new models of sweeping federal legislation like immigration restrictions, state surveillance, and a weaponized bureaucracy, would be more viable solutions. In the years following the disbanding of the first Italian Squad, Woods continued to work his way through the ranks. In 1914, his ascension to the job of commissioner led to a four-year tenure in which his visions of meticulously kept records and well-trained patrolmen equipped to handle any community eclipsed the brief but influential figure of the immigrant detective.[112]

"THEY NEEDED ME AS MUCH AS I NEEDED THEM"

6

Black Patrolmen and Resistance
to Police Brutality, 1900–1913

If the history of white immigrants in New York is the story of people slowly gaining access to the privileges of whiteness, then the history of Black people in the city is the story of centuries of denial of that same social—and often geographic—mobility. Before the gradual abolition of slavery in New York between 1799 and the 1830s, the city was home to a small number of enslaved people of African descent. Although the anonymity of urban living held some advantages for enslaved people, surveillance by white city residents was almost constant and aided by eighteenth-century lantern laws. Under these laws, any free *or* enslaved Black person was required by law to carry a light after nightfall to make them more visible to pedestrians and authorities. Even after the 1840 census revealed that New York City no longer contained a single enslaved person, the small Black population of Manhattan continued to live under constant threat of state-aided mob violence. Anti-Black racism in the wake of the 1863 Emancipation Proclamation, as well as protests against Union Army drafts, made Black New Yorkers a particular target of white violence. Following the Draft Riots, a large number of New York's Black citizens left the city and moved to less densely populated Brooklyn, or more diverse cities like Philadelphia.[1]

By 1900, there were just over sixty thousand Black New Yorkers, many of whom had migrated following the collapse of Reconstruction and the withdrawal of federal troops from the American South. By 1920, the number of Black residents of the city had more than doubled as Southerners participated in the Great Migration and Caribbean-born people of African descent migrated to New York in larger and larger numbers. However, during this time the white political elite, both Anglo and Irish American political factions, conspired to keep Black New Yorkers away from municipal participation.[2]

In the years following the riot of 1900, Black and white activists from across New York called for more oversight of the police force, more recourse for victims of police violence, an end to state and media "whitewashing" of racial violence—and also demanded representation on the police force. Beginning in 1909 and building on almost ten years of organizing against police brutality, Rev. Reverdy Ransom of the Tenderloin used his pulpit to advocate for the appointment of Black patrolmen in order to curb state violence. In the same way that middle-class Italian Americans had called for more Italian police as a method of coercing their working-class kin into becoming law-abiding citizens, Ransom and other advocates of respectability politics also believed that Black police would be central to ending "the prevalence of lawlessness among certain classes of negroes in New York City."[3] However, whereas other races were enthusiastically recruited to the police force because of the perceived necessity for their bodies and knowledge, Black New Yorkers had to demand that their communities be made more knowable and policeable by way of Black officers in an attempt to access the state's protection.

When Samuel Battle, the first African American on the NYPD, was appointed in 1911, his advocates felt that they had won a symbolic victory for representation, as well as practical shift in the relationship between their community and the state. Samuel Battle bore on his shoulders the expectation that his presence would reduce crime in Black neighborhoods and curb the ubiquity of police brutality, while simultaneously proving the worthiness of African Americans to participate in the mechanisms of civic governance. Battle rose through the ranks, eventually becoming New York City's first Black parole commissioner in 1941, and paved the way for dozens of Black officers to join the NYPD by the 1930s. As a result, he has been popularly canonized as a civil rights pioneer. But there is more to the story.

Locating him within the complex racial landscape of New York illuminates his complicated relationship to immigrant policing and the way Blackness and ethnicity intersected with hierarchies of racial citizenship in the early twentieth century.

Stories of arrests of Black women or beatings of Black men appeared in newspapers regularly read by both white and Black New Yorkers. The assaults were concentrated in the two neighborhoods covering the sprawling West Side of Manhattan: the Tenderloin, and north of that, San Juan Hill. Spanning Fourteenth Street to the mid-Seventies, and the Hudson River to Sixth Avenue, this area housed the vast majority of Manhattan's small Black population, which amounted to about thirty-six thousand people in 1900.[4] Despite news coverage that perpetuated notions of Black criminality and often celebrated anti-Black police violence, internal documents produced by the department rarely left the same imprint as attempts to police other racial and ethnic groups.

Underrepresented in Paperwork, Overrepresented in Jail

The published yearly reports of the New York City Police Department are among the few documents generated within the department in the early twentieth century to survive its draconian policies on record retention and destruction. Each year, the NYPD released data on arrests, expenditures, station house repairs, hires and retirements, and recommendations for the following year. Because the Office of the Commissioner collected the materials for each year's reports, contents from year to year varied drastically depending on the availability of data or the particular priorities and biases of the commissioner.

The 1895 end-of-year police report is one of the earliest to break down arrests by race. In 1890 there were only 23,601 African Americans living in New York City, about 1.5 percent of the population. Despite this, Black men (1,895 arrests) made up 2 percent of arrests (out of 92,669 arrests for all men) and Black women (974 arrests) made up around 5 percent of all women arrested (20,328 arrests). And while the overall number of arrests of women citywide dropped between 1894 and 1895, arrests of Black women increased by almost two hundred arrests. If no one was arrested more than once, which is unlikely, close to one in every eight Black New Yorkers would have been arrested at some point during that year.[5]

In the reports for 1904 and 1905, Commissioner William McAdoo, who had overseen the founding of both the short-lived German Squad and the

Italian Squad, compiled the report so that it broke down arrest records by precinct, profession of the suspect, crime committed, and nation of the suspect's origin. The category "Black" appears only twice in the report: as a subcategory of people who were arrested that were born in the United States, and as a category of "missing persons" and "foundlings." For all other records, including accidental deaths, the data is devoid of racial or national categories and is separated only into males and females.[6]

The Black population of Manhattan nearly doubled between 1900 and 1910, from 36,346 to 60,534, which put it between 1.8 percent and 2.5 percent of the borough's entire population during those ten years. Although they represented such a small group on the island, in the year 1904 African Americans comprised almost 8 percent (8,506) of all arrests in the city, and in 1905, African Americans accounted for 5 percent (9,718) of all arrests in the city, quadruple and double their representation in the general population respectively. The inclusion of the accused's occupation allows some room for speculation as to the race of the individual. In 1905, for instance, 274 jewelers—a field generally associated with Jewish immigrants—were arrested. Similarly, 347 "ragpickers," a job associated with Italian men, were arrested in the same year. In terms of historically Black professions in New York City, the 1,159 porters or 2,392 servants might provide a vague notion of policing and arrests made within Black communities.[7] The level to which African Americans were disproportionately arrested becomes even more apparent and stark when considering the arrest rates of Black women. In 1905, 4,070 Black women were arrested in New York City compared to 960 Italian women and 3,391 Irish women, both of which came from populations at least five times larger than the Black population of Manhattan.[8] Black women were more vulnerable to the whims of police than immigrant women and were often arrested for nothing more than being in public, as is shown by the experience of Mary Enoch, whose attempted false arrest for soliciting prostitution sparked the riot of 1900.[9]

From 1906 to 1909, Commissioner Theodore Bingham and subsequent police commissioners no longer reported arrest data broken down by nationality, race, or profession, but continued to exhibit arrest numbers by crime, precinct, and gender. Although more direct count of the number of African Americans arrested in a specific year disappeared after the crucial 1905 report, arrests by precinct provide some indication of an overrepresentation of Black New Yorkers. Precincts along the West Side of Manhattan with large Black populations, like the Twentieth Precinct where the 1900 riot occurred, saw more arrests of men and women than majority working-class, native-born communities downtown, although not substantially higher.[10]

The disappearance of "Black" as a category for recording arrests after 1905 did not mean, however, that the authors of these reports were entirely disinterested in policing along racial lines. The police department's report for 1908, compiled by Commissioner Bingham, begins with a complete demographic breakdown of all residents of New York based on "nationality." Unlike the previous practice, Black Americans are not separated out from white and other native-born people under the heading of "United States." The same document reaffirms the police's overarching concern about nationality and crime by providing lengthy reports on the moral scourge of "alien pimps" and decrying Italians as "medieval criminals."[11]

Although police disproportionately arrested African Americans, especially African American women, Black New Yorkers did not seem to constitute a "police problem" worthy of the intellectual labor dedicated to policing illegible immigrants. Unlike the thousands of memos and reports in which administrators puzzled through the problem of how different styles of policing could account for and mitigate racial and cultural difference among immigrants, Blackness received little attention. Yet it is hard to ignore documents like the NYPD's end-of-year report for 1912; it lists the multiracial San Juan Hill, which contained a majority of Manhattan's Black residents, as the precinct with the second most arrests in the city, with 5,630 arrests. San Juan Hill, or the Twenty-Sixth Precinct (as of at least 1908), was outnumbered only narrowly by the white working-class and supposedly gang-ridden Gas House District on the East Side waterfront north of Fourteenth Street, which saw 5,808 arrests that same year.[12]

The disappearance of "Black" as a category within the police reports can be seen as what members of the Citizens' Protective League called "whitewashing," or purposely erasing evidence of the omnipresence of police brutality and an overrepresentation of arrests in Black neighborhoods. It was also a "negative space," a neglected topic that allowed for the documentation of an imagined New York City in which police officials did not feel responsible for policing or protecting Black New Yorkers. Outspoken advocates against racial policing and state violence, like those who took part in the Citizens' Protective League, attempted to undermine the department's "whitewashing" and created a counter archive to undermine the NYPD's narrative.[13]

Respectability, Black Police, and the *New York Age*

In the wake of the 1900 riot, New York's oldest Black newspaper, the *New York Age*, emerged as a considerable force in disseminating information about police brutality and the disproportionate policing of Black New Yorkers. Under the ownership of T. Thomas Fortune, a close friend, confidant, and political ally of Booker T. Washington, the *New York Age* had been the nation's largest Black newspaper since 1887.[14] Both Fortune and Fred Moore, Fortune's political rival and successor to the ownership of the *Age*, served on the inaugural board of the Citizens' Protective League and oversaw the first meeting at St. Mark's Church and the Carnegie Hall rally. (See chapter 3.) Their voices were increasingly necessary as large-scale racial conflicts between white mobs, police, and African Americans on the West Side of Manhattan continued yearly between 1900 and 1910.[15]

During the next few summers, repeats of the events of 1900 played out in the Tenderloin and San Juan Hill as Black residents took up self-defense to contend with mob and police violence. In July 1905, after a particularly brutal outbreak of racial violence, the *Age* reported Commissioner McAdoo's call for "the colored people of the riotous district to surrender their weapons." African Americans, the piece continued, "are entitled to inquire why they should be compelled to disarm, and not the riotous white people around them as well ... but Mr. McAdoo seems to have jumped to the conclusion that the Negroes are held responsible without further inquiry." The real cause of the violence was not armed Black residents, as the police commissioner constantly reasserted, but rather the "low condition of both whites and blacks in the district between Sixtieth and Sixty-Fourth streets between West End Avenue and Tenth avenue."[16] Poor living conditions and recurring violence in the Tenderloin and San Juan Hill had two important results. The first was that it expedited the migration of Black New Yorkers from the diverse neighborhoods of the West Side to Harlem, a sprawling area to the north of Central Park at that time inhabited by Italian, Jewish, and other working-class immigrants. The second result was a growing chorus of Black voices dedicated to integrating the New York City Police Department in the hopes that it would, among other things, mitigate the ubiquity of police violence against African Americans.

On Sunday, August 1, 1909, Rev. Reverdy C. Ransom took to the pulpit of the Bethel A.M.E. Church on West Twenty-Fifth Street between Seventh and Eighth Avenues, in the heart of the Tenderloin, and began the city's most effective drive for Black appointments to the NYPD. In addition to seeking a solution to the problem of clashes between Black New Yorkers and police, Ransom also saw Black police as a remedy for what he saw as crime and lawlessness in Black communities. Like Booker T. Washington and many others who saw respectability as an avenue toward social and economic mobility, Ransom believed that the existence of Black crime threatened to confirm the worst stereotypes about the relationship between Blackness and criminality. "The time has come," he pronounced, "when the decent self-respecting and law-abiding members of the race should take a strong stand against the lawless negroes of New York City . . . we who are continuously denouncing the whites should show our honesty, broad-mindedness and sincere desire to see that the laws are not broken." Because Black police would allegedly understand the neighborhood better and be more familiar with local troublemakers or dangerous locations, they would be better equipped than white officers to clean up, rather than just brutalize, Black communities. "Chicago has three hundred Negro police," Ransom continued, "We need in New York City at least two hundred to be distributed as patrolmen, plain clothes men and detectives. They can do more to help the situation than under present conditions. This should be done in the interest of public morals."[17] Upper- and middle-class respectable members of the Black community framed bringing the supposedly "lawless" elements of the neighborhood under police control as a civic responsibility and a net positive in the fight for social and economic equality in New York.

This was a not-uncommon tactic in the fight for civil rights. For a large subset of middle-class African Americans across the United States, but particularly women associated with the Black Baptist church, contesting notions of biological racism and inalterable inferiority meant defying the expectations of white observers and setting an example for working-class Black laborers. Black men and women created spaces like churches and community groups from which to organize and voice opposition to racist violence and legal and state-sanctioned discrimination. In building a movement and shared vocabulary to criticize working-class African Americans for their supposed rejection of "hard work, piety, cleanliness, sexual purity, and temperance," respectability reformers like Ransom often reinforced stereotypes and invited more heavy-handed police intervention into Black neighborhoods.[18]

This tactic also made sense within the context of ethnic policing. Groups like the Italians thought that their kin on the police force would lead their community into respectability, inclusion, and whiteness by modeling respectable behavior and forcibly demonstrating a separation between good and bad immigrants. Ransom's plea made the same case—allow African Americans on the police force as a way to exemplify for white society how different respectable Black New Yorkers were from their allegedly criminal neighbors. The attempts of Ransom, the *New York Age*, and their allies were, in a way, an attempt to convert the exclusionary violence policing did in Back neighborhoods to the inclusionary violence they saw in immigrant communities—the type of policing that, according to the police themselves, was making model citizens out of the recently arrived.

Advocates of respectability politics, like Booker T. Washington, were especially enthusiastic about any measures that could crack down on Black urbanites' use of intoxicants. In a 1912 essay in the *Journal of Criminal Law and Criminology*, Washington claimed that after conversations with over a dozen police chiefs he concluded that alcohol and drugs such as cocaine were the chief catalysts for African American criminal behavior. He believed that personal responsibility, public policy that could prevent the consumption of these substances, or perhaps morals policing would be the best way to reverse the unfortunate fact that "two-thirds to three-fourths of the prisoners in the penitentiaries, jails and chain gangs in the South are Negroes." The rhetorical use of substances to stereotype African Americans became an important tool of racial criminalization by white police and reformers alike.[19]

Ransom and his allies also had the recent triumphs of the Italian Squad and other immigrant police to draw upon when imagining a model of policing that accounted for racial difference and the cultural knowledge needed to patrol specific communities. African Americans in New York did not need to be multilingual like Petrosino; instead they drew on their own special experiences and their journey toward political and economic mobility to argue for inclusion in civic life. "It has been cited," wrote one reporter, "that in the district occupied by Italians, fights with police were frequent until Italians were made members of the police force."[20] In his 1895 speech at the Cotton States and International Exhibition in Atlanta, Booker T. Washington famously called upon the sense of shared history between Southern whites and African Americans to advocate for the employment and hiring of those who were familiar and comprehensible, rather than those of "foreign birth and strange tongue."[21]

In New York, however, African Americans found themselves arguing the opposite. It was not their historic familiarity to white mechanisms of power that warranted their inclusion in the NYPD, it was, like recent immigrants, their difference. In an article for the *New York Evening Post* and reprinted in the *New York Age*, one reporter remarked, "There are Italian and Hebrew policemen, as well as Russian, Irish and German; in fact, all classes have their representation." Pointing out that many African Americans had, as in immigrant neighborhoods, become useful as informants, the reporter continued, "Negroes have proved comparatively as useful as was Lieutenant Petrosino among his countrymen."[22] Despite the diversity of the current NYPD and the supposed successes of race-conscious policing, in 1909 the department employed only five African American men as precinct doormen and drivers.[23]

The story of African Americans in US law enforcement began with the nation's acquisition of the Louisiana Territory and the preexisting regime of "free men of color" who served as New Orleans constables, lamplighter-watchmen, and city guards in the first decades of the nineteenth century. Half a century later, under the auspices of Reconstruction and the Republican sweep of local elections in the postwar South, Black police became commonplace in the cities of Alabama, Mississippi, and Louisiana. Their appointments with those police departments were short-lived, however, and most were dismissed after Democratic control was restored to the South after 1877.[24] During the 1870s and 1880s, mayors and police commissioners in Northern cities like Chicago, Philadelphia, and Cleveland found the appointment of Black police essential for providing protection to underserved communities vulnerable to mob violence, as a way to address Black criminality, and as a spoil of patronage to ensure Black votes for a specific party.[25]

In Brooklyn before its consolidation with Manhattan in 1898, a Black population that had grown in the years following the targeting of Black residents in Manhattan during the 1863 Draft Riots necessitated the employment of multiple African American patrolmen.[26] By 1909, activists in New York City had many cities, big and small, to look to as examples when proposing the appointment of Black police officers. "New Bedford, Newport, Pittsburgh, Chester, Harrisburg, Boston, are other cities in which the experiment has long since worked," reported the *Age*. "In some of these cities, where there was at first some prejudice, all friction has disappeared."[27] With the "experiment" of Black police supposedly succeeding in minimizing racial friction in other cities, the writers and editors dedicated themselves to its continuation and expansion.

The *Age* also dedicated many columns between 1909 and 1910 to highlighting other cities' crusades for Black police. After an election in St. Louis, Missouri, local Black residents demanded that newly elected officials keep their campaign promises to appoint African Americans to the police force. "Although they have colored police officers in many of the large Northern and Southern cities," wrote the reporter, "the position has been handled with kid gloves by those who have such appointments in charge ever since."[28] The following year, the

Age also recounted for its New York City readers the crusade undertaken by African Americans in Charlotte, North Carolina, to integrate its police force. "Negro special officers furnish the only satisfactory solution of the problem presented by bad Negroes in cities," one reporter wrote in the *Charlotte Daily Observer*. As evidence of this claim, the report cited the recent good work being done by Black officers in Charleston, South Carolina.[29] Although Black police were already patrolling streets in cities across the country by the time of Reverend Ransom's drive to integrate the NYPD in 1909, the issue was of national concern and captured the attention of the Black press across the country.

The response from NYPD sympathizers to Reverend Ransom's campaign echoed Police Commissioner Bingham's earlier concerns about expanding the Italian Squad. He claimed that during his tenure it was increasingly difficult to find new Italian recruits due to their unwillingness or inability to pass the civil service exam. Black and white critics of Ransom parroted similar concerns. "The absence of Negroes from the police force of Greater New York is not due to color prejudice," contended Chief Edward Lee of the United Negro Democracy, "but because in the past members of the race have been backward and unwilling to take the examination. Within the past four years but two Negro applicants have taken the examination and they failed to prove equal to the test."[30] As discussed in chapter 2, between 1896 and 1897, the department under Commissioner Theodore Roosevelt reworked the civil service exams in a way that excluded nonnative English speakers and working-class people with little formal education. Because the civil service exams valued certain types of (decidedly white) knowledge and skills, it seems moot to ask if Black applicants were actually failing their exams or were being purposely failed by members of the department in order to exclude them from the NYPD. However, under constant and mounting pressure from the *New York Age* and continuing clashes between police and Black New Yorkers, one African American man was finally able to break through.

Many of the writers who have discussed the appointment of Samuel Battle to the NYPD have focused their studies on how his hiring was a brief triumph in the long fight for Black civil rights in the city. Rarely if ever is his career with the NYPD, which began in 1911, understood within the broader context of ethnic and racial policing, and the efforts on the part of the police department to exert control over immigrants and racial others.[31] Although the NYPD did not voice much concern over the legibility of African American subjects, and Battle was appointed under different circumstances than immigrant police in the same era, his deployment to Black majority neighborhoods, and his own understanding of himself as an interpreter and translator of Black life for the NYPD, came to mimic the regime of policing that became the department's hallmark in immigrant neighborhoods.

Samuel Battle

Samuel Jesse Battle was born on January 16, 1883, in the small segregated town of New Bern, North Carolina, about 115 miles southeast of Raleigh. His parents, Thomas and Anne Battle, were born into slavery not far from New Bern. Thomas had worked as a preacher and a bricklayer and was, in time, able to earn enough money to purchase his freedom and that of his fifteen-year-old bride-to-be.[32] By his own recollection, Samuel Battle spent his early years getting into trouble for fighting and petty theft. He recalled being particularly disturbed when an employer caught him stealing and said, "Young man, before another year rolls over your head you'll be in a state's prison."[33] In May 1899, fearing that the young Battle would get into trouble with New Bern's white police beyond his usual youthful scuffles, his sister sent for him to live with her and her family in the North.[34]

Battle then spent some time living and working in Connecticut, first for a judge in Hartford and then for a boarding house in Glastonbury, where he claimed he had experienced "no color line in New England at all."[35] Finally, in 1901, he made the trip to New York, staying with his sister and his brother-in-law, Moses Cobb. Cobb had been a member of the Brooklyn police since 1892, just one year after the department had been desegregated by the appointment of Wiley G. Overton.[36] Because the Brooklyn police would not be consolidated with the more renowned NYPD until 1898, Cobb and his fellow African American Brooklyn police were never given the distinction of being the first Black members of the New York City Police Department.

By 1905, Battle had taken an apartment in Manhattan and was working as a redcap, or porter, carrying luggage for mostly white passengers at Grand Central Terminal. Although the pay was satisfactory, Battle foresaw a time in his life when he would not want to lift heavy bags for a living. Government and municipal work filled a place in Battle's imagination as a career that provided steady income, easy labor, and social mobility. Although young Battle stayed with the Cobbs for at least a few months, he credits another police officer with his decision to consider taking the civil service exam. His entrée into the world of policing ultimately came from the block where he lived.

Later in life, Battle recalled that he often saw "this Irish policeman, a little fellow, a fine old fellow," standing on his street corner, "I never saw him do anything except stand around and talk." More than just this patrolman's seeming laziness, it was his foreignness that convinced Battle that he would make a better policeman. "When he'd talk," Battle said, "sometimes you couldn't understand what he was talking about, it sounded like he had marbles in his mouth, with that Irish brogue of his."

Given the Irish police officer's sometimes impenetrable accent, Battle's own Americanness seemed to be all the qualification he needed. "If this kind of man can qualify as a policeman," Battle reasoned, "Couldn't I? I was born here, I'll volunteer."[37] Five years later, in 1910, Battle took the civil service exam for the first time in hopes of making it into the NYPD.

Battle ranked 199 out of the 683 people who took the exam, which officially made him eligible for an appointment. However, when it came time for the Surgeon General to give him the all clear, Battle was rejected for an alleged heart murmur. It was then that he called upon Fred Moore and the *New York Age* to take up his cause. Moore connected Battle with a white doctor on Sixty-Fourth Street who gave him a clean bill of health, and the two forwarded the report to New York City's mayor, William Gaynor. In addition to conveying Battle's situation to the mayor, Moore took the opportunity to restate the importance of appointing Black officers. "As you know," the letter to the mayor read, "there are colored policemen in Brooklyn who have rendered most efficient service, and I think you looked with friendliness at the time they were appointed."[38] According to Battle, Moore's letter so enraged the mayor that it contributed directly to his decision to fire the acting police commissioner, James Cropsey. Gaynor replaced the ousted Cropsey with the city's embattled Fire Commissioner Rhinelander Waldo, who at the time was still dealing with the fallout of the Triangle Shirtwaist Factory fire. Finally, under Waldo's tenure and after months of direct advocacy on the part of Fred Moore and the *New York Age*, Samuel Jesse Battle became Manhattan's first black patrolman on June 28, 1911.

That morning, the new police commissioner addressed a group of eighty newly uniformed police officers and forty-four probationary officers before their first day on the job. "You have passed the probationary period and now you go from the school to the street," the *New York Times* recorded him saying, adding, "I want you to understand that your appointments came about through your ability to get on the civil service list and not from any outside influence."[39] This statement was designed to dissuade those in the audience who may have thought Battle had gotten his posting through activism alone. *The Crisis*, the newly founded publication of the NAACP edited by W. E. B Dubois, also covered the ceremony, writing that Waldo went on to say, "I am glad to see that there is a representative of the Negro race trying to become a policeman. He was on the civil service list, and no color or race condition could have prevented his appointment."[40] According to Battle's own recollections, Waldo also spoke with him privately on the day of his appointment; "You will have some difficulties," he said, "but I know you will overcome them.[41]

"The Age Wins Its Long Fight for Negroes on the Police Force," blazed across the front page of the *New York Age* the following morning. "More than two years ago," the reporter proclaimed, "The New York Age took up the fight for representation of colored men on the police force of this town. By persuasion, by letter, by visits, by requests, and by demands we have kept up this fight."[42] This crusade by Black activists to force the NYPD to appoint one of their own could not have been more different than the immediate and deliberate appointment of Italians or German-speakers to the force during the early 1900s. Although members of immigrant communities had advocated for their inclusion in the police force, they never needed to mount prolonged campaigns, and were never resisted to the same level at which white police and politicians combated Black integration of the department. By the time of the Italian Squad's formation in 1905, most immigrant communities in New York had representation on the police force as a result of pragmatic necessity or political patronage. For its concerted efforts in the fight to desegregate the NYPD, the *Age* was showered in thanks and congratulations. "No job is too big for the *Age* to tackle," wrote the editor of the *Charlotte Advertiser*, "so we are not surprised that it has undertaken the policing of New York."[43] Battle himself wrote to the *Age* on July 18 to thank his friends and acquaintances for their activism and their congratulations.[44]

Battle also possessed qualities that enabled newspapers and the police department to justify his presence on the force without talking about his race. Whereas Petrosino and others were considered necessary because of their race and language abilities, the familiarity of monolingual Black subjects meant Battle's ability was assessed by different rubrics than other racial police. Battle's size and stamina became a constant legitimizing factor when discussing his appointment. In the *New York Times*, Battle was described as a "big brawny negro" who had "never been ill a day in his life."[45] Similarly, *The Crisis* had made a show of touting Battle as "Six feet tall, weighs 230 pounds, and is twenty-eight years old."[46] The size and prizefighting physique that connoted effective policing to Commissioner Theodore Roosevelt and others did not fully disappear during the age of immigrant detectives. In an era when the department needed "small" and "artistic" detectives just as often as it needed brawlers and pugilists, bodily standards of good policing were applied inconsistently based on what the department expected from a specific individual, often based on their racial identity. NYPD administrators, for example, rarely commented on the size and fighting ability of Italian or Jewish police who were believed to be physically smaller than their Irish, or ultimately Black peers. As eugenic logic rose in popularity among academics and social scientists of the era, optimizing the performance of the police department often meant administrators relied on a scientific discourse of race and bodies that trafficked in stereotypes and crude assumptions.[47]

Battle's personal mobilization of respectability politics also became one of his much-discussed characteristics. His history as a porter, which required him to wear a clean and pressed uniform and treat white patrons with deference, garnered him a reputation of propriety. Captain Palmer, the commanding officer of Battle's first precinct, described him as "a good sensible negro, and his conduct is above reproach."[48] Amid concerns that fellow officers in the station house and in the bunkroom were hazing Battle, police officials emphasized again and again that Battle was "not complaining" but taking the abuse without resistance. Any agitation on his part for better treatment or acceptance could possibly have been read as ungratefulness, unprofessionalism, or even aggression and criminality.

The months following his first posting to the multiracial San Juan Hill neighborhood inspired the Black community, as Battle later said, "as nothing had done in many days not excluding the time Jack Johnson defeated James Jeffries for the heavyweight championship of the world."[49] Like Petrosino, Warren Charles, and other "firsts" of a specific racial or ethnic group, Battle became a recognizable celebrity with people coming to his first posting on the very visible corner of Seventy-Second Street and Central Park West to cheer, jeer, or just to stare.[50] This rise to fame meant that Battle was, practically from the start, too famous and recognizable to go undercover. As he told it, for years sightseeing groups would walk past Central Park West and announce, "Here's New York's first colored policeman." Tour guides, and sometimes children from Harlem looking to make a quick buck, would bring flocks of curious tourists to see him on his patrols. This scene played out similarly to what Warren Charles, the first Chinese American NYPD officer, anxiously foresaw when he turned down a posting in Chinatown for fear of becoming a tourist attraction. [51]

Like the Italian Squad and others, Battle was deployed to a neighborhood where he would be policing members of his own race and setting about his mission to reduce police brutality against Black New Yorkers. Although his assigned corner on Central Park West was hardly the epicenter of danger, Black residents a few avenues west were frequent victims of mob and police violence. It was only a few weeks into his initial posting that he was called to his first riot. "We were ordered by our superiors to clear the streets and use our night sticks, it seemed to me that even though the negroes were fewer, more of them were beaten than whites, of course I really went to town on all."[52] Later in his life, Battle recalled that "the whites and the Negroes were battling. I saw the white cops beating up the colored people, and I thought, 'Here's my chance to get even with them.' I saw them whipping black heads, and I was whipping white heads. I'll never forget that."[53] In these instances, and in many others recorded in both an oral history taken in the 1960s and in the notes he took for Langston Hughes as part of a never-finished biography entitled *Battle of Harlem*, Battle recalled learning the lesson that his advocates had hoped to disrupt: "there was more law + order in the end of a night stick than the statute books."[54] Although Battle's appointment remained a symbolic victory for other African Americans hoping to join the ranks of the NYPD, police violence in Black communities continued unabated.

After two years of "whipping heads" in San Juan Hill, the NYPD moved Battle to the neighborhood where he and an increasing majority of Black New Yorkers were quickly migrating: Harlem. African Americans had been moving to Harlem en masse since the riot of 1900, and by 1913, when Battle received his new posting, parts of the neighborhood were almost entirely Black. Battle himself had been living on 136th Street since his time as a redcap. Although newspapers continued to focus on the racial street violence that still occurred with regularity along the west side of Manhattan, New York's Black population was steadily moving north. "Many were of the opinion," wrote one reporter for the *Age*, "that the colored police officer would be sent out in Harlem," in the same way that Italian police were sent into Little Italy, and German police to Little Germany.[55]

Sure enough, by 1913, the NYPD was unable to ignore the demographic shifts. Not only was Samuel Battle moved to the newly constructed station house on 131st Street, but the NYPD also hired its second African American officer, the Howard University-educated Robert Holmes.[56] Battle seemed to think this move, and the Holmes's appointment, were necessary as many white officers in Harlem "worked in an all-Negro neighborhood." In much the same way immigrant officers with linguistic capabilities often described their value to the department as translators, Battle also understood himself as an interpreter and ambassador for the police department in Harlem.

Describing the white officers in his precinct, Battle said, "they needed me as much as I needed them and sometimes more because some of them were on posts where there were all Negroes."[57] According to Battle, white police still felt as if they were patrolling a population that could not be understood. Although Battle's deployment to the Tenderloin, and then to Harlem, resembled the NYPD's strategy in immigrant neighborhoods, the department's leadership never articulated that they *needed* Battle in the same way that they needed multilingual immigrant police. Occasionally, however, they were proven wrong. In certain neighborhoods of the city, there were places to which Black police could supposedly gain access that white police could not.

For decades, police officers had attempted and failed to gain access to saloons, gambling houses, and other spaces frequented by a majority Black clientele. Although Black-and-Tans, which catered to all races and facilitated social and sexual interaction between Black and white customers, were known to and loathed by police higher-ups, white officers could infiltrate them. More homogeneous spaces were less easily policed. There was also the question of whether police had any interest in infiltrating entirely Black spaces. As historian Jennifer Fronc has argued, Progressive Era private anti-vice groups like the Committee of Fourteen and its colored auxiliary, the Committee of Seven, were primarily interested in shutting down establishments that enabled interracial fraternizing to protect intoxicated white women from the perceived threat of Black men's sexual advances. This meant these private investigators saw homogenous spaces as less of a threat to social and moral order because, unlike white women, "black women did not need to be saved from black men."[58] Private surveillance groups employed Black and white undercover investigators and sent detailed reports about establishments to the NYPD. Often, detectives of both races were sent to gain admittance to all-Black spaces. If the white investigator could gain admittance, it was used as evidence that the saloon catered to white as well as Black clientele, grounds for a raid and closure in the eyes of the police. In those instances where white investigators were met with suspicion, some resorted to calling themselves

"Cuban" in order to explain away their light skin. If this ploy worked, their admission could still be used as evidence of interracial mingling.[59]

For some time even after Battle's appointment, the NYPD had to rely on informants because there were few people capable of undertaking undercover work in majority Black spaces. For instance, despite his ability to infiltrate German-, Dutch-, or even Yiddish-speaking establishments, officer Cornelius Willemse remembered being denied entrance to a Black-owned saloon in the Tenderloin.[60]

By refusing to recruit Black officers, the NYPD allowed anti-Black racial bias to undermine its need to police parts of the city deemed inaccessible. Even though police failed to articulate an "African American problem" in the same way they repeatedly expressed concern over a perplexing "Italian problem," Battle's deployment to majority Black neighborhoods shows how the "native police" model had become the department's default for policing racial others. His understanding of himself as an interpreter for the state within Black neighborhoods further emphasizes that his role on the police force was filtered through the lens of the preexisting regime of immigrant policing. Battle was a translator the department didn't know it needed in a community it either thought it understood or did not think was worth understanding.

Samuel Battle, and his close associate Robert Holmes, blazed the path for dozens of other African Americans, including Black women, to join the NYPD in the two decades that followed.[61] By 1920, and the following generation of Black officers, however, it was clear that the criteria for good policing were changing.

After 1911, the department transitioned away from valuing officers who could utilize their backgrounds. Police commissioner Arthur Woods and his successors promoted a model of policing that valued qualities that could be taught or trained into officers, rather than characteristics they already possessed. Even though the "brawny" Samuel Battle was not an immigrant detective like Joseph Petrosino, Warren Charles, and others, his value as an officer came from a style of policing that valued a person's embodied and inherited traits.

With an increasing emphasis placed on classroom learning, scientific management, and well-trained and disciplined bodies, the NYPD saw new recruits of all races as unmolded clay that they could turn into effective officers. For example, Emanuel Kline, a Black officer appointed to the department in 1920, became fluent in Chinese, Spanish, and Italian while attending Columbia

University. Similarly, Louis Chisholm, a Black officer who joined the NYPD in 1921, became an acting lieutenant after producing a sociological study entitled "Rising Tide of Crime and Delinquency in Harlem."[62] The emerging trend of using the social sciences to understand the roots and causes of criminal behavior exemplified the scientific thinking that came to dominate law enforcement management in the years after 1910. These two incredibly successful officers followed in Samuel Battle's footsteps but entered a very different department: one that was being remade in the image of technocratic European police departments.

"POLICE ARE RAW MATERIALS"

7

Training Bodies in the World War I Era

In 1914, the year that World War I began in Europe, the NYPD released its most thorough police handbook since the department's founding. *Police Practice and Procedure*, by Cornelius F. Cahalane, the inspector in charge of the NYPD's new training school, covered everything an officer would need to know on the job including first aid, legal advice, techniques for collecting fingerprints, identifying different models of motor vehicles, and the proper technique for dispatching a rabid dog with a service revolver. The book was so beloved by the department's new commissioner, Arthur Woods, that it was distributed to every member of the force, regardless of rank or experience.

Police Practice and Procedure came to define the evolving objectives of the NYPD in the years following the 1909 dissolution of the Italian Squad and the phasing out of purposeful immigrant policing. "Police," wrote Commissioner Woods in the book's introduction, "must grapple, without hesitation, with any situation that arises, no matter at what risk to life."[1] The new guidebook was intended to train police officers who could handle any situation, no matter what arose, and no matter the demographics of their beat. It furthered a vision, shared by Commissioner Woods and other police technocrats, of a fully interchangeable and standardized police force where no ethnic group had a monopoly on any type of knowledge or specialized policing. Central to this project were department administrators' attempts to standardize not only the knowledge base and skill set of officers but also the bodies and physical capabilities of all the men on the force.

In 1917, at the behest of the Rockefeller-backed Social Hygiene Bureau, former NYPD administrator Raymond Fosdick conducted a survey of police departments in seventy-two medium and large cities across the United States. While embedded with those departments, he observed that officers "must be prepared to understand the criminal propensities of Sicilians and Poles, of Chinese and Russians. They must *become* expert in detecting crime characteristics as shown by twenty races.... They must have a ready knowledge of national customs and habits so as to be forearmed against an Italian festival, a Polish wedding, or a Russian holiday." Fosdick's word choice is telling. In the years since Joseph Petrosino's death, or even the deployment of Samuel Battle to the increasingly homogenous Black areas of Harlem, the NYPD overruled its default tactic for mitigating racial difference by using officers with specific backgrounds. Now with the prospect of a major war abroad looming, Fosdick suggested that police departments should find recruits who could "become" experts rather than those who had a lived knowledge of immigrant cultures. Informed by his years studying Europe's modern and technocratic police procedures, Fosdick's solutions to this problem were based, in part, in the NYPD's ability to classroom train, discipline, and educate police officers. These newly trained patrolmen and detectives were, in the eyes of NYPD leadership, qualified and prepared to be deployed into any community, not just their own.[2] *Police Practice and Procedure* was just beginning to shape this new generation of police.

This chapter argues that campaigns on the part of police intellectuals and politicians to prepare the city for an eventual US entry into World War I fueled the department's attempts to train and standardize the bodies and minds of police officers. It was expected that wartime officers should be as ready to defend the home front as they were to suppress petty crime. Standardization meant more than just uniforms and exercise regimens—it also meant a standardization of racial, ethnicity, and race-based knowledge. Even as police administrators attempted to build institutional support for a standardized response across all populations of the city, the wartime obligations of the NYPD made it hard for detectives to fully jettison specialized consideration of race, ethnicity, and language.

During the war, including the years preceding the United States' entrance into the conflict in 1917, immigrants, Black Americans, women's rights advocates, civil rights and labor activists, pacifists, and those labeled as sexual threats to soldiers became targets of the fledgling national security state. These individuals and communities were deemed suspicious by police, politicians, and military officials because their assumed foreignness and lack of patriotism, their radical, gender, or sexual politics, or their critiques of American imperialism and capitalism were thought to undermine any potential war effort by lowering national morale or practicing sabotage. For women and same-sex-desiring men, asserting economic agency through sex work or the right to spaces of leisure and vice ran the risk of being labeled a threat to the moral and physical well-being of soldiers, specifically out of fear of venereal disease. Central to this project was the renewed police harassment and surveillance campaign, both official and vigilante, against people of German descent living in the United States. Although language skills would still prove useful in sussing out possible German spies, wartime "preparedness" meant much more to police administrators than maintaining a detective bureau that relied on niche specialized squads to ensure national security; it also meant having a police force uniformly loyal, patriotic, and skilled. Ethnic and nationalist homogeneity and uniformity could be forged by requiring that officers, as in the Roosevelt era, cast off their ethnic markers and skills, cast away the hyphen between Polish American or Italian American, and commit to the department's attempt to remake them.[3]

For many years officers of Southern and Eastern European descent were the department's solution for reliably policing immigrant crime. Under that regime, NYPD administrators never made a sustained effort to teach Anglo-Irish officers how to more effectively patrol non-English-speaking immigrant communities. The 1914 training manual overturned that model by assuming that that Anglo-Irish or native English-speaking officers could be conditioned and educated enough to work within immigrant communities. "When you are on post in a section of the city populated by a foreign element," Cahalane wrote, "you will find that you are expected by the people to be their doctor, their lawyer and their interpreter." In Cahalane's view immigrants would treat police, the closest and most readily accessible proxy of the US state, as a directory for all government services.[4]

The explicit instructions to "render assistance in all good faith and confidence," with the qualification that, "such confidence should not be betrayed or abused," conjured the constant and ongoing threat of American-born police taking advantage of an immigrant's imagined lack of cultural knowledge for the purposes of exploitation or an easy arrest.[5] This new generation of police not only would be taught to help immigrants learn about the United States, they were also required to learn (formally rather than on the streets) something about immigrant New Yorkers as well. This knowledge, now disseminated by the department in books like *Police Practice and Procedure*, was still told through the lens of American-born officers. While discussing "general attitudes and habits," particularly those that imply guilt or nervousness, the manual's author warned that "gesticulation is very marked in some persons," and is not always a sign of nervousness. Hand gestures while talking, particularly in "Frenchmen, Italians and Hebrews," were so common that, "many of them would have great trouble in expressing themselves if their hands were tied behind them." Again, *Police Practice and Procedure* seemed invested in training American-born officers in how best to do their jobs in the presence of foreign-born New Yorkers.[6]

For a decade or more, systems like Taylorism, Fordism or the more broadly defined field of industrial science offered methods to make laborers of all sorts as effective and efficient as possible. Fosdick, Cahalane, and Woods all committed to the new objective of *creating* officers effective at policing immigrant communities where once they had to *find* them. Michel Foucault described a similar process when he wrote about the training of efficient and dependable soldiers, "[soldiers] have become something that can be made; out of formless clay, an inapt body, the machine required can be constructed; posture is gradually corrected ... ready at all times, turning silently into the automatism of habit."[7] Like the eighteenth-century soldiers Foucault discussed, the new bodies that signified good policing in the eyes of the NYPD administration were cultivated to be fit, ready, and interchangeable. The mechanical metaphors of the eighteenth century gave way to scientific and eugenic discourse in the early twentieth. The New York City Police Department gave a home to the Progressive project of using academic knowledge and scientific management to achieve mental and physical perfection.

Woods's focus on putting Anglo-Irish or second-generation immigrant-American officers through intensive physical and classroom training prompted the development of a number of new institutions. These included a training school, library, and partnerships with local universities to provide officers with classes in law, criminal science, and foreign languages. In Fosdick's words, "police are raw materials to be molded and shaped into efficient officers."[8] Mimicking both the world of industrial production and the growing class of white-collar bureaucratic laborers, the NYPD administration sought to prepare workers who were fully interchangeable and devoid of individualized or specialized skills, knowledge, or even physicality.[9] Commissioners and police intellectuals attempted to create officers who could be effectively deployed and redeployed in disparate neighborhoods without worrying about an individual's racial or ethnic background, or that of the community.

The "New" Spirit of the NYPD

From December 31, 1913, until April 1914, the NYPD had been in the hands of Douglas McKay, a thirty-five-year-old West Point graduate with a dwindling reputation. McKay operated on a no-nonsense "common sense" approach to policing that entailed repeated arrests of all suspicious persons. "It's no use hitting these fellows on the head," he told the *New York Times*, "They expect that kind of punishment, and they are probably used to it. . . . What they fear most is imprisonment. If they get to understand that it is a choice between prison and hiking, they'll hike."[10] However, on January 10, less than two weeks into his tenure, a gunfight between the Jewish "Dopey Benny" Gang and a rival Italian group erupted outside of Arlington Hall, a dance venue on St. Mark's Place. Despite multiple arrests the following day, the openness and brazenness of the violence were enough to deflate the reputation of the new commissioner.[11] By late February, newspapers began to speculate that a more experienced and older man would replace McKay. Rumors circled around many names, including Raymond Fosdick, a former NYPD deputy currently running the Social Hygiene Bureau, and Col. George Washington Goethals. Goethals, the clear front-runner, had served as the chief engineer during the construction of the Panama Canal, and weeks earlier had been named the new governor of the Panama Canal Zone.[12] It appeared once again that politicians and administrators in New York valued skills developed in the US imperial project as requisite experience for running the police department in America's most diverse city.

After Goethals declined the job in New York in order to stay in Panama, Mayor John Mitchel turned to someone familiar with the NYPD: Arthur Woods. Before joining the NYPD in 1906, Woods had been a reporter for the *Evening Sun* with deep ties to Progressive politics. He also served as a member of the delegation led by former president William Howard Taft that reported on the status of the colonial government in the Philippines. Among the Taft report's many findings was the observation that American soldiers were ill-equipped to be policemen on the diverse archipelago. Upon returning, Woods joined the department as deputy commissioner under Theodore Bingham. At the NYPD, he championed reforming the detective bureau as well as using legislation, specifically immigration restrictions, to prevent crime by deporting or forbidding potential criminals from entering the country.[13] His first stint in the department only lasted a few years, because in 1911 he went to England to study police procedures there before becoming the superintendent of a mining camp in Mexico.

By the spring of 1914, McKay's position at the NYPD had become untenable. After weeks of press speculation about an impending firing and replacement, he tendered his resignation to the mayor. "The reasons why I want to get out of the Police Department . . . I shall not discuss them," he told the *Evening World*.[14] Eight days later, on April 8, 1914, Woods was sworn in and immediately launched a campaign to boost the morale of the police department. Interested in how a poor quality of life for police officers negatively impacted their ability to patrol the city, Woods increased vacation time from ten to fourteen days a year and improved the cleanliness of station houses.[15]

For the rest of his tenure, Woods remained fixated on his reputation, both among the daily newspapers of the city and among the rank and file of the department. To that effect, a seemingly clandestine operation tasked officers with reporting what they overheard around police station houses. There were over a dozen unnamed and unsigned reports containing notes on this eavesdropping. "Woods is a pillar to the department," one report recorded two veteran officers allegedly saying on December 21, "I don't want to appear sentimental, nor sanctimonious but it . . . would take ten years to undo the constructive work that Woods has built up in a year and a half."[16] Hundreds of newspaper clippings compiled in multiple scrapbooks allowed Woods to keep track of the good and bad press coverage of his new initiatives. Like the positive reinforcement Woods received from many of the overheard conversations, much of the New York press also validated the rapid improvements and changes he was making in the department.

Dubbed the "New Spirit of the New York Police Force" by the *Sun*, Woods's early tenure was characterized by its preoccupation with quality of life for officers and with the integration of scientific discourse in order to show the modernity of policing in New York. Scientific rhetoric dominated conversations about department reforms as Woods "experimented" with the effectiveness of the fixed-station method and walking a beat. The NYPD also announced it would double the resources put into criminal identification procedures and technologies based on the "best experience and practice obtainable here and in Europe." Finally, early in his tenure Woods became a champion of classroom training and drilling new recruits so that no situation would catch them off guard. On March 17, 1914, he doubled the length of the training school from six to twelve weeks, and introduced training for such scenarios as, "rescuing drowning person," "carrying unconscious persons up and down ladders," and "descriptive portrait identification."[17] This renewed focus on training and conditioning police officers also informed the publication and distribution of *Police Practice and Procedure*.

Yet despite the "new spirit" of the NYPD and the increased training for officers, for many people on the ground, particularly African Americans, labor organizers, and other working-class New Yorkers, the new police looked and behaved an awful lot like the old police. In the years they served together, Mayor Mitchel and Commissioner Woods developed a mixed reputation for police brutality and the excessive use of clubbing. Both Woods and Mitchel, dubbed the "boy mayor" because of his election at age thirty-four, were inconsistent in their contradictory public calls both to curb brutality and to "restore the club" to its full glory after the previous administration's attempts to restrain police.

During his campaign for reelection in 1917, Mitchel was forced to contend with jeers and taunts from the crowd during campaign events. "Why did you let the police beat the East Side women up at the food riot?" shouted a Harlem heckler. This came after years of NYPD participation in the brutal breakup of strikes, union parades, and radical political meetings across New York. Even in moments when Woods praised the type of policing that happened without heavy-handedness, he also often cited work in neighborhoods where police regularly used violence against residents. "The handle of certain elements of society, particularly where there is a mixture of white and colored people is a police problem of no small proportions," he said in a statement to the *New York Age*. Particularly, Woods claimed that San Juan Hill, which had been rocked by riots yearly for over a decade, was now peaceful. He claimed that "intelligent supervision" and a "change of tactics" were enough to allow officers to be "just as firm" but without the use of clubs or revolvers. This statement from Woods came only months after police had shot three Black neighborhood residents, killing one, in a street brawl between San Juan Hill residents and civilian members of the Home Defense League.[18]

There remained a large disconnect between the rhetoric of the politicians at the head of the department and the daily operations of police. While Mitchel and Woods grappled with the moral and political implications of encouraging rampant clubbing on the streets, police were observed "assaulting and threatening to shoot a citizen in a subway train and brutally clubbing a *Tribune* reporter." And while some welcomed the changing rhetoric of politicians—even if it had no bearing on the behavior of patrolmen—some of the employer class balked at the idea of a more benign police force. "The free use of the nightstick, . . . is a positive necessity," wrote the president of Brooklyn's Commerce Club in the *Brooklyn Daily Eagle,* a sentiment also common in letters to the *Times* editor.[19] Although there is no evidence that Woods's and Mitchel's mixed signals on clubbing had any impact on the amount of police brutality in the city, their politics did have a manifest effect on the lives and bodies of officers.

Training the Minds and Bodies of Officers

The expanded NYPD training school was only one small piece of Woods's initiative. Beginning in late 1914 with the precinct downtown, the department added gymnasiums to station houses throughout the city. Woods also oversaw the creation of a police library in collaboration with the New York Public Library. In addition to dictionaries and encyclopedias, the library's focus was on the foundational books of criminology including the first book by Raymond Fosdick. Notably, the library also contained the 1911 inaugural English translation of Italian criminal anthropologist Cesare Lombroso's groundbreaking *Crime, Its Causes and Remedies.* For a department attempting to train Anglo-American officers to decipher potential criminality written on the bodies of immigrants, Lombroso's work seemed an obvious text.[20] During Woods's tenure, the NYPD at an institutional level attempted to replace street smarts or the lived experience of officers, also known as *metis*, with expertise disseminated in books and lectures, or *techne*.

Between 1915 and 1917, the NYPD continued to invent more reasons to put officers into classrooms. On most days between 1 p.m. and 2:30 p.m. and from 7:30 p.m. to 9 p.m., the department now ran a preparatory school for any patrolman looking to acquire the skills necessary to make him eligible for a promotion to sergeant. In addition to its own classrooms and schools for teaching motorcycle riding, criminal identification, detective work, and so on, the NYPD also developed a number of crucial partnerships for instructing

7.1 A cartoon satirizing a new regimen of officer training, clipped and placed in a scrapbook by NYPD commissioner Arthur Woods in December 1914. "Rollo's Rambles," *New York American*, December 1–14, 1914.

officers in topics not directly related to policing. In June 1915, the Eighty-Sixth Street branch of the YMCA, in the heart of the German Yorkville neighborhood, arranged for classes in French, Spanish, and German specifically for police officers. South Brooklyn Evening High School, with an attendance of almost four hundred, began to offer police-specific classes that focused on, among other things, developing "the power to express fully, briefly and clearly." In February 1917, Columbia University announced the creation of a sixteen-week program to teach police about criminal law, evidence, criminology, and municipal government.[21] It would be at least forty years before the city of New York would establish the John Jay College of Criminal Justice, a public university designed to give bachelor's degrees to future police.

These efforts drew a backlash, however, as political cartoons began lampooning the department's new emphasis on officer education. Clipped and scrapbooked by Commissioner Woods, one cartoon shows a group of policemen attending a lecture in a college hall. The lecturer tells the men in the audience about the proper application of a disguise and that if they encounter a criminal they must "tell him he ought to be ashamed of himself." Outside the building, a dozen men with guns shoot at each other and rob civilians unabated. The implication is that, in addition to forgetting the actual priorities of police work, the force has become decidedly less manly. Where once patrolmen would have clubbed wrongdoers, the cartoonist sees police as pampered college students more concerned with fanciful disguises and being polite than with public safety. In the corner of the cartoon, Uncle Sam and a young man labeled "The Common People," survey the scene. Uncle Sam's grin makes it unclear if he is looking on approvingly, in laughter, or in horror over the new style of police officer.[22]

Police themselves were sometimes reluctant to endure the amount of classroom schooling expected by Woods. Some complained, in the press as well as in private, about being treated like schoolchildren. At Woods's newly founded recruit-training school some administrators were finding that "all study and no play would have made Kelly a dull recruit," so recruits were encouraged to participate in physical training and pistol practice twice a day. However, even these activities, which were supposedly different from the classroom drilling, were still guided by experts. Expertise became a hallmark of the Woods administration, and no skill officers developed went into the field untested and uninspected.[23]

Not only did the department's new regime teach recruits their job one skill at a time, but they also proposed to rebuild each man from the ground up. Mundane activities that officers had been performing their entire lives, such as walking and eating, were now subject to critique and modification in order to make them more effective officers. The new initiatives that followed Woods' reforms reflected the popularity of Taylorism and scientific management in industrial labor, which taught workers how to move in ways that would maximize production. "In standing," *Police Practice and Procedure* suggested, "a policeman should not have his hands or arms folded or hanging in front of his body. This position throws the shoulders and head to the front."[24] Because officers spent most of their days stationary, the NYPD made an effort to train officers out of their usual ways of standing. The *Police Bulletin,* a monthly magazine that circulated within the department between January 1915 and April 1917, also gave officers regular reminders of the ways their daily habits might hinder their performance. "At the request of the Police Commissioner,"

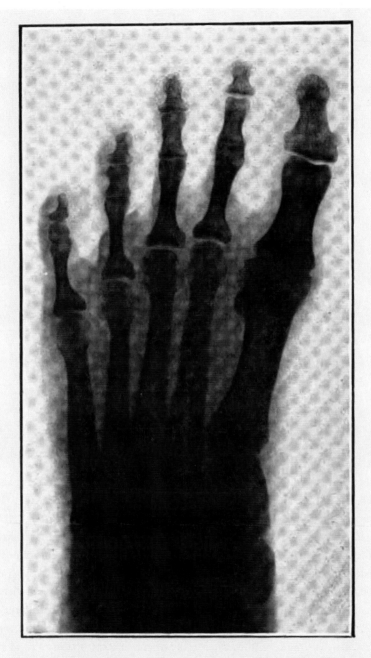

An X-Ray of a good type of police foot (bare foot).

7.2 X-ray of a healthy foot. "Foot Troubles: Their Cause and Prevention," part of the NYPD's attempt to build officers from the ground up. *Police Bulletin* 1, no. 7 (July 1915): 5.

7.3 "Cure for Obesity," image demonstrating proper exercise for police. Cahalane, *Police Practice and Procedure*, 6.

CURE FOR OBESITY

one entire issue in July of 1915 was dedicated to "foot troubles: their cause and prevention." With a doctor's precision, the article painstakingly articulated how an officer should stand and walk, and the consequences of long-term missteps. "Shoe-wearing people are taught to toe out, so that they get little use from the fourth and fifth toes, and so throw their weight on the inner, or weak side of the foot . . . their foot muscles get very little exercise and are put to waste more rapidly." These warnings and descriptions signaled to officers that any and all lifelong behaviors were subject to review by the department.[25]

Other technologies also aided the modernizing mission. Photographs in particular became central to the project of creating the bodies of modern police. The NYPD, like factory owners and industrial scientists, turned to photographs as instructional materials to both guide the movements of men and provide images of bodies to emulate. "Through photographs," writes historian Elspeth Brown, "the body's fluid and organic movements could be frozen, broken down, and reassembled into a more efficient combination of individual movements." During the period between 1880 and 1930, photography was a tool in the modernization of labor, as employers subjected their employees to instruction manuals almost identical to *Police Practice and Procedure*. The policing guide used images to break down exercises that could ward off obesity the same way employers used images to demonstrate the proper technique for cutting metals. Discovered in Germany and brought into practical use in 1895, X-rays similarly became a vital tool for shaping the bodies of police officers. The *Police Bulletin* relied heavily on X-rays to provide evidence that, even if police felt that they were standing correctly, their bones told another story.[26]

For officers, their bodies and minds were not all that was broken down to constituent parts, standardized, and retrained. On September 1, 1917, word got out that Commissioner Woods was considering requiring that each officer wear a wristwatch, in part to ensure proper recording of the time on incident reports. One detective was aghast at the idea of a police officer being forced to "wear an alarm clock on his arm." "Just imagine the men of twenty years ago" he said, "or even ten years ago for that matter—wearing wrist watches. Officially I am for it if the suggestion becomes an order, though personally I will wear mine above the elbow . . . times certainly do change."[27] Although objection to the watch campaign came from officers feeling threatened by having to account for their time down to the second, organizing a policeman's day around diligent record keeping was indeed a far cry from the freewheeling style of previous generations. Watches, according to historian Alexis McCrossen, were "adjuncts to armies, bureaucrats, and other agents of state building." In the decades that followed the Civil War, the importance of time keeping to military discipline had only increased to the point that police in 1917 would have seen a decidedly martial regimentation in being forced to wear wristwatches. It was not enough that the bodies and minds of officers had to be shaped according to new departmental standards, their chronologies had to be as well.[28]

There were, of course, limits to the top-down approach to police professionalization and discipline, especially where police violence was concerned. In 1917, at the height of World War I-era attempts at standardizing police performance, one violent incident illustrated where racial violence, xenophobia, and wartime policing collided to raise doubts about how "new" the "new spirit of policing" *could* really be. On May 26, 1917, a Black resident of San Juan Hill, Benjamin Hamilton, was showing a white friend around the neighborhood when the two entered a saloon on the corner of Sixty-Fifth Street and Amsterdam. The two ordered lemon and seltzers but were met with hostility from both the bartender and the white patrons. One report noted that the bar's location was just "passed the unmarked limits of the black belt" marking the unofficial boundary dividing white San Juan Hill from the Black blocks of the neighborhood, which meant Hamilton was not welcome.[29]

Another summary of events recounted that the white bar patrons were already on edge and agitated because of the authorities that patrolled the neighborhood that day. While many police officers were in the military during these years, cities and states organized Home Guards, volunteer semiprofessional men enlisted to keep the peace in the absence of more patrolmen. While in some places, like Connecticut, the majority American-born and Protestant Home Guard often bothered Catholic immigrants in cities like Bridgeport and New Haven, in San Juan Hill things were quite different. On May 26, the men of the Home Guard patrolling San Juan Hill were reportedly "Hebrews," although accounts of the day also mention men with Italian surnames serving in the area—either of which irritated the saloon patrons who took out their anger by jeering at and harassing Benjamin Hamilton and his friend.[30]

Hamilton fled from the bar, pursued by its patrons. When nearby Home Guard member Gabrielo Gilotti and Patrolman Michael Mirglia attempted to arrest Hamilton, believing him to be a thief, his white pursuers and police attacked Black onlookers. One man, Richard Hill, ran from police who chased him to Sixty-Third Street, where Patrolman Francis Meade began spraying bullets at him. When the shooting stopped Hill was dead, and Meade's bullets had also shattered the window of a Black-owned grocery store. Meade had shot the grocer, Eustace Graves, in the leg while his thirteen-year-old niece, Dorothy Graves, had been hit in the right thigh. The Black newspaper *New York Age* noted that, "while the race riot occurred on Amsterdam Avenue, from Sixty-first street to Sixty-fifth street, the police did all the killing and injuring on Sixty-third street, which is occupied by Negroes." Five people were arrested, all Black, including Benjamin Hamilton, whose disorderly conduct charge was eventually dismissed.[31]

Despite the lessons of firearm discipline and responsibility drilled into officers by extensive training and the department's new bible, *Police Practice and Procedure*, the realities of life in New York often made top-down reforms if not impossible, then hugely inconsistent. At least a decade of racial violence aimed at Black residents in San Juan Hill, white residents' defense of racial boundaries within the neighborhood, and the contested authority of immigrant men in wartime New York all eroded any semblance of police professionalism. The department remained what Black New Yorkers and reformers worried it would always be.[32]

Weight, Calories, and the NYPD Diet Squad

Chewing and eating also became an important reoccurring topic in the *Police Bulletin*. "Twenty-eight per cent of all cases of illness in the Police Department," one article read, were caused by issues concerning chewing, eating, and the choice of foods. The *Bulletin* warned against the vogue for "soft" foods, which it described as a source of "a degeneration of the 'civilized' mouth and teeth," which could lead to "chronic disease and degeneracy into old age."[33] More than anything else, reconditioning men to be more aware of their chewing, eating, and digestion was a way to address the NYPD's multiyear preoccupation with the weight of officers.

Throughout the first decades of the twentieth century, police administrators attempted to fight a growing concern that "after appointment to the force, the arms and body get comparatively little exercise and therefore become stiff and accumulate fat." Supposedly this excess fat not only led to "a slovenly appearance and, very often, carelessness in dress," but it also hurt the department's endeavor to prevent crime and apprehend suspects. In addition to being more effective at chasing or subduing people, fit and well-dressed officers were also seen as being able to "command respect" among citizens to such a degree that they wouldn't commit crimes or flee from police.[34]

For over two decades, NYPD administrators and a critical press voiced concerns about overweight police. In 1899 a letter to the *New York Times* provoked the paper's readers. In "Our Fat Policemen," author F. C. characterized the situation as a "disgrace of having such grossly overfed specimens of humanity on exhibit at our street corner.... Fancy this man, or any of the others for that matter, in pursuit of a malefactor! Do we need to look further for the reason so many criminals go uncaught?" In the eyes of the writer, overweight policemen presented a threat to society through their ineptitude as well as their alleged laziness. "If we do not reduce the girth of our guardians, we shall find that they will become more and more dependent on the ever handy revolver for 'holding up' an unwilling prisoner, a course which will make our streets even more exciting than they are now."[35] Critics and supporters alike often read virtue or moral failings onto the bodies of the officers. Trustworthiness, laziness, and even a proclivity for bribery were all supposedly legible based on the physique of an officer. These embodied characteristics were often intertwined with race and ethnicity. Starting with the rise of nutritional science and education in the 1880s, a person's commitment to gastrointestinal health and their choice of a diet was read as a reflection of their "ignorance or bad choices." For immigrants and people of color, including racialized and ethnic police, the lack of personal responsibility supposedly visible in robust waistlines or choice of food reflected a flaw in their psyches that could be overcome by education, Americanization, and conforming to imposed standards of masculinity and health.[36]

Some objected to the idea that overweight officers needed to change. Two days later, the *Times* ran a critical letter responding to "Our Fat Policeman." Rather than seeing overweight police as embodying inefficient policing and slovenliness, reader William Strang retorted that "Fat men are always jolly; they rarely pull a pistol on anyone. Fat men are never vicious preferring always to pacify rather than antagonize ... the greyhound policemen of to-day very often becomes the heavyweight of to-morrow."[37] But this defense of the embodied characteristics of "fat policemen" became increasingly unpopular as NYPD administrators continued their attempt to reform the bodies of men along with the structure and operations of the department. In the years following 1899, this attitude continued to shift along with popular headlines, many of them clipped and scrapbooked by reform police commissioners like Francis Vinton Greene and Rheinlander Waldo. For example, "Fat Policemen Hurt in Spill," "Waldo Will Make Fat Policemen Train," and "Fat Policemen Must Walk" all represented a growing consensus that overweight officers carried negative connotations, not only about their cleanliness, morality, and their effectiveness as individual officers but as representatives of the NYPD.[38]

The decades-long battle against obesity in the department came to a head in 1917 during Woods's tenure as commissioner. Both the manual he championed and the short-lived *Police Bulletin* promoted the idea that strict training and conditioning would allow any man to achieve an ideal police body. This ideal body was tall, slim, toned, and clean, with a straight posture and an uncreased uniform. Woods aimed for uniformity in physique and ability, and anyone whose body violated those expectations was subject to a strict regime of conditioning. On the first days of the year, Woods' NYPD

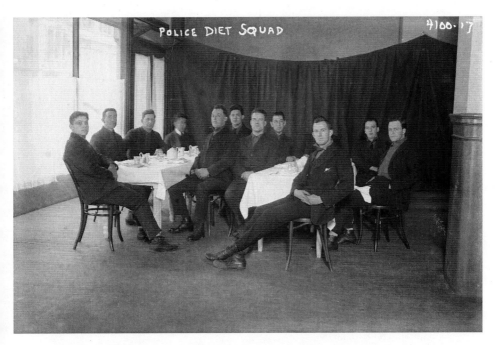

7.4 Perhaps the only photograph of the NYPD Diet Squad. Bain Collection, Library of Congress.

announced its most direct experiment to date in conditioning men's bodies: the NYPD Diet Squad.

The Diet Squad consisted of twelve "husky" bachelors from the new recruitment class who would live on twenty-five cents a day. The squad had a number of objectives in addition to teaching men how to eat more healthily. First, the experiment sought to teach their families (and by extension others) thriftiness in light of stagnant wages and an increasing cost of living. Second, it provided an opening for broaching the subject of rationing should the US government decide to enter the ongoing war in Europe.[39] There does not appear to be any institutional connection between the Diet Squad and the war effort, but it was framed in the New York City press as a vital experiment under the umbrella of preparedness. Calories were the fuel that fed the soldier-machine, and finding ways to put the proper number of beneficial calories into the body was vital to the health of the nation and the integrity of the war effort.[40]

In lieu of higher-ranking police officers, the Diet Squad reported to a team of doctors and professors. These experts included Henry Sherman of

Columbia, Irving Fisher of the political economy department at Yale, and Dr. Eugene Fisk of the Life Extension Institute. The transition, toward the full integration of academic knowledge into policing was now extended to the management of police diets.[41]

The men, referred to in the press as "brawny aspirants," "voluminous undergraduates," and people who, "might be looked to to put up a gallant struggle in an old-fashioned eating contest," were subjected to scrutiny by the department, their professorial handlers, and an enthusiastic media that recorded nearly every morsel of food they ate. A full-length mirror was placed in the room in which their meals were served, the "Café de Diet," so that they could study the effects of the diet on their bodies. Daily newspapers reported on the gains and losses recorded in their regular public weigh-ins. Whether the Diet Squad proved a failure or a success depended on one's perspective. On the one hand, the men gained between six and seven pounds in one week, but on the other, the experiment had demonstrated clearly that it was possible to purchase and consume a necessary number of calories on an extremely limited budget.[42]

Militarizing Militarized Police

Teaching police about rationing was not the only aspect of the war effort folded into the department's culture. As politicians weighed the necessity of US involvement in the European war, the influence of the many former military men in high-ranking positions in the NYPD became increasingly apparent. During 1916 and early 1917, "preparedness" became a central concern of Woods's department, whether it be for "fire, flood, cyclone, tidal wave, earthquake, or even foreign invasion."[43]

Many New Yorkers looked on with anxiety as preparedness transformed the NYPD into something that began to resemble a militarized occupation of the city. In one training exercise, police were sent to Staten Island in companies of 350 men, given military rifles and tactics training, and forced to defend a fort during a "sham battle."[44] On October 17, 1916, the NYPD paraded down Fifth Avenue in a fashion they never had before. Gone were the signature blue uniforms, or the batons hanging from their belts. Now New Yorkers saw their neighborhood police officers clad in khaki military-style uniforms with rifles on their shoulders and mounted machine guns pulled on tripods. "We ask Commissioner Woods—WHAT IS THE REASON FOR THIS ARMY EQUIPMENT," read one letter in *The Call*, "New York's police are becoming more militaristic all the time. They are becoming more like cossacks. With the mounted cops, the machine-gun cops, the cops with rifles, New York cops are getting to look more like an army than a police force. WHAT FOR?"[45] One thing that had supposedly set the United States apart from its adversaries in Germany and Austria-Hungry was the alleged benevolence of its police force. Some units of the multifaceted German police looked more like soldiers than beat cops and it was often their job to maintain order by use of violence, indefinite detention without a trial, and sanctioned torture. Although the lived experience of many Black New Yorkers may not have been much different from that of the most brutally treated German citizens, law enforcement in the United States was still symbolically, if not legally, opposed to such extreme and militaristic tactics.[46]

A song entitled "Soldiers All the Time" was published in the *Police Bulletin* in November 1915 in light of the ramping up of "preparedness" in New York. The poem's purpose, as evidenced by its emphasis on how "commissioners are changin' fast," was to show how militarization and modernization of the police force were entwined. Progress came in the form of new uniforms, fitter men, and larger equipment. The third refrain in particular emphasized how far the police had come:

Time was when they was heavyweights and
Did their little stunt
In a sort of German Helmet and a big, bow window front.
They turned a corner like a truck; they
Couldn't beat a dray,
But that was some before the flood—just
Look at 'em to day.
A-foot, a-horse, a-wheel the force is turned
Out spick and span.
They're prideful of their uniforms as any
Army man;
They're drilled and quick and straight and
Slick—it's good to put in rhyme
That they're the city's U.S.A. and soldiers
All the time![47]

Implicit in the song is the constant refrain that what made modern police modern was their physique. Gone were the days of "heavyweight" prizefighting bodies that "turned a corner like a truck." The new police were "drilled" in clean military uniforms.

Although "Soldiers all the time" emphasized the newness of the militarization of the police and its modernity, a militaristic posture had been one of the defining characteristics of the NYPD during the past two decades.[48] The militarization of the police under the guise of preparedness was, in many ways, the culmination of a process that had begun in 1898 and even earlier. The Civil War provided an opportunity for fledging municipal police departments to consider wartime preparedness and defend infrastructure from would-be saboteurs. For decades after that, the NYPD had absorbed men, tactics, and technologies from the farthest reaches of the American imperial project. This included adopting "native policing" and the anti-insurgency mentality that came with it. Combined with a large-scale crackdown on civil liberties, the passage of the Sedition Act of 1918 and resulting arrests, and the official as well as state-sanctioned enforcement of nationalist jingoism, the militarism of the police took on a form that was more recognizable, obvious, and ultimately troubling to many New Yorkers.[49]

American Police, Foreign Suspects

Conditioning the bodies of men was also about demonstrating Americanism and patriotism. In an ethnically and racially diverse department where physical martial preparedness was synonymous with patriotism and belonging, one's body became an important signifier of allegiance. In the months after the United States declaration of war against Germany, many New York notables and NYPD alumni such as Theodore Roosevelt and the current mayor, John Mitchel, declared hyphenated identities—and the physical traits in which they were embodied—an affront to American patriotism. In 1917, Mitchel ran for reelection on a platform of scientific management and xenophobic jingoism and created a climate where some immigrant groups felt the need to endorse the young Republican or be branded unpatriotic foreigners. At Temple Beth-El, Rabbi Samuel Schulman clarified his position: "Jews will cast their votes as Americans, and not as Jews." Similarly, concerns that German immigrants would sway Irish New Yorkers by arguing that "the cause of Irish freedom would be furthered by a German victory on the battlefield or of their apologists in the present municipal campaign," worried some in the city. Although he received the endorsement of the like-minded Roosevelt, Mitchel lost the Republican primary.[50]

"I stand for straight Americanism unconditioned and unqualified, and I stand against every form of hyphenated Americanism," Roosevelt declared in a 1916 speech. "All I ask of the immigrant is that he shall be physically and intellectually fit, of sound character, and eager in good faith to become an American citizen." This vision of an American style of masculinity is definitively tied to a preferred type of male body with its signifiers of heterosexuality, unquestionable whiteness, and productivity. Any deviation from the ideal American masculine form could be read as sick, deviant, criminal, or unpatriotic.[51]

Whether patrolmen took the department's training regimen seriously or not, the NYPD's focus on trying to create bodily uniformity among officers by definition did so in a way that replicated "American" bodies. Fit bodies were ready for war, and people ready for war were without conflicted national allegiances. Although years earlier, Roosevelt in his "Ethnology of the Police" had attempted to literally rank the ability of police officers based on their ethnicity, he now said, "We are false to this country if we rank ourselves as 'German-Americans' or 'English-Americans,' 'Irish-Americans' or 'French-Americans.'" In the eyes of nationalists like Roosevelt, war required physically turning immigrant officers into unquestionably American soldiers, and the integration of scientific management gave police administrators the tools with which to do it. But what about those New Yorkers, especially those of German descent, who were suddenly regarded with extreme suspicion?[52]

Although the standardization of policing had incorporated a "de-ethnicizing" of formerly identity-based squads, the war effort and the hypernationalism it engendered presented its own challenges for police in a multiethnic and multiracial city. Because the Italian Squad, phased out in 1909, had been tasked with handling the supposed bomb-based crimes associated with both organized crime and anarchists, many of its members became the core of the NYPD Bomb Squad, officially formed by Arthur Woods in 1914.

Because of the war effort and the fear that immigrant radicals and German sympathizers might attempt to destabilize the city with explosives, the deracialized squad, officially valued for their ability to defuse bombs, was still primarily tasked with monitoring those deemed foreign or un-American. "As time wore on," reflected Woods on the formation of the new bomb unit, "the Squad's energies became directed solely against the nefarious activities of Germans among us." For this reason, the Bomb Squad was temporarily renamed the Bomb and Neutrality Squad, because of their responsibility not just to defuse bombs but also to ensure no bombs threatened to upset the nation's neutrality in a war that President Woodrow Wilson was determined at the time not to enter. After the United States' entrance into the war, the squad's mission shifted from maintaining neutrality to sniffing out spies and saboteurs, which often meant either recruiting informants inside radical, antiwar, or pro-German circles, or sending in officers who could speak the language. The squad's go-to detective spoke only English, "a good language for social intercourse, but not the key to affairs of the group," who would revert to their native tongue and make it "impossible for our man to eavesdrop." The police department administrators were very much in need of officer-translators who could infiltrate spaces most Anglo-Irish officers could not. The department-level policy might change and priorities shift, but policing's relatively small toolbox meant no tactic was ever retired permanently.[53]

In February 1917, a member of London's Metropolitan Police Force at Scotland Yard warned the NYPD that anti-imperialists objecting to Great Britain's continuing occupation of India had been conspiring with Germany to carry out "dynamite plots" throughout England and the United States—placing the force on a continuum of race, empire, and global circuits of violence. As a result, members of the Bomb Squad surveilled one particular Indian anti-imperialist in New York for an extended period of time from an apartment across the street from his home on West 120th Street. Now Indians too, like Germans, suffragists, civil rights and labor advocates, working-class women, and many other groups were added to the list of people whose mere presence was deemed to challenge the geopolitical and socioeconomic status quo and thus threaten national security.[54]

White Americans, following the lead of the British, also feared that the peoples they had subjugated through formal and informal violence, as well as legal discrimination and segregation, might become a liability in the war effort and vulnerable to infiltration and influence by an enemy foreign power. For much of the war, local police worked in conjunction with military intelligence and other federal law enforcement agencies to investigate and surveil Black activists and publications and monitor Black soldiers for signs of disloyalty. Police had always treated Black New Yorkers with a heavy hand—but that brutality and harassment took on a new dimension because of the war effort and other imperial powers' fears of foreign-stoked dissent within the metropole.[55]

In a diverse city where foreignness or non-whiteness itself was understood as a potential threat to national security, police intellectuals in the years during and after World War I searched anxiously for ways of scaling up their ability to track and subordinate large groups of people. It was not enough that the police themselves had trained and standardized their skills—now the same thing had to be done with the general population. Aided by new techniques, technologies, and ways of thinking about policing developed by European police and their colonial counterparts, NYPD administrators found themselves in the years following World War I with a new desire for information.

GLOBAL KNOWLEDGE / AMERICAN POLICE

8

Information, International
Collaboration, and the Rise of
Technocratic "Color-Blind" Policing

On July 17, 1919, New Yorkers opened their copies of the *Evening World* to find a humorous anecdote nestled between articles about returning soldiers convalescing at the Yale Club and an unemployed man who leaped from the Queensboro Bridge. The story concerned the Essex Market Police Court's move to a "palatial" new building and, more important, how its dusty basement had become the new home for decades of police files chronicling the arrests and criminal cases brought against residents of the predominantly immigrant Lower East Side. The story narrated how the documents were under attack from a large family of rats that were gnawing their way through boxes of files. Special sheets were attached to the floors and walls to collect "fingerprints" from each rodent in an attempt to identify the guilty parties. Once the individual rats were differentiated by their paw prints, they were assigned names and mock summons were written for them. The article triumphantly quoted the court's so-called fingerprint expert: "There is no doubt that we shall get 'em. You may quote me as saying authoritatively that science and the law never fail. I have the fingerprints and the rest is easy."[1]

The article may have been a parody of police methods, but it conveyed a real sentiment being pushed by academics and police administrators, not just in the United States, but also around the world: The continued merging of science, technology, and policing could produce results even when used on creatures as uncompliant, inhuman, and elusive as rats. To identify, trace, and summon these rodents, the police did not need witnesses or even interaction with the suspects. It didn't matter that they did not speak English or looked indistinguishable from one another. By virtue of their slightly different paws and the science that unlocked them, the "rest is easy."

During the first decades of the twentieth century, police administrators had been searching for ways to make the diverse and multiracial populations living in New York City more knowable to the government. Absent wide-scale community cooperation, a near-constant police presence, or officers who could effectively infiltrate racially and ethnically insular social spheres, technology emerged as a primary method of making sure no neighborhoods or communities could avoid police scrutiny. In the years immediately preceding and following World War I, police administrators, academics, and the rich industrialists who supported them tapped into the growing network of global police cooperation to bring back technologies designed to aid in subordinating diverse cities. The beneficiaries of bureaucratic and police experiments often essential to the governance of their colonies in South Asia and Africa, European cities became classrooms for NYPD administrators, who went abroad in search of new techniques for pacification and surveillance. By focusing their attention on affixing bureaucratically compatible and simplified identities on people and amassing information on those individuals, police laid the groundwork for a century of surveillance, biometric data collection, and the information later referred to as "identity management" or "identity dominance."[2]

This chapter argues that Progressive reformers and technocrats like Police Commissioner Woods and the former NYPD administrator and member of the Social Hygiene Bureau Raymond Fosdick, attempted to import emerging European techniques of criminal science, suspect identification, and bureaucratic governance as a universalizing method for policing diverse populations.[3] They were aided by a coterie of police professionals and intellectuals across the United States and the world, people like the Berkeley, California, police chief August Vollmer, who maintained extensive relationships and correspondence with professors, politicians, and police chiefs around the globe. Motivated by what politicians saw as decades of NYPD failure and the inability of US police in general to oversee diverse cities, scientists rather than beat cops provided innovative control measures. Technologies like the photograph and police file, which had been deployed in various forms over the past fifty years, suddenly held more sway—and strategies and mentalities like proactive lawmaking, criminology and eugenics, and information hoarding became a more fertile ground for experimentation.[4]

The growing international system of policing collaboration crystalized a global move toward disciplinary technocracy, a system of police governance guided by the formalized discourse of expertise rather than knowledge collected through the everyday lived expertise of officers. Police not only needed to gain more academic and scientific legitimacy through classroom training, academic affiliations, police laboratories, and a heavy reliance on statistics, but they also needed to have their daily experience turned into usable data by having scholars and scientists launder and legitimize their observations. Policing had always been a struggle as departments attempted to balance what James C. Scott has discussed as *metis*—knowledge predicated on "practical experience"—with *techne*, an empirical and academic style of knowledge characterized by "impersonal, often quantitative precision and a concern with explanation and verification." While one mode of thinking about policing never truly eclipsed the other, especially at the street level, technical thinking and expertise dominated police administrations.[5]

Although policing in the 1910s moved away from the style of "native policing" when the NYPD dissolved its ethnic squads, more technology-based colonial and military mentalities and tactics remained central to the operations of the department. The impact of the officers' and administrators' encounters with colonialism remained visible within a post-Italian Squad NYPD in the ways that detectives and clerks utilized bureaucratic technologies and engaged daily with ideas about bodies and identities. Filing cabinets, paperwork, and other technologies that were essential to the growth of the enormous railroad corporations in the nineteenth century also found a home in the coercive management of colonies far from the halls of power in Washington, DC. In New York, technocratic-minded commissioners and police intellectuals deployed these tools as part of a twofold solution to the

American Problem: Develop American-born police more capable of understanding immigrant communities and make immigrant communities more knowable to the US state.[6]

In addition to training American police to read previously illegible subjects through education and standardization of skills, attempts were also made by both the state and employers to make those indecipherable subjects more susceptible to control. Police understood reading the bodies and motives of immigrant residents as if they were trying to read a book written in a foreign language. While officers in the classroom were taught how to read that language, other administrators within the police department were trying to write accessible translations. The rise of new managerial technologies meant that police departments could distill the identity of each alleged criminal or suspect to a well-organized and highly navigable collection of standardized observations. Building on decades of the NYPD's use of technologies like the Rogues' Gallery and the Bertillon system (described below), these innovations in criminal identification created a searchable paper index of subjects that paralleled their more mysterious and guarded analogs walking the street. The process of making foreign-born subjects more understandable happened alongside the process of European immigrants becoming increasingly included in the project of whiteness. Although it would take many decades for people of Southern and Eastern European descent to be integrated into the white middle class, the police decision to ignore ethnicity in its operations was a harbinger of the consolidation of whiteness that was to come.[7]

These files created not "paper cadavers," a term historian Kirsten Weld has used to refer to subjects whose paper selves survived long after their flesh selves were killed by the state, but what I call static "paper suspects."[8] Paper suspects are the version of a person that exists in the records of the police department. Regardless of a person's ethnicity, linguistic ability, or behavior, all paper suspects could be built and organized in such a way that they were comprehensible. On the street, police had long struggled to make sense of the motives, body language, and speech of immigrant suspects; but in the comfort of the police headquarters, everyone could be made unambiguous. Even if a suspect could not speak a word of English, a file containing their fingerprints, a photograph, and a documented modus operandi (the newly invented psychological term meaning a suspect's preferred method of criminal behavior based on prior arrests) could be enough evidence to make an arrest.[9]

The Global Problem of Fixing an Identity to a Person

Assisting in the conditioning of officer's bodies through the use of X-rays and visual training handbooks was only one of the ways that photography and images became central to modernizing the police department. For decades police had organized photographs of arrestees in the Rogues' Gallery, a wall or sometimes a large cabinet filled with straight-on images of hundreds of faces. For much of the nineteenth century, the Rogues' Gallery was the primary means of identifying suspects and noting prior arrests. This method had its obvious downsides. For one, "In searching through large collections of photographs the eye soon becomes fatigued," wrote social scientist A. F. B. Crofton in 1895, "and refuses to notice any but the more striking peculiarities. It is physically impossible to compare any given photograph with each of the portraits in a collection of many thousand."[10] In addition to eye fatigue and the unreliability of comparing too many photographs, relying on pictures as the primary tool for suspect identification also meant relying on the suspect's cooperation to get a good representation. A scrunched face or unnatural curl of the lips would be enough to make the resulting photograph unusable by future detectives. The Rogues' Gallery, developed by American detectives and made popular by Thomas Byrnes, was to be one of the last innovations to come from the United States for a few decades. For new inventions and techniques designed to pin an identity to a person, American police would have to turn toward Europe.[11]

During the 1880s, the arrival of the Bertillon or "French" technique, proved a short-lived and equally problematic alternative to the Rogues' Gallery. Named after Alphonse Bertillon, a Paris detective and collaborator with Cesare Lombroso, the system broke down the suspect's body into a dozen minute measurements that could be used in the future to link the suspect to a specific criminal file. For instance, detectives could measure the length of a suspect's head circumference, height, left middle finger length, or right ear length, and search indexed cards to see if the suspect's measurements matched those of a previous arrestee. Deemed more effective than relying on photographs, the system circled the globe. For colonial troops attempting to subjugate foreign subjects, measuring a head seemed to be easier than attempting to learn a person's identity through the interrogation of informants. Indeed, British authorities first tried it out in India before introducing it in London.

In the United States, municipal police departments were not the only fast adopters as administrators of European colonial powers put the system

8.1 The NYPD Rogues' Gallery, 1909. Bain Collection, Library of Congress.

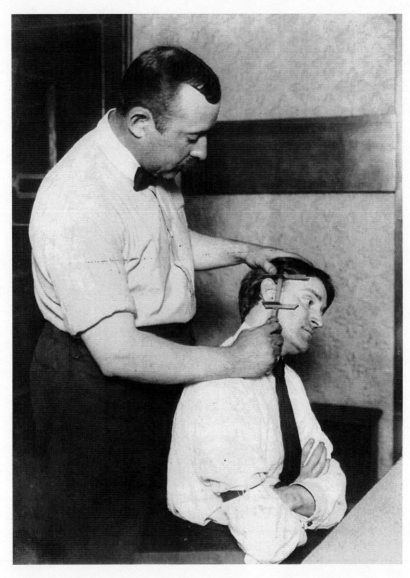

8.2 An NYPD employee demonstrating a Bertillon measurement of the ear, 1908. Bain Collection, Library of Congress.

in place all over France, Britain, Germany, and the entire British Empire. In practice, there were multiple specific techniques that police departments deployed. The police department of Rome, for instance, preferred the "Argentine system" used most commonly in South America, while the Boston and Newark, New Jersey, police preferred the Conlay method developed by authorities in Singapore.[12] In 1907, the US Secret Service Bureau in the Philippines jettisoned the bulky bound books used to store information on individuals in exchange for a Bertillon and file method of organizing information.[13]

However, the Bertillon system required immense cooperation from the suspect. Different officers were also likely to record measurements slightly differently, meaning a single arrestee could possibly generate multiple index cards. And because "no two men will measure a criminal in exactly the same way because of the infinite variety of measurements," this also threatened the department's crusade to create a system in which officers were fully interchangeable. Experts believed the Bertillon method was less reliable when it came to affixing identities to women and children because of children's steady growth and because of women's "hair" and "recurring pathological disturbances." Whether it was long hair or biology that appeared to stump police, it is clear that they had identified something particular about the criminality of women that rendered minute and accurate measurements ineffective. These two technologies, both the Rogues' Gallery and the Bertillon system, contributed to developing a system of knowledge about criminals in which bodies, and representations of the body, became the primary representation of criminality.[14]

The transition from Rogues' Gallery to the Bertillon system and then to the latest imported invention—fingerprinting—all represented moves toward identifying unknown people with less and less necessity for cooperation or interaction with the arrestee. British imperial administrators developed the system as far back as the 1850s as a tool for tracking and verifying identity among colonial subjects in India. It proved an effective means to surveil a large populace where the administrative power differed in language and culture from the general population.[15] Fingerprinting made its public debut at the 1904 World's Fair in St. Louis, which also played host to a convention of US chiefs of police. Famed detective and fingerprint enthusiast John Kenneth Ferrier represented Scotland Yard of London at the convention and educated the American public on the concept and techniques of fingerprinting for use by law enforcement.

"It is not necessary," wrote one Kansas newspaperman after seeing the London police department's 1904 display, "to know a man's age, color, or

8.3 An NYPD officer fingerprinting a German, 1909. Bain Collection, Library of Congress.

any circumstance of his life in order to discover his personality by means of the finger-print method." Simply put, police did not have to learn to communicate with, or even tell the difference between the faces of newly arrived immigrants if they could rely on their fingerprints to do the differentiating for them. "A person's appearance may alter," read the NYPD procedure manual in 1914, "he may become stout or thin, grow a beard or remove one, but the imprints made by his fingers will never differ." Unlike taking a photograph of a suspect for the Rogues' Gallery, or measuring a head for their Bertillon file, collecting fingerprints no longer required the body of the suspect. Detectives could dust for prints at a crime scene hours or even days after a crime had been committed. Fingerprints not only held a key to making foreign bodies understandable, recognizable, and easy to reliably index, but they also allowed police to make *absent* bodies recognizable.[16]

By the late 1910s, fingerprints were only one component of the technology used by police to create "paper suspects" in the police station. The criminal file, which, according to Raymond Fosdick, came into being in the mid-nineteenth century in European police departments, was a modular technology that could expand or contract to contain as many different and important pieces of information as needed. Photographs, fingerprints, and each new innovation could be incorporated into the file and stored in easily searchable filing cabinets. Throughout the early twentieth century, both in Europe and in the United States, criminal files were constantly standardizing, incorporating new technologies and jettisoning obsolete ones. By 1916, Bertillon measurements in police files were replaced with a new page for a person's modus operandi or "known methods of operation." If an arsonist was at large in the city, police need only search through files of known arsonists to find what they believed was a likely suspect. A person's MO combined with a fingerprint at the scene now meant that, even without witnesses, a file could provide reason enough to land someone in police custody. Even if an actual suspect had not been apprehended and was in hiding somewhere in the city, police could "interrogate" a corresponding paper suspect and find enough probable cause to order an arrest.[17]

The centrality of these files to police work altered the way the patrolmen and detectives did their jobs. Similar to the backlash over officers spending their days sitting in classrooms rather than preventing crime, images of policemen spending their days filling out paperwork and filing became commonplace. On August 18, 1916, only two years after Woods took command, the *New York Times* ran the headline, "Every Policeman a Card Indexer." The article read: "Every policeman has become a sort of walking card index. He must now record on cards the arrests he makes, and the accidents and other cases in his line of duty he handles from time to time." Even though department statisticians had become overwhelmed by the amount of data coming in, Woods believed meticulously kept records had the potential to reveal trends and patterns that anecdotal evidence could not. For instance, the police practice of recording every automobile accident they came across supposedly revealed that diagonal street crossings were more dangerous than those that met at right angles. Requiring officers to constantly contribute to the department's massive archive of information on the city also meant more discipline.

For the average arrested person, there were always downsides to this retention of information. Starting with the widespread adoption of the Rogues' Gallery, some New Yorkers objected to having police retain their photographs after arrest. Even if police eventually let a person go or they were acquitted at trial, their photograph remained in police custody—meaning that any witness coming in to identify a burglar or arsonist had the chance to review photos and test their memory against the faces of people who may have been found innocent of all charges.

"Once a photograph is hung in the gallery there is no removing it," wrote a reporter in one newspaper. "A police of that kind is utterly indefensible. It is a cruel injustice and a constant bar to reform. Youthful indiscretion is put on the same plane with murder. . . . Nobody is going to employ a young man or a young woman whose picture adorns the rogues' gallery." Newspapers around the country read about the case of George B. Duffy, a nineteen-year-old Brooklyn boy arrested on the charge of being a "suspicious person." When he was finally released, Duffy became the face of a campaign to end the retention of photographs and Bertillon measurements of unconvicted people who had had encounters with police. The campaign went all the way up to the governor, then the New York State Supreme Court, and ultimately led to the ouster of NYPD commissioner Theodore Bingham for operating under "no legal restraints." Duffy was a white man from a respectable family that was able to summon the sympathy of a white public and politicians that other people whose photographs adorned the Rogues' Gallery were clearly unable to conjure. When it came to collecting information on individuals, government oversight and backlash against police overreach extended only to the damaged reputations of white men with a certain background, just like George Duffy.[18]

Writers hoping to combat the constant renewal of age-old associations between criminality and specific races also took issue, not just with the retention of information by police departments but also the willingness of the mainstream white press to regurgitate those specific facts. The Rogues' Gallery may have been a collection of photographs of arrested individuals, but they were kept inside station houses. For the famed orator and civil rights leader William Pickens, daily crime reporting stressing the race of suspects built a kind of public Rogues' Gallery, allowing readers to make inferences about what types of people were most likely to commit crimes. "We cannot play up RACE with the same display with which we play up CRIME, without causing the *race* of the criminal to be equally culpable with his crime—in the psychology of the average man. This is what causes innocent Negroes or innocent Jews to be mobbed when a crime is committed by a member of their race with whom they do not even have personal acquaintance," he wrote in 1922. "It is because the race itself has been mixed into the idea of the blameworthy." Essentially, the alleged harm the Rogue's Gallery did to the reputations of individuals, crime reporting and police data were doing for entire races.[19]

American Police in Europe

The file, fingerprinting, and modus operandi all had one thing in common: They were European technologies brought to New York to aid in the operations of law enforcement. Policing was a central avenue of the intellectual exchange that freely crisscrossed the Atlantic during the Progressive Era. The organization of industrial economies, welfare, municipal governance, and even modern agriculture—all became parts of a collaborative effort between Progressive politicians and knowledge producers in North America and Western Europe.[20] Although it is left out of the most well-known histories of these transatlantic intellectual exchanges, during the years leading up to and immediately following World War I urban policing was one such collaborative effort.[21]

New York City became the model for police departments throughout the United States in part because it was an intellectual gateway to Europe. Modern European policing techniques generally appeared first in New York before spreading to places like Philadelphia or Chicago. In the case of technologies like fingerprinting, in which the St. Louis Police Department had been the earliest adopter in the United States, the NYPD was quick to seize on the innovations and deploy them.

Through this system of collaboration and cooperation a police technique could travel relatively quickly from a European colony in Africa or Asia back to the European metropole and from there to the United States. In 1907, during his earlier career with the NYPD, Commissioner Bingham sent then-Deputy Commissioner Woods on a prolonged trip to London to learn police techniques that could be implemented in New York. When Woods returned, he brought with him the police dog, a technology that the NYPD integrated into the force immediately.

Trips like this were common in the first decades of the twentieth century with deputy commissioners and other NYPD administrators returning from London, Paris, or Berlin with new tools and tricks to improve the department's practice. By the 1910s, however, this exchange was more managed, not just by municipal governments, but also by private Progressive anti-vice organizations that could pour money and resources into attempts to augment American policing with European techniques.[22]

From 1911 until 1934, the Bureau of Social Hygiene, under the generous patronage of John D. Rockefeller Jr., became one of the largest producers of knowledge about policing and criminality in the United States. Concerned with finding new ways of curbing vice in American cities, the Bureau of Social

Hygiene funded a number of studies, books, and even the NYPD Psychopathic Laboratory. Although the focus of the bureau shifted over time to narcotics from its earlier preoccupation with prostitution, the importation of European innovations in science, medicine, and technology seemed to be the organization's key tactic to combat what it saw as social and moral evils.[23]

The third of its major publications was the 1915 book *European Police Systems*. Rockefeller and the Bureau of Social Hygiene sent the former NYPD commissioner of accounts, Raymond Fosdick, to Europe for the better part of two years to undertake a detailed study of the organization and operations of police departments in London, Liverpool, Manchester, Birmingham, Glasgow, Edinburgh, Paris, Lyons, Berlin, Hamburg, Bremen, Dresden, Munich, Stuttgart, Cologne, Vienna, Budapest, Rome, Brussels, Amsterdam, and Rotterdam. In early 1914 Fosdick was already in Europe researching the book when he appeared on lists in the press as a front-runner for the position of New York police commissioner. By traveling to a number of cities, Fosdick believed he could see the "variable" ways that European police departments handled the specific type of criminality native to their own countries and cultures. "The Italian police," he wrote, "are confronted with a situation unfamiliar to the English police; Stuttgart and Königsberg, two typical German cities, require in the way of police activity, somewhat different treatment."[24] In Germany, the "autocratic spirit of the German government is reflected in its imperviousness of the police to public opinion." Under the German model of policing citizens were subjected to random arrests without probable cause, constant surveillance, and unrestrained use of violence on suspects. In England, on the other hand, Fosdick observed "unfailing courtesy" of the bobbies. In London especially, the administration dedicated a tremendous amount of intellectual labor to forging a balance between autocratic necessities and a pristine public reputation among the upper classes.[25]

The choice for US police departments, Fosdick thought, was whether they wanted to conform to the German model or the English. Despite his concerns about the unrestrained autocracy of German-style policing, after his return to the United States he clearly voiced his opinion that the path toward modernization rested on the ability of the NYPD to conform to the Berlin approach. On March 16, 1915, two hundred inspectors, captains, and detectives gathered to hear Fosdick speak about what he had learned in Europe. In particular, Fosdick expounded upon the possibilities for New York police if they mimicked their German brethren. "The obvious disadvantage of the fingerprint system is that in America we have no clearing house for the exchange of the finger prints of criminals," he pronounced to the lecture hall of police administrators. "A burglar can commit a crime in Boson, go to Philadelphia or come to New York and if he should be apprehended here and his finger prints taken, nothing would be found on file against him." Despite the push for a national fingerprint index, the first federal archive, the Bureau of Investigation fingerprint warehouse, did not come into existence until 1924.[26]

A generation earlier, NYPD commissioner Thomas Byrnes had attempted a similar feat by publishing a hardcover version of New York City's Rogues' Gallery. Byrnes intended *Professional Criminals of America* to serve a similar role: a resource for individuals and police departments to cross-reference the identities of suspects with previously arrested individuals in the country's largest city. By 1915, Germany already had a working system of intercity communication between police departments. "Here's how it works," Fosdick recounted: "In Stuttgart such a man got into some stores under peculiar circumstances. The news reaches Berlin. Perhaps the Berlin police know something about this man. It is the same kind of crime that has recently committed in Dresden," and so the Dresden, Stuttgart, and Berlin police already have the protocol and infrastructure to share this information on the suspect.[27]

The interconnectedness of German police departments seemed twice as effective when considering their extensive communication in conjunction with expansive recordkeeping. In Germany, Fosdick had seen firsthand how useful it could be for police to retain detailed files on nearly every citizen. He asserted that when a person traveled from city to city, they carried their police file with them and promptly presented that file to the local police department within twenty-four hours of arrival. The file was supposed to contain military papers, criminal records, marriage certificates, and other documents of identification including work and insurance papers. Not only did this traveling file allow police to know exactly who was in the city at any given time, but once copied it also went into their own archive, thus allowing each city to replicate a kind of national database. Under this system, it was incredibly easy to figure out if someone had lied about their name or where they were from.[28]

Fosdick laid out a hypothetical for his audience. "Here is a man named William Jones who registers in Berlin under the name John Smith. He says he came from Cologne. The Berlin police communicate with Cologne and say: 'Here is a man named John Smith, who says he came from your city.' If the Cologne police say that he did not, he is arrested for perjury and sent to jail for five years." Although Fosdick conceded many times throughout the speech that many of these systems could never be instituted in the United

States, the "German method" of policing had an oversize influence going forward in shaping the department's policy on the collection and retention of information. It was true that unlike the German police, the NYPD would never be able to "go into a park like our Coney Island and gather up everybody," for example, and detain them without charges for twenty-four hours. However, thanks to Fosdick's Atlantic crossings, German-style policing largely impacted the direction of the department under Arthur Woods.[29]

The Law as Proactive Policing

The emerging police university programs stressed the pressing necessity for police to understand the law. It was not enough that they understood specific street-level arrest-worthy charges. The law, in the hands of a proactive and politically inclined officer and police department, could be a powerful weapon.

During his four-year tenure as commissioner, which was longer than any other police administration since the 1880s, Woods reformed and reshaped the NYPD so that it was almost unrecognizably different from the department of his predecessors. However, no matter how modernized, Europeanized, or effective New York policing became, by the end of his time as commissioner Arthur Woods had come to believe that police could really do nothing to stop crime. In a lecture delivered at Princeton University in 1918, Woods began his talk on crime prevention by announcing: "We learned that most crimes are not hindered by the conventional methods of police protection, and we tried." No matter how adequately the streets were patrolled, no matter how technologically advanced detectives became, the police could not be expected to be on the scene every time a "lady's jewels are stolen by a dishonest servant girl."[30]

For Woods, increasing police presence or ramping up arrests did nothing if jail time failed to turn criminals into law-abiding citizens. Recalling his training in the US imperial project and the type of problem-solving central to American colonialism, Woods likened criminals in New York to flies in a tropical locale. "It is good to arrest and convict them just as it is good to swat the flies, but we shall never go far toward ridding the community of criminals until we get at the breeding places. *We must drain the swamps of crime as they drained the swamps in Cuba to get rid of yellow fever mosquitoes.*" He saw criminals as a potentially lethal nuisance, indigenous to New York as mosquitoes were to Cuban swamps, but the persistence of both was not inevitable. Both could be eradicated, he claimed, through structural and fundamental alterations to the social and physical landscape.[31] His proposals for how to prevent crime in New York not only extended to legislation but also to radical ideas about how to change the structure of American society itself.

In keeping with the Progressive political aim of constructing a robust social safety net in the United States, Woods believed that large-scale national solutions could remedy the three major causes of crime: poverty, mental illness, and drugs. "We must of course recognize," he said, "the fact that police forces cannot be expected to abolish poverty." The ultimate solution to crime in New York City lay in the hands of politicians in Washington, and not with any given detective, patrolman, or even commissioner. Woods came to similar conclusions on other issues. When it came to treatment of the mentally ill, Woods felt they could not be "turned loose on the public" but also should not be committed to a sort of prison. Similarly, he believed in a prohibition of the sale of alcohol, which he called a potential "god-send to any community" from a "police point of view."[32]

Sweeping legislative solutions had been a growing response to panic over immigrant crime since at least the 1890s, if not earlier. Despite a number of restrictions, including the Immigration Act of 1903, which gave the NYPD the ability to recommend immigrants with criminal records for deportation, police intellectuals continued to push for a ban on immigration to the United States.

It was during this same era of technocratic revolution in governance that Congress passed the most draconian immigration law since the Chinese Exclusion Act of 1882. The so-called Emergency Quota Act or the 1921 Immigration Restriction Act, restricted arrivals such that no more than 3 percent of the number of people from a given country already living in the United States could immigrate. This meant that rather than the 100 percent or even higher per year increase in the Eastern or Southern European population in the United States in the previous decades, the Italian or Polish population in the United States could now only increase 3 percent per annum. Three years later, the 1924 Immigration Restriction Act curbed immigration even more. The 1924 act limited immigration to 2 percent from a specific nation based on the 1890 census. If only three hundred thousand Italians lived in the United States in 1890, then after 1924 the United States would admit no more than six thousand Italians a year. These acts were, in many ways, the logical outcome of a collision between two decades of panic over immigrant crime and a Progressive politics that looked toward structural and technocratic national solutions to local problems.

Back in 1909, directly after the assassination of Joseph Petrosino, Arthur Woods, the deputy commissioner, had also promoted a tightening of immigration laws nationally as a solution to concern over immigrant crime rates in New York. Writing about the insufficiencies of the 1903 immigration restrictions Woods wrote: "The law already specifies that persons who have been convicted of a crime are ineligible for admission to this country. Careful consideration should be given to the question whether it would be wise to exclude also persons with bad police reputation." He continued, "Besides such measures as may be necessary to keep these people out, powerful and far reaching forces must be set in motion."[33] The "powerful and far reaching" forces Woods had in mind were serious legal changes like systematic shutdowns of immigration admissions, solutions far beyond the scope of any one politician or police official in New York.

For Woods the law itself, both as a disembodied manifestation of the power of the state and as a tool for curbing crime locally, contained the key to the future of crime prevention. Police could be in only so many places at a time. Woods often wondered what incentives there were to keep people from committing crimes when the watchful eyes of the neighborhood patrolman were focused elsewhere.

The law, powerful enough to dissuade wrongdoers and omnipresent and pervasive enough to induce paranoia, was his solution. "If the prisoner can escape the legal punishment which has been specified as the due of one who does what he has done, the conclusion cannot be escaped that the law is weak and that one can afford to take a chance against it," Woods wrote earlier in his career. "The law," he continued, "should stand in the community as an impersonal power that inexorably deals out to offenders the penalties that have been set."[34] The new technocratic regime of policing sought to build on this exact idea—the "impersonal" and omnipresent power of policing. Discouraging patrolmen's identifying characteristics like ethnic identities or varying sizes created the illusion of the police force as a uniform and monolithic institution. Not only did technocrats intend this institution to be faceless, it was also, like the law, seamless, raceless, and omnipresent. When it was possible to find fingerprints days or weeks later, police work was uninhibited by hurdles of time and space. Woods hoped that police, like the law itself, could be everywhere and operate through everyone. These changes would be Woods's defining legacy as commissioner and as a police intellectual.

The law, however, is not created nor does it govern in a vacuum. Laws are enforced in a society rife with inequalities, dishonesty, and implicit prejudices that are more likely to be felt or known by its victims than read about on the pages of newspapers or official records. That was one thread that Black intellectuals and writers in New York in 1922 could not help but tug on as they felt vexed by the trial and execution of Luther Boddy for the killing of two NYPD detectives. After a period of eluding police, Boddy was finally caught in Philadelphia. He was apprehended, as the *Daily News* made sure to point out, by a Black magistrate. No one had doubted that Boddy had committed the crime, although there seemed to be a consensus among observers that his confession had come during rampant abuse at the hands of police. As Boddy put it, "They kick and knock you about for two or three hours in the station house," a note that rang true to many Black New Yorkers. But despite his guilt, some Black writers felt his story revealed harder truths about a legal system and society supposedly in the process of becoming more impartial. Boddy had been arrested many times before his final arrest, and as W. E. B. Du Bois wrote in his magazine, *The Crisis*: "It has been said that Boddy himself had been beaten by the police a dozen times when they could prove nothing against him. It is said the dead detectives have beaten and killed unconvicted Negroes, and slapped and insulted black women." But his biggest concerns, as well as those of several writers in the *New York Age,* were about the larger society and legal system that the Boddy trial surfaced.[35]

"He has been in jail; he has been in the penitentiary; he has been in the army; he has stolen; he has killed. Now society is going to kill him. Why? Whose fault is it? Who made this boy what he is? Society assumes that he is to blame, but he is not wholly to blame and it is barely possible that he is not a bit to blame. How fair a chance to live has he had?" Du Bois asked in a heartfelt piece about white society's contempt as felt by Black New Yorkers, and especially Black veterans. "His city and his country have laughed at him, insulted him, hated him, given him few places for play or recreation, and filled his ears with too true stories of outrage and lynching. We can kill this boy, and perhaps in the horrible muddle of our penal code there is nothing else to do." The law may have seemed impersonal and impartial to people like Commissioner Woods, but to Du Bois, it seemed more like a cliff's edge that the state was pushing a whole race toward. "And finally," he wrote, "when this boy is dead, remember that the same forces which made him what he was are alive and in power and working to make others like him."[36]

In December 1920, Woods's successor, Commissioner Richard Enright, attempted to increase the time between shifts from thirty-six hours off every nine days to thirty-six hours off every six days. In his own words, making the patrolman's job a little less grueling was an effort to make policing a "white man's job."[37] Enright's assertion simultaneously equated overwork as a condition suited only for New York's nonwhite population and reasserted the supposed middle-class whiteness of policing as a profession. By 1920, the NYPD was more ethnically and racially integrated than ever before, yet his assertion erased the diversity within its ranks. Declaring policing a "white man's job" also, in many ways, bolstered the project of anti-Blackness that NYPD administrators began when the department was frantically recruiting immigrants but denying the repeated attempts of African Americans to join the force. Despite some tenuous moments when the place of Southern and Eastern European immigrants within the department was in question, the uniformity and conditioning of the new era had acknowledged white immigrant belonging.

The University as a Site of International Collaboration in Policing

The explosion of knowledge about crime and policing in the first few decades of the twentieth century happened both inside and outside of police departments. Police training academies, manuals, partnerships with universities, social welfare charities, as well as growing police libraries were several of the important places where academic and formalized scientific knowledge was dispersed into everyday police practice in addition to the lived understanding of officers. For decades, Europe had sustained a thriving academic field of scholars attempting to identify the biological and social causes of crime as well as policing innovations from which the United States benefited. But by the 1920s, the United States had caught up, with privately funded research institutes, police laboratories, and academic programs aimed at training police. The growing twentieth-century trend toward classroom and university training for police was a project intertwined with, but somewhat separated from early criminology—then a growing interdisciplinary study of criminal patterns and behavior.

Criminology as a field of study was seen by police intellectuals as a well of emerging knowledge that could enrich and inform police departments and criminal justice policy, but one that only supplemented officer classroom training in other topics like the law, forensics, foreign languages, and so on. Criminological scholarship made its way into the lives of police officers in a number of forms, including university or departmental training courses, and the departmental library that stocked the most influential titles from the United States and Europe on the topics of criminals, criminality, and police procedure. The relationship between academics who thought about crime and criminals and the state actors tasked with monitoring and punishing them should not, as one scholar put it, "be conceptualized as a one-way street but as a close relationship of mutual influence." Rather, the knowledge was circular, self-fulfilling, and mutually constitutive. Police continued to play the role of the state's ground-level observers and knowledge producers about crime and criminals, and that data fed universities and professionals who in turn created studies that could be fed back into police departments so that they might seem academically or empirically informed.[38]

Eugenics, like the interdisciplinary field of criminology, was another tool in addition to the law that police believed could circumvent some of the decades-long problems of policing a multiethnic and multiracial society. The law could suss out or prevent crime before it occurred, and criminology could supposedly identify the social and psychological conditions that gave rise to criminality, but the controversial field of eugenics, some scientists believed, could prevent wrongdoers from being born. "The police power of the state, however powerful, has only resulted in temporary control" of crime, wrote one independent monitor of prisons in Illinois. "In view of this failure of statesmanship in dealing with the problem of crime, the scientists have more recently essayed various solutions." Even though "the best scientific knowledge indicates there are no born criminals," a break with the criminal anthropology that had swept New York's police intellectuals a decade or so earlier, a number of states were still willing to sterilize habitual offenders out of fear they would transmit some kind of hereditary predilection for crime. This was hotly debated among so-called "crime doctors," especially where the improvement of entire races was concerned. For many of these white doctors and academics a race's predilection for criminality and its need for uplift and civilization were not in question—but debates about whether these goals could be achieved through cultural and economic means or via eugenic methods of sterilization filled academic journals of the era. "Education of the individuals who compose a community," wrote one eugenic-skeptic psychology professor, "must be secured before any other agencies for the improvement of the race can be effective." Like many of the coercive and paternalistic methods used to Americanize, civilize, and enforce heteronormative sex lives and gender norms, eugenics and its medical interventions were often used punitively against those who did not conform to societal and respectable expectations.[39]

The rise of social sciences in the 1910s and 1920s coincided with police professionalization and a renewed focus on classroom training for police. What started as ad hoc agreements between police departments and universities to offer useful classes soon became specialized programs. For this reason, it is not surprising that in the years following World War I, universities in the United States and around the world developed curriculum specifically for future or current police officers.[40]

By the end of the 1920s, August Vollmer, police chief of Berkeley, California, and one of the most celebrated police innovators in the world, began working on a program for police education at the University of California at Berkeley. Revered as a champion of professionalizing and militarizing policing, Vollmer used his position at the University of California to collaboratively develop a multiyear academic curriculum that would offer all the skills and knowledge officers needed in a rapidly modernizing field. An avid correspondent of police chiefs around the globe, Vollmer wrote to some of the most celebrated department administrators to get their opinion on what police ought to learn to make them as prepared as possible for the job. Police intellectuals wrote to suggest courses like public speaking, military science, psychology, and foreign languages. Police administrators and academics, some from as far away as Japan, wrote with some regularity for updates on the progress of the program and the most recent bibliographies related to policing and crime.[41]

Vollmer and many of his closest collaborators recognized the limitations presented by police academies and their narrow focus. For one thing, concentrating on skills needed in the "apprehension of criminals" would be too circumscribed, as the officer is "in effect a social worker and should be continually on the alert for community conditions that prove a fertile breeding ground for crime." Preparation for that responsibility included studying "poverty and control of immigrants," as "a disproportionate percentage of major crime is traceable to immigrants or the first generation of immigrants." Academic training in history, anthropology, and psychology would be enough, Vollmer and his colleagues believed, to train officers so that they could police any community without the native-born knowledge of ethnic police. Because many of the classes would be taught not just by academic experts but by officers like Vollmer himself, these courses could also legitimize and sanitize knowledge generated by police. If an officer taught a roomful of cadets that immigrants, for instance, were socially predisposed to crime—many, especially those in immigrant communities, might object to that as xenophobic. But if a professor-officer taught the same thing from a lectern, the material carried an air of legitimacy and might be more readily accepted.[42]

Others, like the deputy commissioner of the NYPD, scoffed at the wide-ranging nature of the education Vollmer proposed for police. "I also believed too much emphasis has been placed on chemistry...less than one per cent of those in supervisory positions in police departments will need this specific knowledge and the same objections might be made with reference to the requirements of two years of work in physics and one year of work in zoology." Instead, he proposed the new program in Berkeley take a page out of the more practical curriculum books of the New York police academy by offering Problems of Juvenile Delinquency and a lecture series given by the chief medical examiner. Of these lectures, intended to familiarize detectives with medical knowledge necessary for homicide investigations, he wrote to Vollmer, "I believe this course surpasses the series that has been given at the Medico-Legal Institute of the University of Paris. In any event there is more practicality to it for police purposes." Vollmer's program at Berkeley was one of many throughout the world, and while some police objected to the overly broad curriculum the international revolving door between academia and law enforcement was really only just beginning.[43]

There had always been "police intellectuals," people inside and outside police departments who had developed knowledge about crime, criminals, and what constituted effective policing. But, as the twentieth century rolled on, those sometimes organic and sometimes classroom or laboratory-made intellectuals increasingly became "scientists." More and more institutions and legitimizing discourses gave police intellectuals avenues through which they could promote their theories under the banner of science. Basic tenets of policing once informally or colloquially shared from officer to officer or codified in departmental handbooks could now be published, lectured on, and labeled as modern and empirical. For centuries physicians and other professionals respected for their expertise had explored connections between race, the mind, the body, and criminality—but for most of policing's early years, police were exempt from using those legitimizing discourses. There were general understandings among Anglo-Irish officers, who knew from the popular and even scientific knowledge of the time which races were more prone to violence or sexual deviance, but their knowledge was not scientific—not yet. There were notable exceptions. Propelled by stories like that of scientist-detective Sherlock Holmes, famous detective-inventors in the United States and Europe like Thomas Byrnes and Alphonse Bertillon attempted to challenge popular (and in the United States, often anti-Irish) notions of officers as corrupt and brutal.[44]

The professionalization of policing, along with the growing view of police as experts with university classroom training and access to libraries and laboratories, had a familiar self-replicating effect. Police generated knowledge about Italian or Chinese crime and criminality, which became the basis of policy and academic investigations, which in turn, informed police procedure with more empirical backing, completing the cycle. This type of knowledge, writes anthropologist James C. Scott, "is characteristic, above all, of self-contained systems of reasoning in which the findings may be logically derived from the initial assumptions," as long as those findings can be read as impersonal and universal. Scholars and police disagreed with each other and among themselves over definitions and roots of criminality and its relationship to people, bodies, and heredity. But the accelerated rise of technocratic policing gave them new forums and legitimate avenues through which to carry on those debates.[45]

CONCLUSION

Policing's Small Toolbox and
the Afterlives of Ethnic Policing

Where Lafayette Street intersects with Spring Street near what was once the heart of Manhattan's Little Italy, there is a small triangle of land. Since 1987, it has carried the name Lt. Joseph Petrosino Square. Named after New York's first Italian detective and leader of the New York City Police Department's Italian Squad, the public ground serves as a reminder of his contemporary status among police as a pioneer and a martyr. The blackened bronze plaque that faces the street declares Petrosino an enduring "symbol of justice and social responsibility."[1]

In the tumultuous era of the late 1980s, as police departments across the country struggled to maintain legitimacy and develop new strategies for contending with what they saw as a decade-long rise in crime, the park's renaming is a window into understanding how the NYPD tells stories about itself. At a moment when polls suggested that as many as 30 percent of New Yorkers believed race relations had gotten worse in the previous decade, putting a white immigrant, a neighborhood hero, and a hearty dose of "social responsibility" at the center of the history of policing made a specific argument about belonging and benevolence that obscured the complicated multiracial politics that Petrosino navigated every day.[2] After 1987, this version of Petrosino, the one that acted as a vessel into which the NYPD could pour its own political motivations and anxieties, remained a permanent landmark in the city's physical and historical geography. This story articulated that stopping crime was not just the responsibility of the city—it was the obligation of that community to take an active role in crime reduction. Petrosino, in essence, became a symbol of the neoliberal order, in which the job of policing and surveillance was dispersed to the public and anyone who rejected that role was not worthy of protection by the state.

Nine miles north, in Harlem, the sprawling intersection at 135th Street and Lenox Avenue displays the name of another pioneering figure. Established in 2009, Samuel Battle Plaza commemorates Samuel Jesse Battle who, in 1911, became the first African American appointed to the NYPD.[3] Dedicated by embattled NYPD commissioner Ray Kelly, the ceremony came at the height of the protest movement against the department's harassment of young men of color in the city. Under the long-standing stop-and-frisk policy, police could detain anyone they deemed suspicious and pat them down. In Kelly's second tenure as police commissioner, between 2002 and 2013, these stops increased from just over 97,000 in 2002 to 685,724 in 2011. Like the dedication of Petrosino Square, creating a visible tribute to Samuel Battle at this pivotal moment preserved a narrative of symbiosis between the people of Harlem and the NYPD.[4]

The attention to these landmarks during tumultuous times in the 1980s and 2010s was an attempt on the part of the NYPD to inscribe an imagined century of good police-community relations onto the visible landscape of the city. The parks and street signs people walked past every day now reinforced a historical narrative that often disrupted popular understandings about social relationships in the city. At two moments when encounters between New Yorkers and police seemed particularly fraught, the department retrofitted history in ways that were politically expedient.

But why did the NYPD choose these two specific figures from the Progressive Era? How did narratives of policing from that time take on a new political meaning and utility?

Remaking the Progressive Era detective once called the "Sherlock Holmes of Italy" into a pillar of police-community relations operated as more than just the department's attempt to lift its sagging approval ratings. Remembering Petrosino also allowed NYPD administrators to manufacture parallels between the quality-of-life policing in the 1980s and the nostalgic golden era of the beat cop. Likewise, at a moment when Black New Yorkers increasingly voiced a sense of alienation and protested their brutalization at the hands of police, commemorating Samuel Battle played an important role in attempting to pacify critics.

By celebrating these ethnic and racial minorities' willing participation in police power, the NYPD attempted to "manufacture" the consent of the policed. Not only did these immigrants and African Americans agree to the project of policing their own communities, they often fought for the privilege of being able do it. By recalling the constructed narratives of Petrosino and Battle on the racial and ethnic animosity they faced and the labor they performed, these landmarks attempted to connect the police of the past with the civilians of the present. These monuments made it clear: Immigrant and Black police, and not civilians, were the real victims of prejudice that deserved attention and commemoration. For the NYPD of the late twentieth century, if the new community police could be made into the spiritual successors of Petrosino and Battle, they would also be the beneficiaries of the goodwill generated by these historical retellings.[5]

Community policing, however, was not an invention of the Progressive Era but rather an outgrowth of the quality-of-life policing in the 1970s and 1980s. In 1989, in an effort to lower crime rates and improve police-community relations, the Houston Police Department tried something they believed was new. "The new philosophy," as the *New York Times* described it, "called community policing or problem-solving policing is controversial among some residents long suspicious of the police." The supposedly new approach involved having police get out of their patrol cars and walk their neighborhoods. More than that, community policing often dictated that police departments recruit new police from the communities that seemed most difficult to patrol. Departments marketed the strategy as the future of policing: a new regime of governance more benevolent and mindful than the one that came before it. As many police departments, including New York, integrated these "new" tactics that simultaneously conjured and retrofitted Progressive Era origin stories for these new models of policing.[6]

The process of creating and legitimizing community policing exemplifies the functional relationship police have to their own history. Administrators and police intellectuals, people who create knowledge about policing, often engage in simultaneous acts of forgetting, remembering, and (re)inventing. Now dubbed community policing, this new tactic was simultaneously cutting-edge and as old as policing itself. Bringing Joseph Petrosino and Samuel Battle back into the news and reshaping the official narrative of the history of the NYPD to center their stories made the department seem ahead of its time. For the timeless NYPD, these new monuments were contradictory— they made the department both nostalgic and prophetic. Along with the useful narrative came a specific reading of how Progressive Era officers did their jobs.

These figures endure on the urban landscape in part because police still need them and in part because the style of policing they represented has never really been deleted from the department's playbook.

Enduring Problems, Recycled Solutions

In 1920, the nationwide ban on selling, importing, and producing alcohol created a new strain on law enforcement in the United States. In an era when the Bureau of Investigation had only 650 employees total, the Treasury Department's new Prohibition Unit became the country's largest federal law enforcement agency, with 1,550 field agents and 1,500 support staff. Prohibition policing was, in many ways, the culmination of the ideas pushed by police intellectuals in New York during the Arthur Woods years. The legislation that made Prohibition possible, the Volstead Act, was a large nationwide solution to local law enforcement problems. In much the same way police intellectuals in New York believed that a national ban on immigration would make the streets of Little Italy safer, Progressives and temperance advocates pushed for a prohibition of alcohol on the grounds that it would curb gambling, prostitution, and public and domestic violence in communities across the nation.[7]

Federal solutions to local problems were not the only way Prohibition was an exemplar of Progressive Era policing. The Prohibition Unit, and later the Prohibition Bureau, became the earliest fruit of Raymond Fosdick's vision of a behemoth federal law-enforcing agency. Not only did it cooperate and oversee the anti-alcohol work at the federal and state levels, it also took an active role in the daily operations of local police. However, even in this new age of post–World War I militarization and federal funding, policing the vast geographical and demographic terrain of the United States came with familiar difficulties.[8]

In 1929, almost a decade into Prohibition, the National Commission on Law Observance and Enforcement asked for a report on how effectively federal, state, and local police were enforcing the laws associated with Prohibition. Known as the Wickersham Report after the commission's chairman, former attorney general George Wickersham, its conclusions, published in 1931, were less than satisfying for people in favor of a continued moratorium on alcohol. Not only was enforcement lacking in many areas of the country, but the report questioned whether, in a practical sense, any such law was enforceable in a consistent way. Discussing the inability of government propaganda and enforcement to break local habits around alcohol, the report's authors wrote, "Few things are so stubborn and unyielding as habits and conceptions of personal or political conduct which have their roots in racial instincts or social traditions." Biologically ingrained racial instincts, it seemed to the committee members, played a large role in the inability of the government to stamp out drinking. For over a decade, police intellectuals tried to construct a law enforcement regime in the United States that cloaked implicit anti-Black racism in a technocratic refusal to explicitly consider race in its operations and in the organization of departments. During Prohibition, racial difference once again reasserted itself as the defining difficulty of exerting state power in America.[9]

"As a consequence of this truth—so often ignored—the development of that social and institutional cohesion which is essential to the spirit and fact of nationality is always a matter of slow and painful evolution," the report noted, going on to argue that this national, ethnic, and racial cohesion "cannot be hurried by mandate of law." Simply put, law enforcement was hindered by the lack of a cohesive national spirit. If the "different races and nationalities" in the United States were represented as a topographic map, then navigating and enforcing laws in that terrain would "present an aspect as rough, and with variations as acute, as the physical surface of the country." The writers continued: "If we should undertake to fit one rigid plane to every part of this highly irregular and unyielding surface, it would give some idea of the difficulties of adjusting national law of this character to every community and to each individual of the United States." Like the NYPD commissioners of 1904 or the Progressive technocrats of 1914, police intellectuals in 1931 were still grappling with the seemingly unsolvable American Problem. Even with the benefit of hindsight and the results of years of experimentation, Prohibition police spent the better part of a decade wondering how to enforce the law in a nation consisting of so many different races, languages, customs, and cultural sensibilities.[10]

Between the mid-nineteenth century and the 1930s, racial and ethnic difference in the United States presented a challenge to the project of policing as it had existed within a European Enlightenment framework. In its pursuit of protecting the accumulation of wealth among Anglo property owners, the police served as one of the main institutions whose goal was to identify and subordinate threats to the rights associated with capitalist liberalism. Aided by scientific discourse, colonialism, and the intellectual work that for centuries had propped up chattel slavery in the United States, police often viewed and cataloged those threats in racial terms. How these racialized threats were treated by police could sometimes vary drastically. For Black New Yorkers, the state's attempt to pacify imagined threats meant police and state-sanctioned mob violence. Because of well-established racial discourse that portrayed African Americans as familiar, police intellectuals did not dedicate time or energy to determining exactly how Black New Yorkers should be policed. After all, racialized pacification by force had been a central project of US state-building since the nation's founding. However, the introduction of European, Chinese, and other non-English-speaking immigrants to industrial cities in the United States presented a new problem. Pacification by force alone could not bring about the desired results in the same way white police believed it had in Black communities. Police intellectuals sought to provide solutions for Anglo-Irish police who were routinely stymied by the linguistic and cultural differences of the neighborhoods they patrolled.[11]

Thus police in New York City began to develop new ways of extending the coercive power of the state into communities that could use their foreignness as a tool of noncompliance. By examining the period of experimentation covered by this book, I have argued that the problem of mitigating racial difference in the modern city was one of the primary engines that drove the modernization of the New York City Police Department, producing the institution that it is today.

As whiteness slowly and unevenly enveloped many European immigrant groups after the 1920s, the state targeted newly arrived groups and continued to overpolice those presumed to be either unassimilable or excluded altogether from the processes of whiteness. In other words, as cycles of migration and demographic shifts continued—as each generation's immigrants became more socially and economically mobile—the NYPD found new populations to slot into the "problem" end of the American Problem along with its permanent inhabitants.[12] This increasingly meant police had to learn to contend with nonwhite immigrants during the mid-to-late twentieth century as large-scale military conflicts brought large populations from Southeast Asia, Latin America, the Caribbean, Africa, and the Middle East to the United States.

In the twenty-first century, a large amount of evidence suggests that the American Problem continues to concern the NYPD. In an initiative that seems borrowed from the era of the Italian Squad, the NYPD after the terrorist attacks on September 11, 2001, created a squad called the Demographics Unit, whose purpose was to spy on Muslims in New York. "Understanding certain local demographics," said the department's chief spokesman in 2014, "can be a useful factor when assessing the threat information that comes into New York City virtually on a daily basis." As at various other times in the department's history, in the years following 9/11 police intellectuals felt that action was required to understand decades-old communities they now saw as illegibly foreign and potentially dangerous. The eventual revelation of the group's existence caused outrage among the city's Muslims and in 2014 the squad was rebranded with the innocuous and vague title Zone Assessment Unit. The NYPD's spokesman assured the public that "in the future, we will gather that information, if necessary, through direct contact between the police precincts and the representatives of the communities they serve." In other words, collaboration and not surveillance; partnership rather than infiltration. As the history of the NYPD's ethnic squads shows, however, there is a fine line between coercion, exploitation, and collaboration.[13]

This book only begins to scratch the surface of contemporary policing's connection to the Progressive Era. The international collaboration that allowed police departments from around the world to communicate and share methods in the late nineteenth and early twentieth centuries is still with us. As of 2016, the NYPD boasts a permanent presence within the police departments of at least thirteen cities around the world through its International Liaison Program (ILP). Officers in the program live and operate in London, Paris, Jerusalem, Amman, and Sydney, among other locations, with the aim of improving cooperation and sharing intelligence that might contribute to the safety of New York City.[14]

Like the footprint that NYPD officers and commissioners left on US imperial possessions in the years following 1898—and that colonial experiences left on the NYPD—the revolving door between the NYPD and US-controlled territories still turns. In recent years, the police-military relationship has been exemplified by the US Department of Defense's 1033 program, which gives surplus military equipment to police departments across the country. Since 1990, almost five billion dollars' worth of armored vehicles, assault rifles, sniper rifles, bomb-defusing robots, and even grenade launchers have been given to local and state police departments from the Department of Defense's stockpiles of equipment intended to be deployed in Iraq, Afghanistan, and other places around the globe. Not only do the optics of this equipment give citizens the impression that their communities are being occupied by a military force, it has also altered policing tactics so that they closely resemble counterinsurgency operations abroad. One statistical analysis conducted by social scientists concluded that "the receipt of more military equipment increases... the expected number of civilians killed by police." The spread of the us-versus-them "warrior mentality" of militarized policing is as old as policing itself, but the impact of sophisticated equipment on local police departments has made modern militarized policing an especially corrosive force on communities.[15]

The increased material and intellectual connection between the NYPD and Iraq and Afghanistan has had an impact in both locations. After the 2003 US invasion of Iraq, NYPD commissioner Bernard Kerik briefly became the interim interior minister of Iraq. Once in Baghdad, his primary task was to organize and train the nation's police force. In 2004, he was named George W. Bush's nominee for secretary of homeland security, but ultimately withdrew his nomination after rumors surfaced that he had employed an undocumented nanny. Like NYPD officials' reorganization of municipal governance in the Philippines and Cuba after 1898, Bernard Kerik's stay in Iraq accelerated the process by which Baghdad's police department became more like the NYPD—and the NYPD came to resemble the US military occupation of Iraq in its mentality, tactics, and equipment.[16]

Even as departments integrate new technologies into their work, police intellectuals in the twenty-first century retain a fairly small toolbox for contending with urban diversity. Many of the tools employed by police today were forged in the Progressive Era and returned to the streets every few decades with new names and new branding. There are, however, some things that definitively do change. Race and racism now operate in more insidious ways within American law enforcement. To contend with racial diversity in New York at official levels, the NYPD standardized the treatment of the police and the policed regardless of race. While race was once an explicit factor in how police recruited and organized their departments, race and racism now operate implicitly and below the surface. Rather than address the American Problem as police intellectuals had hoped it would, technocratic "color-blind" policing merely provided plausible deniability about racialized subordination and profiling. But the NYPD's implicit consideration of race was and remains central to its operations and the horizons of its imagination, not only in the development of modern police science but in the foundational principles of "color-blind" law-and-order politics.

ACKNOWLEDGMENTS

To research a book, let alone write one, is to accrue a massive debt to countless individuals and institutions. The fact that you are holding this book at all is a testament to the support of so many people who allowed me to bounce off ideas, read drafts, offer advice, or discuss the concepts and arguments that make up this work while we sat over a coffee or a bourbon. A line in the acknowledgments can never repay what so many of these people have done for me, but it is a start.

First, I have to thank all of the archivists and librarians who made accessible the body of documentation on which this work rests. The interesting connections this book is able to make are a testament to their knowledge and the patience they showed a young researcher. Particularly I am indebted to the archivists at the New York Municipal Archive and Ken Cobb, the New York Public Library, the Library of Congress, and John Jay College of Criminal Justice. I also owe a great debt to the thoughtful and supportive staff of Duke University Press, and especially Ken Wissoker, who spotted the potential in this project very early on.

This book was incubated when I was an undergraduate playing around with Freedom of Information Act requests and reading too much Foucault and to that end, I owe particular thanks to Karl Qualls, Matt Pinkser, Jeremy Ball, Elizabeth Lee, and the late Kim Lacy Rogers, who once told me that I could transition seamlessly from student to colleague. That meant the world to me. Special recognition belongs to Christopher Bilodeau who in particular put me on this path. This project was originally conceived under the instruction and education of the New York University History Department, and especially Andrew Needham, who directed me to the books that became the core historiographical foundation of this one.

This book would not exist without the history department at the University of Connecticut and in particular Peter Baldwin, Frank Costigliola, Nina Dayton, Mark Healey, Christopher Clark, Jeffery Ogbar, Melina Pappademos, Sylvia Schafer, Fiona Vernal, and Jason Chang. I could not have become the historian or writer I am today without the special guidance, community, and space given to me by the UConn Humanities Institute and the friendship and mentorship offered to me there by Michael Lynch, Alexis Boylan, Brendan Kane, Nasya Al-Saidy, and Jo-Ann Waide-Wunschel.

I am especially grateful to Melanie Newport, who has been my window into the larger world of carceral studies and a tireless advocate of my work; Jelani Cobb, whose support of me as an author and a writer for the public have been unquantifiable; and Micki McElya, whose genius, support, generosity, and historiographical wizardry is evident on every page of this book.

My colleagues and friends whose help with this project I will never be able to repay are Gabrielle Wescott, Graham Stinnett, Maggie Stack, Mary Mahoney, Allison Horrocks, Jorell Meléndez-Badillo Carolyn Levy, Danielle Dumaine, and Nathan Braccio.

Thanks go to the Immigration and Ethnic History Society for the generous support and recognition, especially Julian Lim and Maddalena Marinari. I would also like to thank the Urban History Association for giving me a chance to write for the public about the history of policing and for connecting me to a much larger community of incredible writers and thinkers. Ryan Reft and Avigail Oren are tremendous editors and friends.

I also have to thank my colleagues at the UC-Berkeley, UC-Hastings, and the Electronic Frontier Foundation for providing such an intellectually stimulating and supportive environment for continuing my academic work. Under their watchful eyes have I been able to create a cohesive vision for my scholarship.

The larger community of carceral studies have given me more than I will ever be able to say, but I owe so much to Carl Suddler, Marisol LeBrón, Alex Vitale, Jennifer Fronc, Daniel Czitrom, Heather Ann Thompson, Elizabeth Hinton, Brendan McQuade, and Khalil Gibran Muhammad, many of whom took time out of their busy schedules to talk to me about this project, even at its very early stage. There is no way to fully articulate how grateful I am for the comradery and generosity of Anna Lvovsky, Simon Balto, Max Felker-Kantor, Stuart Schrader, Anne Gray-Fischer, Emily Brooks, and Charlotte Rosen for reading drafts, giving me advice, and making me feel included in a growing field.

My friends and family have had to endure so many dinners, parties, and long walks listening to me talk about this project that they all deserve special ribbons and awards, especially Drew Rivard, Kyle Horton, Timmy Semenza, Patrick Reiher, Zack Garlitos, Bryna Hautau, Ryan Carey, and Andrew Guy. I owe special thanks to my in-laws, John and Mildred, as well as to Jack Spalding and the whole Spalding-Cross family for being big supporters. My siblings and their spouses, Sarah, Noah, Emily, Harrison, uncles Roy and Keith, and my *bubbe* Barbara and Norbert have been cheering me on since the beginning, and this book is dedicated in part to them. My parents, Louis and Beth, have made every word written possible and made me the thinker I am today.

None of this would be possible without the help and support of my number one sounding board and co-conspirator, my wife, Holly. Her patience, curiosity, and encouragement inspired me to write even in the moments when I did not have the patience, curiosity, or encouragement to motivate myself.

Finally, I want to dedicate this book to the people for whom none of this knowledge is new or surprising. Intergenerational survivors of state violence will always viscerally know the interior labors of power, and how to resist it, better than I ever will in an academic or personal way. This book is an oath, of sorts, that I will continue the work.

Introduction

1. "Tear Down the Dens of Chinatown and Make a Park of New York's Darkest Spot," *Evening World*, February 28, 1906, 3; Heap, *Slumming*, 118–21, 146–47.

2. Lui, *Chinatown Trunk Mystery*.

3. "Tear Down the Dens of Chinatown and Make a Park of New York's Darkest Spot," *Evening World*, February 28, 1906, 3. "Local Board Calls Public Hearing on the Chinatown Park Plan," *Evening World*, March 6, 1906, 5.

4. "Local Board Calls Public Hearing on the Chinatown Park Plan," *Evening World*, March 6, 1906, 5. "Mysteries of New York's Chinatown," *Buffalo Courier*, July 4, 1909, 6; "Detective Is Real Thief: Chinatown Writes to M'adoo Begging for Mercy," *Sun*, April 4, 1905, 6.

5. Seigel, *Violence Work*, 11. The best discussion on the intellectual justifications of police violence specifically against African Americans remains Muhammad, *Condemnation of Blackness*.

6. The idea that the state may need "anthropologists" to learn about ethnic and religious minorities comes predominantly from Ginzburg's *Clues, Myths, and the Historical Method*.

7. "War on the Black Hand," *Alexandria Gazette*, June 16, 1909, 2.

8. McCoy, *Policing America's Empire*, 21; Rodgers, *Atlantic Crossings*, 7; Unterman, *Uncle Sam's Policemen*, Finn, *Capturing the Criminal Image*, 6.

9. Fosdick, *American Police Systems*, 8; "Elsie Siegel's Slayer Fled," *New York Times*, December 9, 1911, 1; "Chinese Prisoners Let Go," *Sun*, February 14, 1905, 12.

10. Czitrom, *New York Exposed*, 35.

11. Peel, "Principles of Law Enforcement"; Harring, *Policing a Class Society*; Hadden, *Slave Patrols*; Browne, *Dark Matters*, 7.

12. Rodgers, *Atlantic Crossings*.

13. Heclo, *Modern Social Politics*, 305.

14. "Harlem Murder Full of Mystery," *New York Age*, March 20, 1913, 1.

15. Bederman, *Manliness and Civilization*, 13.

16. Watkins-Owens, *Blood Relations*, 12–13; Wilkerson, *Warmth of Other Suns*, 9; Hicks, *Talk with You Like a Woman*, 51; New York City Police Department, *Report of the Police Department of the City of New York for the Year Ending December 31, 1905*, 48; Muhammad, *Condemnation of Blackness*, 54.

17. Fosdick, *American Police Systems*, 9.

18. Barrett, *Irish Way*, 20; Ignatiev, *How the Irish Became White*, 112; J. Guglielmo and Salerno, *Are Italians White?*, 57; J. Guglielmo, *Living the Revolution*, 16, 33; T. Guglielmo, *White on Arrival*, 7–8; Roediger, *Working toward Whiteness*; Wilder, *Covenant with Color*.

19. J. Guglielmo and Salerno, *Are Italians White?*, 57; J. Guglielmo, *Living the Revolution*, 16, 33; T. Guglielmo, *White on Arrival*, 7–8; Roediger, *Working toward Whiteness*; Wilder, *Covenant with Color*.

20. T. Guglielmo, *White on Arrival*, 7–8; Roediger, *Working toward Whiteness*; Wilder, *Covenant with Color*.

21. McAdoo, *Guarding a Great City*, 146.

22. Battle, "Reminiscences of Samuel J. Battle," 33.

23. Heap, *Slumming*, 118–21, 146–47.

24. Lee, *At America's Gates*.

25. Lew-Williams, *Chinese Must Go*, 36; Benton-Cohen, *Inventing the Immigration Problem*, 196–97.

26. Wu, *Color of Success*, 7; López, *White by Law*, 56.

27. This is a sprawling and growing historiography, which has particularly impacted me: Flowe, *Uncontrollable Blackness*; Taylor, *Fight the Power*; Haley, *No Mercy Here*; Felker-Kantor, *Policing Los Angeles*; Balto, *Occupied Territory*; Agee, *Streets of San Francisco*; Hinton, *From the War on Poverty to the War on Crime*; Suddler, *Presumed Criminal*.

28. Many important books have been written in recent years about the role that sexuality and racism have played in justifying the expansion of police power and violence, particularly in immigrant and Black neighborhoods. Specifically, Pliley, *Policing Sexuality*; Fischer, *Streets Belong to Us*; Blair, *I've Got to Make My Livin'*; Odem, *Delinquent Daughters*; Gross, *Colored Amazons*; Hicks, *Talk with You Like a Woman*; Mumford, *Interzones*; Lvovsky, *Vice Patrol*; Canaday, *Straight State*; Canaday, Cott, and Self, *Intimate States*; Somerville, *Queering the Color Line*.

29. Most useful for understanding police corruption, party politics, and elections in the nineteenth and early twentieth century has been Czitrom, *New York Exposed*; also enlightening are Broxmeyer, *Electoral Capitalism*; Murphy, *Political Manhood*; Schrag, *Fires of Philadelphia*; Harring, *Policing a Class Society*; Anbinder, *Five Points*; Burrows and Wallace, *Gotham*.

30. Hernández, *City of Inmates*, 5; Singh, "Whiteness of Police," 1097; Hirota, *Expelling the Poor*, 43.

31. Lambert and Gilmore, "Making Abolition Geography in California's Central Valley."

32. Lambert and Gilmore, "Making Abolition Geography in California's Central Valley"; Singh, "Whiteness of Police," 1096; Molina, *How Race Is Made in America*, 6–7.

33. Lui, *Chinatown Trunk Mystery*, 17; Murakawa, *First Civil Right*; Seigel, *Violence Work*; Hernández, *City of Inmates*; Gilmore, *Golden Gulag*; Felker-Kantor, *Policing Los Angeles*; Balto, *Occupied Territory*; Agee, *Streets of San Francisco*; Hinton, *From the War on Poverty to the War on Crime*; Suddler, *Presumed Criminal*; Lebrón, *Policing Life and Death*; Schrader, *Badges without Borders*; Kohler-Hausmann, *Getting Tough*; Thompson, "Why Mass Incarceration Matters," 703–34.

34. Scott, *Seeing Like a State*, 17; Cronon, *Nature's Metropolis*, 148.

35. For a discussion of the legal absolution of racial profiling, the fantasy of standardization and deracializing policing, and the difficulty of proving racist intent in policing in the 1980s and onward, see Hinton, *From the War on Poverty to the War on Crime*, 326; Murakawa, *First Civil Right*, 4–11.

36. Childs, *Slaves of the State*, 11.

Chapter One. Becoming Blue

1. *Civil Service Roster for the City of New York*, 1902; Carey, *Memoirs of a Murder Man*, 3.

2. Carey, *Memoirs of a Murder Man*, 3.

3. Key texts in this early debate are: Miller, *Cops and Bobbies*; Levett, "Centralization of City Police in the Nineteenth Century United States"; Richardson, *New York Police*; Monkkonen, *Police in Urban America*.

4. Singh, "Whiteness of Police," 1093; Schrag, *Fires of Philadelphia*.

5. Harris, *In the Shadow of Slavery*, 264.

6. Anbinder, *City of Dreams*, 193; Roosevelt, "Municipal Administration"; Broxmeyer, *Electoral Capitalism*.

7. Rosenwaike, *Population History of New York City*, 36–42.

8. Von Skal, *History of German Immigration in the United States*, 25.

9. Nadel, *Little Germany*, 1; Von Skal, *History of German Immigration*, 29; Barrett, *Irish Way*, 20; Harris, *In the Shadow of Slavery*; Sacks, *Before Harlem*.

10. Dickens, *American Notes and Pictures from Italy*, 76.

11. Dickens, *American Notes and Pictures from Italy*, 70.

12. Wild, *Street Meeting*, 3; Barrett, *Irish Way*, 7; Ignatiev, *How the Irish Became White*, 112; Anbinder, *Five Points*.

13. Busey, *Immigration*, 143.

14. Czitrom, *New York Exposed*, 35; Busey, *Immigration*, 127.

15. Walling, *Recollections*, 54.

16. Walling, *Recollections*, 54–55; Burrows and Wallace, *Gotham*, 838.

17. Burrows and Wallace, *Gotham*, 839; O'Malley, "Protecting the Stranger," 138–39.

18. "Fourth of July," *New York Tribune*, July 6, 1857, 6.

19. "Late Riots," *New York Tribune*, July 7, 1857, 4–5; Burrows and Wallace, *Gotham*, 839.

20. "The Mayor's Rebellion," *New York Tribune*, June 18, 1857; Walling, *Recollections*, 57; Burrows and Wallace, *Gotham*, 840.

21. "Daniel F. Tiemann Elected Mayor by over 3,000 Majority," *New York Times*, December 2, 1857, 1.

22. Walling, *Recollections*, 23, 54.

23. Walling, *Recollections*, 54.

24. Baptist, *Half Has Never Been Told*, 376–79.

25. May, *Fugitive Slave Law and Its Victims*, 130.

26. May, *Fugitive Slave Law and Its Victims*, 22–23; Malka, *Men of Mobtown*, 24–25, 110–12; Wilder, *Covenant with Color*; "The American and Foreign Anti-Slavery Society," *New York Herald*, May 12, 1852, 7.

27. "The News," *New York Herald*, January 14, 1860, 6.

28. May, *Fugitive Slave Law and Its Victims*, 11, 22, 24, 87.

29. Harris, *In the Shadow of Slavery*, 264–65; Foner, *Gateway to Freedom*.

30. Barnes, *Draft Riots in New York*, 6; Brownson, "Catholics and the Anti-draft Riots," 385.

31. Barnes, *Draft Riots in New York*, 9; Walling, *Recollections*, 85.

32. Stoddard, *Volcano under the City*, 1; Smith, *Urban Disorder and the Shape of Belief*, 107.

33. Stoddard, *Volcano under the City*, 168.

34. Barnes, *Draft Riots in New York*, 13.

35. Anbinder, *City of Dreams*, 253; Burton, *Melting Pot Soldiers*, 152; Öfele, *True Sons of the Republic*, 70–71; Stoddard, *Volcano under the City*, 67, 275, 276; Barnes, *Draft Riots in New York*, 19.

36. Barnes, *Draft Riots in New York*, 29–30.

37. Harris, *In the Shadow of Slavery*, 280.

38. Barnes, *Draft Riots in New York*, 91, 42, 47.

39. Walling, *Recollections*, 79–80.

40. Stoddard, *Volcano*, 156–58. For more on the 1871 Orange Riot and political violence involving Irish New Yorkers, see Gordon, *Orange Riots*.

41. Czitrom, *New York Exposed*, 35; Burrows and Wallace, *Gotham*, 1006.

42. "The Mob in New York," *New York Times*, July 14, 1863, 4; Stoddard, *Volcano*, 20, 251, 233, 89.

43. Nast, "Charge of the Police on the Rioters of the 'Tribune' Office," 652.

44. Nast, "The American River Ganges."

45. Carey, *Memoirs*, 1. This is one of many police memoirs written in the late 1920s and early 1930s to recount the last two decades of the nineteenth century. These books reveal a deep feeling of nostalgia for policing before Prohibition contributed to the rising perception of danger and organized crime in US cities.

46. Carey, *Memoirs*, 2.

47. Carey, *Memoirs*, 4.

Chapter Two. Racial Hierarchies of Crime & Policing

1. Hicks, *Talk with You Like a Woman*, 154; Odem, *Delinquent Daughters*, 26–32, 96; Appier, *Policing Women*; Schulz, *From Social Worker to Crime Fighter*.

2. Walling, *Recollections*, 194; Bederman, *Manliness and Civilization*; Emsley, *Gendarmes and the State in Nineteenth-Century Europe*, 2–3.

3. Rosenwaike, *Population History of New York City*, 78.

4. Walling, *Recollections*, 432, 419.

5. Walling, *Recollections*, 418.

6. Walling, *Recollections*, 423–29.

7. Walling, *Recollections*, 427.

8. Stansell, *City of Women*, 89; Heap, *Slumming*, 10; Odem, *Delinquent Daughters*; Mumford, *Interzones*. One illustrative story on the relative respectability of Irish and German women is that of Elsie Sigel, the granddaughter of a German-born Civil War general who met a Leon "William" Ling, a Chinese immigrant, while she did missionary work. When police found evidence that Sigel had been murdered, New Yorkers were transfixed by daily news of the manhunt and new evidence of a prolonged romantic relationship. The story fit into a popular narrative of fallen women seduced or brainwashed by the sexuality and/or illicit substances provided by immigrant men. Lui, *Chinatown Trunk Mystery*.

9. Escoffier, Strub, and Colgan, "The Comstock Apparatus," 41–59; Gilfoyle, *City of Eros*, 104, 82–83. See also Odem, *Delinquent Daughters*; Stern, *Trials of Nina McCall*; Brandt, *No Magic Bullet*; P. Cohen, *Murder of Helen*; and Fischer, *Streets Belong to Us*, introduction and chapters 1 and 2.

10. Walling, *Recollections*, 424; Fronc, *New York Undercover*, 53–56.

11. Walling, *Recollections*, 487; Fronc, *New York Undercover*, 61; Lvovsky, *Vice Patrol*, 124–27; Chauncey, *Gay New York*, 108–10.

12. Walling, *Recollections*, 321.

13. Bederman, *Manliness and Civilization*, 23–25. For more on the relationships between race, sexuality masculinity, criminality, civilization, and science see Carter, *Heart of Whiteness*; Flowe, *Uncontrollable Blackness*; Moore, *I Fight for a Living*; Stein, *Measuring Manhood*; and Murphy, *Political Manhood*.

14. Stein, *Measuring Manhood*, 68; Agyepong, *Criminalization of Black Children*, 35.

15. Walling, *Recollections*, 331; Pick, *Faces of Degeneration*, 54, 106.

16. Crosby, "Crime and Punishment in New York," 168–69.

17. Parkhurst, *Our Fight*, 5.

18. Parkhurst, *Our Fight*, 5; Czitrom, *New York Exposed*, xi; Gardner, *Doctor and the Devil*, 22, 52; Fischer, *Streets Belong to Us*.

19. Parkhurst, *Our Fight*, 8, 13.

20. "The Master of the Club: Captain Williams," *Brooklyn Daily Eagle*, February 13, 1885, 4.

21. "Williams, 'Ex-Czar' of Tenderloin, Dies," *New York Times*, March 26, 1917, 11.

22. District Attorney to Police Commissioner William McAdoo, December 27, 1904; "Williams, 'Ex-Czar' of Tenderloin, Dies," *New York Times*, March 26, 1917, 11; "Capt.

Williams Promoted." *New York Times*, August 10, 1887, 1, "Captain Williams Questioned," *Sun*, October 14, 1885, 4; Gilfoyle, *City of Eros*, 65.

23. Parkhurst, *Our Fight*, 21.

24. Parkhurst, *Our Fight*, 32.

25. Frances Willard, "Annual Address before the National Woman's Christian Temperance Union."

26. *Tammany Times*, May 11, 1895, 892.

27. Carey, *Memoirs*, 3; Kammen, *Mystic Chords of Memory*, 248–49.

28. Owen, W. D. (William Dale), US Select Committee on Immigration and Naturalization, *Report of the Select Committee on Immigration and Naturalization: and Testimony Taken by the Committee on Immigration of the Senate and the Select Committee on Immigration and Naturalization of the House of Representatives under Concurrent Resolution of March 12, 1890* (Washington, DC: Government Printing Office), 31, 319; Lew-Williams, *Chinese Must Go*, 159; Lee, *At America's Gate*, 64–65.

29. Willard, "Annual Address before the National Woman's Christian Temperance Union," 171.

30. "Police Matrons at Last," *Evening World*, March 21, 1891, 4; "Entraps Bandits: Earns Promotion," *Star-Gazette*, March 8, 1912, 12.

31. Willard, "Annual Address before the National Woman's Christian Temperance Union," 171.

32. Willard, "Annual Address before the National Woman's Christian Temperance Union," 96; "Arrests without Evidence," *Sun*, August 4, 1904, 10; Evens, "Plainclothes Policewomen on the Trail," 49–66; *People of New York v. George Glucksman*, Trial Transcripts of the County of New York, 1883–1927.

33. *People of New York v. Dora Miadowicz*, Trial #1373, Trial Transcripts of the County of New York, 6–7.

34. *People of New York v. Dora Miadowicz*, Trial #1373, Trial Transcripts of the County of New York, 11.

35. *People of New York v. Dora Miadowicz*, Trial #1373, Trial Transcripts of the County of New York, 11.

36. Hicks, *Talk with You Like a Woman*, 61; *People of New York v. Robert Jefferson*, Reel 488, Trial Transcripts of the County of New York.

37. Kornmann, *Our Police*, 39–40; Walling, *Recollections*, 593.

38. Wexler, *Tender Violence*, 22–23.

39. Parkhurst, *Our Fight*, 240; New York State Senate, Lexow Committee, *Report and Proceedings of the Senate Committee Appointed to Investigate the Police Department of the City of New York*, vol. 1, 30.

40. New York State Senate, Lexow Committee, *Report and Proceedings*, vol. 5, 5466.

41. New York State Senate, Lexow Committee, *Report and Proceedings*, vol. 5, 5533–36, 5431, 5437.

42. New York State Senate, Lexow Committee, *Report and Proceedings*, vol. 5, 4969, 4979.

43. "Paid $500 to Schmittberger," *New York Times*, October 12, 1894, 4.

44. "Paid $500 to Schmittberger," *New York Times*, October 12, 1894, 4; New York State Senate, Lexow Committee, *Report and Proceedings*, vol. 1, 86.

45. New York State Senate, Lexow Committee, *Report and Proceedings*, vol. 1, 81.

46. "Farewell to Williams," *New York Times*, May 25, 1895, 1.

47. "Chief Byrnes Retired," *New York Times*, May 28, 1895, 1.

48. New York State Senate, Lexow Committee, *Report and Proceedings*, vol. 1, 87.

49. Parkhurst, *Our Fight*, 285.

50. "After the Battle," *Sun*, November 8, 1894, 6.

51. "The New Mayor's Third Day," *New York Times*, January 4, 1895.

52. "Sheehan Out, Andrews In," *Evening World*, February 14, 1895, 1.

53. "Roosevelt Will Accept," *Democrat and Chronicle*, April 24, 1895, 1.

54. "Roosevelt Takes a Night Tour," *New York Herald*, June 8, 1895.

55. "The Combination Was Too Much for the Cops," cartoon, *New York Recorder*, July 12, 1895.

56. "Among The Victims . . ." *Tammany Times*, September 14, 1895, 5.

57. "Awful Possibility under Our Blue Laws," cartoon, *New York World*, July 15, 1895.

58. "Roosevelt," *Tammany Times*, January 25, 1897, 6.

59. Letter from Theodore Roosevelt to Alphonse Major, January 28, 1896.

60. Letter from Theodore Roosevelt to G. Fraser, British Consulate General. August 11, 1896.

61. Bederman, *Manliness and Civilization*, 187.

62. Moore, *I Fight for a Living*, 11.

63. Letter from Theodore Roosevelt to Sir Cecil Spring Rice, August 5, 1896.

64. Letter from Theodore Roosevelt to Sir Cecil Spring Rice, August 5, 1896.

65. Roosevelt, "The Ethnology of the Police," 398.

66. Roosevelt, "The Ethnology of the Police," 396, 398.

67. Roosevelt, "The Ethnology of the Police," 397.

68. Roosevelt, "Administering the New York Police Force," 184.

69. Ripley, *Selected Bibliography of the Anthropology and Ethnology of Europe*, vii.

70. Ripley, *Races of Europe*, 3.

71. Ripley, *Races of Europe*, 583, 91; Bender, *Sweated Work*.

72. Ripley, *Races of Europe*, 89.

73. New York State Senate, Lexow Committee, *Report and Proceedings*, vol. 5, 5316.

74. *Report of the Municipal Civil Service Commissioner Investigation of Promotions From Sergeant to Captain in the Police Department of the City of New York*, June 19, 1901.

75. New York City Police Department, *Report of the Police Department of the City of New York for the Year Ending December 31, 1895*, 5, 17; *Year Ending December 31, 1904*, 49, 65; *Year Ending December 31, 1908*, 1, 5.

Chapter Three. Colonial Methods

1. Greene, "The Duty of the Church in Our New Possessions," 10.

2. Anderson and Killingray, *Policing the Empire*, 8.

3. Anderson and Killingray, *Policing the Empire*, 9; Go, "Imperial Origins."

4. Jung, *Menace to Empire*, 30–40.

5. Go, "Imperial Origins," 1196; Kramer, *Blood of Government*, 24; Singh, *Race and America's Long War*, 50.

6. Willemse, *A Cop Remembers*, 114.

7. Rosenwaike, *Population History of New York*, 95.

8. William Tecumseh Sherman to Francis Vinton Greene, October 23, 1877.

9. Emory Upton to Francis Vinton Greene, August 18, 1877.

10. Stowell, *Streets, Railroads, and the Great Strike of 1877*, 2–3.

11. William Tecumseh Sherman to Francis Vinton Greene, January 13, 1878.

12. Emory Upton to Francis Vinton Greene, October 3, 1879.

13. Emory Upton to Francis Vinton Greene, October 3, 1879.

14. P. Tecumseh Sherman to Francis Greene, May 12, 1891.

15. P. Tecumseh Sherman to Francis Greene, May 12, 1891.

16. William Tecumseh Sherman to Francis Greene, July 28, 1878.

17. John Hay to Theodore Roosevelt, July 27, 1898.

18. Greene, "Address to the Republican Club in the City of New York," March 20, 1915, 1.

19. Greene, "Address to the Republican Club"; Kramer, *Blood of Government*, 97–98.

20. H. C. Corbin to General E. S. Otis, Manila, December 21, 1898, 858.

21. Joyce, *Rule of Freedom*; Lowe, *Intimacies of Four Continents*.

22. McCoy, *Policing America's Empire*, 17–18; Dphrepaulezz, "Right Sort of White Men," 10.

23. Francis Vinton Greene, "Future of the Philippines," 11.

24. Francis Vinton Greene, "Future of the Philippines," 11.

25. H. C. Corbin, Adjutant General, "Special Order 240," October 11, 1898, 1.

26. *Reports of the Taft Philippine Commission*, 38.

27. General Order 40, March 29, 1900, 1.

28. Greene, *Report*, August 30, 1898, 2.

29. MacArthur, *Annual Report of Major General Arthur MacArthur* 2:40.

30. Beredo, *Import of the Archive*, 9–10; Scott, *Seeing Like a State*, 2; Foucault, *Discipline and Punish*, 195–96.

31. Greene, "The Duty of the Church in Our New Possessions," 2.

32. Greene, "The Duty of the Church in Our New Possessions," 2 (emphasis added).

33. *Reports of the Taft Philippine Commission*, 77.

34. Anderson and Killingray, *Policing the Empire*, 8.

35. Arnold, *Police Power and Colonial Rule*, 45.

36. Ellis, "Reservation *Akicitas*," 186–87.

37. MacArthur, *Annual Report of Major General Arthur MacArthur* 2:5–6.

38. MacArthur, *Annual Report of Major General Arthur MacArthur* 2:5.

39. MacArthur, *Annual Report of Major General Arthur MacArthur* 2:39; "Transport Service to Manilla," *St. Louis Globe-Democrat*, February 15, 1900, 3; Devins, *Observation of the Philippines*, 166.

40. Wood to President Roosevelt, February 25, 1906, quoted in McCallum, *Leonard Wood*, 216.

41. *Reports of the Taft Philippine Commission*, 41–42; Dphrepaulezz, "Right Sort of White Men," 97; Fulton, *Moroland*, 210; Ross, *Inventing the Savage*, 15.

42. "Laying for Taft in the Philippines," *New York Age*, August 10, 1905, 4.

43. Vollmer and Parker, *Crime and the State Police*, 140.

44. Willis, *Our Philippine Problem*, 123.

45. Willis, *Our Philippine Problem*, 123.

46. Jung, *Menace to Empire*, 41.

47. Secretary of War Russell A. Alger to Francis Vinton Greene, November 12, 1898, 5.

48. Secretary of War Russell A. Alger to Francis Vinton Greene, November 12, 1898, 5.

49. Greene, *Report*, December 27, 1898, 9.

50. "McCullagh's Police Plan for Havana," *New York Times*, December 17, 1898, 6.

51. Bolton, ed., *History of the Second Regiment Illinois Volunteer Infantry*, 89–149.

52. "To Greet His Soldier Son," *New York Times*, June 10, 1902, 16.

53. Bernard York, President of the Police Board of Commissioners, to Mayor Robert Van Wyck, May 23, 1899.

54. H. C. Corbin to Francis Vinton Greene, December 2, 1898, 1; H. C. Corbin, "Special Order 307," December 30, 1898, 1.

55. Go, "Imperial Origins," 1213; *Honolulu Star*, June 5, 1923, 6, quoted in Go, "Imperial Origins," 1208; Oliver, *August Vollmer*, 153–54; "August Vollmer Suicide on Coast," *New York Times*, November 5, 1955, 40.

56. Vollmer and Parker, *Crime and the State Police*, 134–35.

57. Vollmer and Parker, *Crime and the State Police*, 140.

58. Vollmer and Parker, *Crime and the State Police*, 8.

59. Pennsylvania State Federation of Labor, *The American Cossack*, 63.

60. Pennsylvania State Federation of Labor, *The American Cossack*, 15.

61. "Filipino Methods," *Statesman Journal*, March 12, 1902, 2; Jung, *Menace to Empire*, 188.

62. Hoff, *Report of the Superior Board of Health of Porto Rico*, 479; Willrich, *Pox*, 145, 159–67.

63. Briggs, *Reproducing Empire*, 46–49; Pliley, *Policing Sexuality*, 28–29; Kramer, *Blood of Government*, 408.

64. Kramer, *Blood of Government*, 89–90.

65. Kramer, *Blood of Government*, 122.

66. Carson, *Settlement Folk*, 102–3; Carlson, *Americanization Syndrome*, 67.

67. Kramer, *Blood of Government*, 147; McCoy, *Policing America's Empire*, 85; Dphrepaulezz, "Right Sort of White Men," 86.

68. "A Filipino's Blade for Wanger," *Bucks Country Gazette*, July 5, 1900, 3; "War Mementoes," *Daily Herald*, June 19, 1900, 4; "A Filipino Ambush," *Brooklyn Daily Eagle*, April 24, 1899; Dphrepaulezz, "Right Sort of White Men," 86.

69. To reference a few: "Used Teeth and Stiletto," *Brooklyn Daily Eagle*, July 1, 1904, 2, "Stabbed with a Stiletto," *New York Tribune*, September 3, 1900, 6; "Duel with Stilettos," *New York Times*, September 17, 1900, 15; "Slashed Wife With Stiletto," *Brooklyn Daily Eagle*, May 23, 1906, 2.

70. "Stiletto Should be Banished," *Evening World*, March 21, 1894, 4.

71. Appleton Morgan, "What Shall We Do With the 'Dago'?"; "Italian Crime and Police Incompetence," *New York Tribune*, August 21, 1904, 1.

72. "Partridge Resigns," *Democrat and Chronicle*, December 13, 1902, 1.

73. "Gen. Francis V. Greene Named to Head Police," *Brooklyn Daily Eagle*, December 23, 1902, 1.

74. Francis V. Greene to Theodore Roosevelt, December 26, 1902.

75. "Quick Shakeup by Greene in Police Department," *Brooklyn Daily Eagle*, March 13, 1903, 2.

76. Hugh McGowan to Francis Vinton Greene, February 6, 1903.

77. Francis Vinton Greene, "The Present Condition of the Police Force," 4.

78. "Bayonet-Imposed Civilization," *Indianapolis Recorder*, March 18, 1899, from Marks, ed., *Black Press Views American Imperialism*, 117.

79. "Filipinos May Have Learned From the Fate of Negroes and Indians," *Broad Ax*, April 8, 1899, from Marks, ed., *Black Press Views American Imperialism*, 121.

80. "Civilize America First," *Illinois Record*, January 14, 1899. from, Marks, ed., *Black Press Views American Imperialism*, 96.

81. J. Johnson, *Black Manhattan*, 127; Fred Newell quoted in Capozzola, *Bound by War*, 55.

82. Hicks, *Talk with You Like a Woman*, 58.

83. Willemse, *Behind the Green Lights*, 51.

84. "Race Riot on the West Side," *New York Times*, August 16, 1900, 1.

85. This is based on dozens of witness accounts recorded in Moss, *Story of the Riot*; "Fifty Wounded, Forty Arrested," *Buffalo Evening News*, August 16, 1900, 1.

86. "Fifty Wounded, Forty Arrested," *Buffalo Evening News*, August 16, 1900, 1.

87. Moss, *Story of the Riot*, 80.

88. Moss, *Story of the Riot*, 4; "Negroes Demand Justice," *New York Tribune*, September 13, 1900, 1.

89. "Negroes' Public Protest," *New York Times*, September 13, 1900, 2.

Chapter Four. The Rise of Ethnic Policing

1. McAdoo, *Guarding a Great City*, 146.

2. McAdoo, *Guarding a Great City*, 160–61.

3. Pliley, *Policing Sexuality*, 35.

4. Hicks, *Talk with You Like a Woman*, 129; Gross, *Colored Amazons*, 126; Fischer, *Streets Belong to Us*, 18–25, 29–33; Flowe, *Uncontrollable Blackness*, 96–97; Flowe, "'Drug-Mad Negroes,'" 509–10.

5. Turner, "Daughters of the Poor," 50.

6. Bingham, *Girl That Disappears*, 39.

7. Canaday, *Straight State*, 19–54.

8. McAdoo, *Guarding a Great City*, 96.

9. McAdoo, *Guarding a Great City*, 100, 154; "Told by Negro's Prisoners," *Sun*, March 22, 1906, 5; Thale, "Informal World of Police Patrol," 183–216.

10. Fischer, *Streets Belong to Us*, 37.

11. Fronc, *New York Undercover*, 102–3; McAdoo, *Guarding a Great City*, 100.

12. *People of New York v. Francesco Sansone*, Trial #1171, Trial Transcripts of the County of New York, 1883–1927.

13. *People v. Leon Jung*, Trial #1385, Criminal Trial Transcripts of New York County, 22.

14. *People of New York v. Francesco Sansone*.

15. Willemse, *Behind the Green Lights*, 26–28.

16. Willemse, *Behind the Green Lights*, 28.

17. Willemse, *Behind the Green Lights*, 76.

18. Willemse, *A Cop Remembers*, 114.

19. Willemse, *A Cop Remembers*, 146.

20. Willemse, *Behind the Green Lights*, 118.

21. "New York's Chinese Policeman a Hero," *Capital Times*, July 25, 1923, 3; "Only Chinese Policeman Passes Up Assignment to Chinatown," *El Paso Herald*, May 5, 1909, 1.

22. "Only Chinese Policeman Passes Up Assignment to Chinatown," *El Paso Herald*, May 5, 1909, 1.

23. "Only Chinese Policeman Passes Up Assignment to Chinatown," *El Paso Herald*, May 5, 1909, 1.

24. "Chinese Police," *Democrat and Chronicle*, November 22, 1896, 7.

25. United States Department of Commerce and Labor, *Report of the United States Commission of Investigation Upon the Disaster to the Steamer "General Slocum,"* October 8, 1904, 9–12.

26. United States Department of Commerce and Labor, *Report of the United States Commission of Investigation Upon the Disaster to the Steamer "General Slocum,"* October 8, 1904, 13, 17.

27. "Heroic Rescuers Afloat," *New York Times*, June 16, 1904, 2

28. United States Department of Commerce and Labor, *Report of the United States Commission of Investigation Upon the Disaster to the Steamer "General Slocum,"* October 8, 1904, 24.

29. Willemse, *A Cop Remembers*, 211–12.

30. Theodore Roosevelt to Francis Vinton Greene, January 21, 1903.

31. New York City Police Department, *Report of the Police Department of the City of New York for the Year Ending December 31, 1905*, 88–96.

32. "Police List of Victims," *New York Times*, June 23, 1904, 5.

Chapter Five. Policing the "Italian Problem"

1. "Slain Man in a Barrel," *Brooklyn Daily Eagle*, April 14, 1903, 1; "Suspects Knew Bendetto, the Barrel Victim," *Evening World*, April 20, 1903, 1; "Man in Barrel War Tortured, then Murdered," *Evening World*, April 14, 1903, 1; "Police Are Certain They Have Slayers," *Evening World*, April 16, 1903, 1; "Indicted for Barrel Murder," *New York Times*, June 26, 1903, 3; New York District Attorney Case File # 42841/1903; "Terror of the Black Hand," *Nebraska State Journal*, September 2, 1904, 3.

Jessica Pliley and others have discussed the racialized meanings of "swarthy" to denote an association between darker-complected European *immigrants* (particularly from Southern and Eastern Europe), promiscuous and predatory sexuality, and the "white slavery" scare of the early twentieth century.

2. Pliley, *Policing Sexuality*, 25; Heap, *Slumming*, 118–19; Bender, *American Abyss*, 82.

3. "Italian Crime and Police Incompetence," *New York Tribune*, August 21, 1904, 1.

4. Pliley, *Policing Sexuality*, 10; Goodman, *Deportation Machine*.

5. McAdoo, *Guarding a Great City*, 160–61.

6. Gabaccia, "Race, Nation, Hyphen," 57.

7. This work builds especially on a growing body of scholarship that links surveillance with subject-making and identity formation. Browne, S., *Dark Matters*, 7; Beachy, *Gay Berlin*, 66; Duggan, *Sapphic Slashers*, 196.

8. Hughes, *Crime, Disorder and the Risorgimento*; Jensen, *Liberty and Order*; Davis, *Conflict and Control*.

9. J. Guglielmo, *Living the Revolution*, 16, 33.

10. J. Guglielmo, *Living the Revolution*, 40; Lombroso, *Crime, Its Causes and Remedies*, xxxiii.

11. Lombroso, *Crime, Its Causes and Remedies*, 16–17, 31.

12. Lombroso, *Crime, Its Causes and Remedies*, 37–39.

13. Lombroso, *Crime, Its Causes and Remedies*, 223; Pick, *Faces of Degeneration*.

14. Ripley, *Races of Europe*, 272.

15. DeSalvo, "Color: White/Complexion: Dark," 25; T. Guglielmo, *White on Arrival*, 7–8.

16. J. Guglielmo, "Introduction: White Lies, Dark Truths," 8.

17. Muhammad, *Condemnation of Blackness*, 10; Roediger, *Working toward Whiteness*, 237; T. Guglielmo, *White on Arrival*, 43; Bender, *American Abyss*, 86–87.

18. Ignatiev, *How the Irish Became White*, 112.

19. Jacobson, *Whiteness of a Different Color*, 57.

20. Morgan, "What Shall We Do With the 'Dago'?"

21. Pliley, *Policing Sexuality*, 50; Harring, *Policing a Class Society*, 33; Scott, *Domination and the Arts of Resistance*; Jacobson, *Barbarian Virtues*, 159.

22. "Made Detective Sergeants," *Brooklyn Daily Eagle*, August 6, 1901, 2.

23. "Memorabilia: A Hero's Story," *Spring 3100*, July/August 1990, 10.

24. Murphy, *Political Manhood*, 99; Pliley, *Policing Sexuality*, 24; Chauncey, *Gay New York*, 137; Canaday, *Straight State*, 19.

25. "Career of Petrosino," *New York Tribune*, March 14, 1909, 3.

26. Gage, *The Day Wall Street Exploded*, 42–44.

27. J. Guglielmo, *Living the Revolution*, 87.

28. Nitti, "Italian Anarchists," 598.

29. Nitti, "Italian Anarchists," 599.

30. William Henry Bishop to Assistant Secretary of State, April 18, 1908, 1.

31. Lombroso, "Illustrative Studies in Criminal Anthropology," 342.

32. William Henry Bishop to Assistant Secretary of State, April 18, 1908, 1.

33. Woods, "Problem of the Black Hand," 43.

34. D'Amato, "The 'Black Hand' Myth," 545.

35. "No Clue to Sack Murder," *Brooklyn Daily Eagle*, July 29, 1902, 16.

36. Morgan, "What Shall We Do," 1.

37. "Assassinated," *Times-Picayune*, October 16, 1890, 1.

38. "District Attorney Files His Report on Italian Lynching," *Times-Picayune*, April 29, 1891, 1.

39. "Italian Crime and Police Incompetence," *New York Tribune*, August 21, 1904, 1.

40. "Italian Crime and Police Incompetence," *New York Tribune*, August 21, 1904, 1.

41. New York City Police Department, *Report of the Police Department of the City of New York for the Year Ending December 31, 1905*, 23.

42. Lowe, *Intimacies of Four Continents*, 8.

43. *People v. Leonardo Broncado*, 1905. From the Criminal Trial Transcripts of New York County Collection, 22.

44. *People v. Francesco Purpura*, 1909. Trial #1170. From the Criminal Trial Transcripts of New York County Collection.

45. "Who Wrote Dynamite Letter," *Sun*, May 11, 1903, 1.

46. District Attorney to William McAdoo, Commissioner of the NYPD, June 22, 1904.

47. "'The Other McAdoo,' Meaning Tammany's New Police Commissioner," *Democrat and Chronicle*, January 3, 1904, 6; McAdoo, *Guarding a Great City*, 154.

48. *Original Italian Squad, 1904*. Photo collage believed to have been created between 1909 and 1910.

49. New York City Police Department, *Report of the Police Department of the City of New York for the Year Ending December 31, 1904*, 49; *Report of the Police Department of the City of New York for the Year Ending December 31, 1905*, 48; *Report of the Police Department of the City of New York for the Year Ending December 31, 1908*, 7.

50. "De Palo Will Be Brought Back," *Brooklyn Daily Eagle*, April 26, 1905, 7.

51. "A Secret Service Squad to Hunt the Black Hand," *New York Times*, December 20, 1906, 16.

52. "Stab Chicago's Petrosino," *Sun*, May 2, 1909, 1.

53. "His Whiskers Fooled Sara," *Pittsburgh Press*, December 12, 1904, 14.

54. "The Police Board," *Times Democrat*, February 15, 1900, 8.

55. "Pinkerton Man to Aid State," *Philadelphia Inquirer*, May 2, 1902, 1.

56. "Theodore A. Bingham," *Buffalo Enquirer*, May 14, 1908, 2; "Commissioner Bingham," *New York Times*, January 7, 1906, 6.

57. "The Black Hand," *International Gazette*, April 6, 1907, 3.

58. Bingham, "How to Give New York the Best Police Force in the World," 703.

59. Bingham, "Foreign Criminal in New York," 383.

60. "Wooden Leg Swings in New Crime Wave," *Evening World*, August 5, 1908, 3.

61. "Most Criminal Nation on Earth, Says Rev. Peters," *Evening World*, August 10, 1907, 3, "Miss White Says 'Straight-Line' Dresses Aid Morality, and That Danger and Demoralization Lurk in Curves," *Evening World*, September 12, 1907, 3.

62. "Most Criminal Nation on Earth, Says Rev. Peters," *Evening World*, August 10, 1907, 3.

63. "The Police Situation," *New York Times*, November 4, 1907, 8.

64. "The Black Hand," *International Gazette*, April 6, 1907, 3, "A Secret Service Squad to Hunt the Black Hand," *New York Times*, December 20, 1906, 16.

65. Pliley, *Policing Sexuality*, 20.

66. An Act to Regulate the Immigration of Aliens into the United States, S. 4403, February 20, 1907, https://archive.org/details/cu31924021131101.

67. "Bingham Takes Office," *New York Times*, January 2, 1906, 5.

68. "Bingham Makes a Speech," *New York Times*, April 19, 1906, 13.

69. Bingham, "Foreign Criminal in New York," 383.

70. "Italians United against Black Hand," *Buffalo Commercial*, February 7, 1908, 9.

71. "Italians United against Black Hand," *Buffalo Commercial*, February 7, 1908, 9.

72. Bingham, "How to Give New York the Best Police Force in the World," 706.

73. "Bingham vs. The Black Hand," *Sun*, February 7, 1908, 2.

74. New York City Police Department, *Report of the Police Department of the City of New York for the Year Ending December 31, 1908*, 5; "Kidnappers May Return Stolen Boy to Parents," *Brooklyn Daily Eagle*, August 13, 1904, 2.

75. "Italian Crime and Police Incompetence" *New York Tribune*, August 21, 1904, 1.

76. "A Secret Service Squad to Hunt the Black Hand," *New York Times*, December 20, 1906, 16.

77. Fiaschetti and Buranelli, *You Gotta Be Rough*, 43, 83.

78. McAdoo, *Guarding a Great City*, 262.

79. McAdoo, *Guarding a Great City*, 265–66.

80. Guariglia, "'Blue Lives' Do Matter—And That's the Problem," *Washington Post*, November 20, 2017.

81. "Slash and Beat Black Hand's Foe," *Chicago Daily Tribune*, May 2, 1909, 3.

82. "Try Again to Kill Longabardi," *Chicago Daily Tribune*, January 23, 1910, 6.

83. "Collection of death threats and threatening notes left on Petrosino's door, 1907–1909."

84. *Civil Service Roster for the City of New York*, 1902–1908.

85. "Warned of Petrosino Death," *New York Tribune*, March 14, 1909, 3.

86. Burrows, "The Need of National Legislation against Anarchism," 733–34; Lodge, "The Restriction of Immigration," 27–36.

87. Lee, *At America's Gate;* Ngai, *Impossible Subjects.*

88. "Aflano Will Be Deported," *Chattanooga Daily Times*, April 23, 1907, 1; Hernández, *Migra!*, 27; Guariglia, "Wrench in the Deportation."

89. Marinari, *Unwanted*, 21–25.

90. "Italian Criminals," *Argus-Leader*, February 22, 1908, 1; *Report of the Police Department of the City of New York for the Year Ending December 31, 1908*, 24.

91. Hernández, *Bad Mexicans*, 166.

92. William Henry Bishop to the Commander of the SS *Minerva*, January 4, 1909.

93. William Henry Bishop to Assistant Secretary of State, March 20, 1909.

94. "A Secret Service Squad to Hunt the Black Hand," *New York Times*, December 20, 1906, 16.

95. William Henry Bishop to Professor Rallo, March 6, 1909.

96. William Henry Bishop to Assistant Secretary of State, March 20, 1909.

97. "Blame Italian Police," *New York Tribune*, March 14, 1909, 3.

98. William Henry Bishop to Tuohy, March 1909.

99. "Italians Who Were Deported," *New York Times*, March 19, 1909, 2.

100. "Arrests in Palermo," *New York Tribune*, March 18, 1909, 3.

101. Vice Consul in Charge to the American Red Cross Society, May 1, 1909.

102. "Italy Police 'Solve' 1909 Petrosino Mafia Murder," BBC, June 23, 2014. http://www.bbc.com/news/world-europe-27971542.

103. "Black Hand Confessions," 1910.

104. "Counterfeiters Guilty," *Brooklyn Daily Eagle*, February 20, 1910, 6.

105. Vice Consul in Charge to the American Red Cross Society, May 1, 1909.

106. "GI'imponenti funerali del luogotenente Petrosino."

107. "Crusade to Restore Italian Detectives to Be Started Here," *Brooklyn Daily Eagle*, July 12, 1911, 2.

108. "Scare of Caruso," *New York Tribune*, March 5, 1910, 1; "Flynn Revolutionizes the Detective Bureau," *New York Tribune*, November 18, 1910, 3.

109. Fiaschetti and Buranelli, *You Gotta Be Rough*, 15, 43; *Civil Service Roster for the City of New York*, 1908.

110. Fiaschetti and Buranelli, *You Gotta Be Rough*, 82, 129.

111. "Bomb Squad Joined With the Italian," *New York Times*, February 5, 122, 9; Fishman, *Dynamite*, 22.

112. Woods, "Problem of the Black Hand," 47.

Chapter Six. "They Needed Me as Much as I Needed Them"

1. Lepore, *New York Burning*, 6; S. Browne, *Dark Matters*, 67–68.

2. Watkins-Owens, *Blood Relations*, 12–13; Wilkerson, *Warmth of Other Suns*, 9

3. Moss, ed., *Story of the Riot;* "Negro Police for New York," *New York Age*, August 5, 1909, 1.

4. Rosenwaike, *Population History of New York City*, 133.

5. Rosenwaike, *Population History of New York City*, 77; New York City Police Department, *Report of the Police Department of the City of New York for the Year Ending December 31, 1895*, 48.

6. *Report of the Police Department of the City of New York for the Year Ending December 31, 1905*, 48.

7. *Report of the Police Department of the City of New York for the Year Ending December 31, 1904*, 49; Anderson, "The Language of Class in Twentieth-Century America," 354; Diner, "The Encounter between Jews and America in the Gilded Age and Progressive Era," 16; *Report of the Police Department of the City of New York for the Year Ending December 31, 1905*, 51–57.

8. *Report of the Police Department of the City of New York for the Year Ending December 31, 1905*, 48; Rosenwaike, *Population History of New York City*, 94.

9. Hicks, *Talk with You Like a Woman*, 53–90.

10. *Report of the Police Department of the City of New York for the Year Ending December 31, 1906*, 136.

11. *Report of the Police Department of the City of New York for the Year Ending December 31, 1908*, 6–23.

12. *Report of the Police Department of the City of New York for the Year Ending December 31, 1912*, 32.

13. Moss, *Story of the Riot*, 1900.

14. Thornbrough, *T. Thomas Fortune*, 95.

15. "Race Riot on West Side," *New York Times*, August 16, 1900; "West Side Race Troubles," *New York Times*, February 23, 1901; "Police Quell Race Riot," *New York Times*, June 14, 1903; "Quiet on San Juan Hill," *New York Times*, July 19, 1905; "San Juan Hill Riots after Bellboy's Ball," *New York Times*, September 13, 1906; "Negros in a Riot on San Juan Hill," *New York Times*, November 29, 1907; "Eight Killed in Fight Riots," *New York Times*, June 5, 1910.

16. "New York Police Brutality," *New York Age*, July 27, 1905, 2.

17. "Negro Police for New York," *New York Age*, August 5, 1909, 1.

18. Quoted here is the classic and most important text on this Black respectability politics and its fluid uses and meanings, Higginbotham, *Righteous Discontent*, 194–95. Other useful discussions include, Hicks, *Talk with You Like a Woman*, 237–52; Blair, *I've Got to Make My Livin'*, 86–122; Haley, *No Mercy Here*, 199–200; Flowe, *Uncontrollable Blackness*, 59–60; Robertson, "Harlem Undercover"; Heap, *Slumming*, 143–44; Mumford, *Interzones*. Also of interest is the critique of the study of respectability in Gross, *Colored Amazons*.

19. Washington, "Negro Crime and Strong Drink," 384; Flowe, "'Drug-Mad Negroes,'" 506.

20. "Negro Police for New York," *New York Age*, August 5, 1909, 4.

21. Washington, "Address before the Cotton States and International Exhibition," 1895. Harlan, *Booker T. Washington Papers* 3:583.

22. "Subject of Negro Police," *New York Age*, August 19, 1909, 1.

23. "Subject of Negro Police," *New York Age*, August 19, 1909, 1.

24. Dulaney, *Black Police in America*, 8–17.

25. Dulaney, *Black Police in America*, 19–21.

26. The first Black police officer in Brooklyn was Wiley G. Overton, who was appointed to force in March 1891 and patrolled the Eighteenth Brooklyn Precinct. "On the Force," *Brooklyn Daily Eagle*, March 5, 1891, 6.

27. "Subject of Negro Police," *New York Age*, August 19, 1909, 1.

28. "Missouri Negroes Slated," *New York Age*, September 16, 1909, 8.

29. "Favor Negro Police," *New York Age*, March 21, 1910, 8.

30. "Will Not Take Examination," *New York Age*, September 2, 1909, 1.

31. Alexander, *Blue Coats, Black Skin*, 10; Dulaney, *Black Police in America*, 25; Browne, *One Righteous Man*, 284.

32. Notes from Samuel Battle to Langston Hughes, 1946.

33. Battle, "Reminiscences of Samuel J. Battle," 6.

34. Battle, "Reminiscences of Samuel J. Battle," 4–9.

35. Battle, "Reminiscences of Samuel J. Battle," 11.

36. "Another Colored Policeman," *Evening World*, April 25, 1892, 3.

37. Battle, "Reminiscences of Samuel J. Battle," 16–17.

38. "New York City Has a Colored Police Officer," *New York Age*, June 29, 1911, 1.

39. "First Negro Named for City's Police," *New York Times*, June 29, 1911.

40. Du Bois, "Social Uplift," *The Crisis*, August 1911.

41. Battle, "Reminiscences of Samuel J. Battle," 20.

42. "New York City Has a Colored Police Officer," *New York Age*, June 29, 1911, 4.

43. "No Job Too Big," *New York Age*, July 20, 1911, 4.

44. "Battle Thanks Friends through *Age*," *New York Age*, July 20, 1911, 7.

45. "Negro Policeman Hazed by Silence," *New York Times*, August 17, 1911.

46. "Social Uplift," *The Crisis*, 10.

47. Carter, *Heart of Whiteness*, 42; Stein, *Measuring Manhood*, 68–69; Ordover, *American Eugenics*, 24–25; Flowe, *Uncontrollable Blackness*, 97; Moore, *I Fight for a Living*.

48. "Hazed by Silence," *New York Times*, August 17, 1911.

49. Notes from Samuel Battle to Langston Hughes, 1946.

50. "Police Officer Battle Now on Regular Duty," *New York Age*, August 3, 1911.

51. Battle, "Reminiscences of Samuel J. Battle," 38.

52. Notes from Samuel Battle to Langston Hughes, 1946.

53. Battle, "Reminiscences of Samuel J. Battle," 23.

54. Notes from Samuel Battle to Langston Hughes, 1946.

55. "Police Officer Battle Now on Regular Duty," *New York Age*, August 3, 1911, 1.

56. "Officer Holmes Assigned to 28th District," *New York Age*, October 16, 1913, 1.

57. Battle, "Reminiscences of Samuel J. Battle," 33.

58. Fronc, *New York Undercover*, 102.

59. Fronc, *New York Undercover*, 106; S. Robertson, "Harlem Undercover," 486–504.

60. Willemse, *A Cop Remembers*. 128.

61. Alexander, *Blue Coats, Black Skin*, 35–39.

62. Alexander, *Blue Coats, Black Skin*, 35–36.

Chapter Seven. "Police Are Raw Materials"

1. Woods, "Introduction," from Cahalane, *Police Practice and Procedure*, iii.

2. Fosdick, *American Police Systems*, 8 (emphasis added).

3. Capozzola, *Uncle Sam Wants You*; Marinari, *Unwanted*; Kornweibel, *Seeing Red*; Kraut, *Threat of Dissent*; Fischer, *Streets Belong to Us*; Sohi, *Echoes of Mutiny*; Pliley, *Policing Sexuality*; Odem, *Delinquent Daughters*; Clement, *Love for Sale*; Fronc, *New York Undercover*; Flowe, *Uncontrollable Blackness*; Hicks, *Talk with You Like a Woman*; Gage, *The Day Wall Street Exploded*.

4. Cahalane, *Police Practice and Procedure*, 4; Anbinder, *City of Dreams*.

5. Cahalane, *Police Practice and Procedure*, 4.

6. Cahalane, *Police Practice and Procedure*, 78–79.

7. Foucault, *Discipline and Punish*, 135.

8. Fosdick, *American Police Systems*, 298.

9. Agar, *Government Machine*, 35.

10. "Common Sense Is to Be the Keynote of the New Police Head," *New York Times*, January 11, 1914, 32.

11. "Four Held for Straus Murder," *Sun*, January 11, 1914, 1; "Fairness to Mr. McKay," *New York Times*, February 21, 1914, 10.

12. "Goethals Will Stay, Unless Forced Out," *New York Times*, January 24, 1914, 1.

13. Theodore Bingham to Arthur Woods, April 12, 1907; Woods, "Problem of the Black Hand," 47.

14. "M'Kay's Resignation Kept Quiet by Mayor for Several Days," *Evening World*, April 1, 1914, 1.

15. "New Spirit of the New York Police Force," *Sun*, August 23, 1914, 26.

16. Unsigned report, December 21, 1915.

17. "New Spirit," *Sun*, August 23, 1914, 26.

18. "Police the Police," *New York Tribune*, October 28, 1915, 10; "No Clubbing Still Mitchel's Orders," *Sun*, October 16, 1917, 4; "Police Club Mob in Cloak Strike Riot," *New York Tribune*, July 27, 1916, 4; "Police Club Big Anarchist Mob," *Sun*, April 5, 1914, 2; "Work of Police Is Discussed by Woods," *New York Age*, November 1, 1917, 1; M. Johnson, *Street Justice*, 111–12; "Home Defense Men in San Juan Hill Riot," *New York Tribune*, May 27, 1917, 18.

19. "Police the Police," *New York Tribune*, October 28, 1915, 10; "No Clubbing Still Mitchel's Orders," *Sun*, October 16, 1917, 4; "The Police Club Should Be Used Freely in Dealing with 'Gunmen' and 'Heelers,'" *New York Times*, January 27, 1914, 8; "Ban Will Let Thaw Roam at Will," *Evening World*, January 12, 1914, 1; "Gangsters Need Clubbing," *Brooklyn Daily Eagle*, October 12, 1916, 5.

20. "The Police Library," *Police Bulletin* 1, no. 8 (August 1915): 4.

21. "The Preparatory School for Promotion to Sergeant," *Police Bulletin* 1, no. 6 (June 1915): 6; "Classes in Foreign Languages," *Police Bulletin* 1, no. 6 (June 1915): 3; "Classes for Police in South Brooklyn High School," *Police Bulletin* 1, no. 9 (September 1915): 2; "Law Course for Policemen at Columbia University," *Police Bulletin* 3, no. 2 (February 1917): 1.

22. "Rollo's Rambles," *NY American*, December 1–14, 1914.

23. O'Brien, "New York's New Police," *Munsey's* (August 1916).

24. Cahalane, *Police Practice and Procedure*, 6.

25. "Foot Troubles," *Police Bulletin* 1, no. 7 (July 1915): 5.

26. Brown, *The Corporate Eye*, 4; Taylor, *On the Art of Cutting Metals*, 4.

27. "Every Policeman a Card Indexer," *New York Times*, August 18, 1916, 14; "Wrist Watch for Police," *New York Times*, September 2, 1917.

28. McCrossen, *Marking Modern Times*, 4, 68.

29. "Home Defense Men in San Juan Hill Riot," *New York Tribune*, May 27, 1917, 18.

30. "District Attorney Swan Order Inquiry Into Brutal Murder of Richard Hill by the Police," *New York Age*, May 31, 1917, 1; Capozzola, *Uncle Sam Wants You*, 124.

31. "District Attorney Swan Order Inquiry," May 31, 1917; "Home Defense Men in San Juan Hill Riot," *New York Tribune*, May 27, 1917, 18.

32. Cahalane, *Police Practice and Procedure*, 12–14; "Officials Cooperate to Punish Police," *New York Age*, June 7, 1917, 1.

33. "Address to the Diet Squad," *Police Bulletin* 3, no. 3 (March 1917): 5.

34. Cahalane, *Police Practice and Procedure*, 5–8.

35. "Our Fat Policemen," *New York Times*, February 2, 1899, 6.

36. Moran, *Governing Bodies*, 11.

37. "Virtues of Fat Policemen," *New York Times*, February 5, 1899, 18.

38. "Fat Policemen Hurt in Spill," *Evening World*, January 13, 1903, 14. "Waldo Will Make Fat Policemen Train," *Evening World*, August 28, 1913, 10. "Fat Policemen Must Walk," *New York Tribune*, May 4, 1905, 10.

39. "Police Start Diet Squad," *Sun*, January 4, 1917; "Police Diet Squad to Show How to Live on 25c. a Day," *American*, January 5, 1917.

40. Moran, *Governing Bodies*, 78.

41. "Police Rookies Brave Cents a Day Diet Test," *New York Tribune*, January 5, 1917; "Cops Begin at Noon on 8 Cent Feasts," *Sun*, January 8, 1917.

42. "Police Rookies Brave Cents a Day Diet Test," *New York Tribune*, January 5, 1917; "Cops Begin at Noon," *Sun*, January 8, 1917.

43. Menkel, "Police Preparedness in New York," 203–5.

44. Menkel, "Police Preparedness in New York," 203.

45. "3,000 Police-Soldiers Parade in Fifth Avenue, Winning Plaudits from Military Achievement," *New York Herald*, October 18, 1916; "New York Police Are Becoming More Militaristic," *The Call*, October 18, 1916.

46. Lüdtke, *Police and State in Prussia*, 124; Spencer, *Police and the Social Order in German Cities*, 102–3.

47. "Soldiers All the Time," *Police Bulletin* 1, no. 11 (November 1915): 12.

48. "Soldiers All the Time," *Police Bulletin* 1, no. 11. November 1915:12; Capozzola, *Uncle Sam Wants You*, 159–60.

49. "The Draft," *New York Herald*, July 25, 1863, 8.

50. "Jews Will Vote as Americans, Says Rabbi Schulman," *New York Tribune*, November 4, 1917, 10. "Hoover Aid Warns Irish-Americans," *New York Tribune*, November 4, 1917, 10.

51. Canaday, *Straight State*, 5; Carter, *Heart of Whiteness*, 43; Slotkin, *Lost Battalions*.

52. Theodore Roosevelt, "America for Americans," speech delivered in St. Louis, Missouri, May 31, 1916; Roosevelt, "The Ethnology of the Police," *Munsey's*, June 1897, 398; Capozzola, *Uncle Sam Wants You*, 45–146.

53. Tunney and Hollister, *Throttled!*, vii, 6, 43.

54. Tunney and Hollister, *Throttled!*, 69–71; Sohi, *Echoes of Mutiny*.

55. Kornweibel, "*Investigate Everything.*"

Chapter Eight. Global Knowledge / American Police

1. "Horace Was a Poet Piker," *Evening World*, July 17, 1919, 10.

2. Although there is a fantastic growing literature on international police cooperation in the years following World War II and during the Cold War and the war on terror, specifically recent books like Schrader, *Badges without Borders* and Seigel, *Violence Work*, the scholarship on international law enforcement cooperation in the nineteenth and early twentieth century remains sparse. Two of the best are Deflem, *Policing World Society*, and Unterman, *Uncle Sam's Policemen*. One text that illustrates the centrality of "identity dominance" in counterinsurgency and colonial pacification is Jacobsen, *First Platoon*.

3. Fosdick, *American Police Systems*, 8.

4. One clear articulation of the ongoing failure of police to achieve long-standing crime reduction, especially without the intervention of medical experts, is by Chicago prison observer F. Emory Lyon. Lyon, "Race Betterment and the Crime Doctors."

5. Scott, *Seeing Like a State*, 6, 320. For scholar Ben Kafka, these ideas are represented by the "personal" versus the "personnel," and to historian of technology and the state Jon Agar, they are represented by the conflict between "technocrats" and "gentlemen bureaucrats" from the eighteenth through the twentieth century. Kafka, *Demon of Writing*, 10; Agar, *Government Machine*, 35.

6. Skowronek, *Building a New American State*; Yates, *Control Through Communication*), 11; Chandler, *Visible Hand*; Chandler and Cortada, eds., *Nation Transformed by Information*; Moore, *American Imperialism and the State,* 17–19; Beredo, *Import of the Archive*, 92; Kramer, *Blood of Government*, 232.

7. Jacobson, *Whiteness of a Different Color*, 57; J. Guglielmo, *Living the Revolution*, 16, 33; T. Guglielmo, *White on Arrival*, 7–8; Roediger, *Working toward Whiteness*, 37; Cohen, *Making a New Deal*, 10; Igo, *Known Citizen*, 2.

8. Weld, *Paper Cadavers*, 2–3.

9. Other stunning exploration of the underlying notion behind "paper suspects" are Verdery, *My Life as a Spy*; and Cole, *Suspect Identities*.

10. Crofton, "Identifying Criminals," 37–39.

11. Finn, *Capturing the Criminal Image*, 6.

12. Fosdick, "Passing of the Bertillon System of Identification," 365; C. Thompson, *Organ of Murder*, 147–49.

13. Fosdick, "Passing of the Bertillon System of Identification," 365; Thompson, *Organ of Murder*, 147–49; McCoy, *Policing America's Empire*, 73

14. Fosdick, "Passing of the Bertillon System of Identification," 364; "Criminal Identification," *Police Bulletin* 1, no. 6 (June 1915): 9; Thompson, *Organ of Murder*, 3.

15. "Fine Police Exhibit," *Times Democrat*, June 18, 1904, 7; Singha, "Settle, Mobilize, Verify," 151–98.

16. Cahalane, *Police Practice and Procedure*, 80; Finn, *Capturing the Criminal Image*, 41; "Finger Prints Blab," *A.H.T.A. Weekly News*, June 9, 1904, 7

17. "Filing Data on Criminals," *Police Bulletin* 2, no. 5 (May 1916): 5.

18. Guariglia, "Facial Recognition Technology Is the New Rogues' Gallery"; "Removal of Bingham," *Chattanooga News*, July 2, 1909, 4; "Owens Picture to Remain," *Brooklyn Citizen*, March 29, 1903, 4. "Oust Bingham, Gaynor Urges," *New York Times*, June 2, 1909, 1.

19. Pickens, "Racialism of Crime," *New York Age*, January 14, 1922, 2.

20. Rodgers, *Atlantic Crossings*, 131–33.

21. Deflem, *Policing World Society*, 103–10.

22. "Brought Police Dogs Here," *New York Tribune*, April 4, 1914, 3.

23. Fosdick, *European Police Systems*, xi.

24. Fosdick, *European Police Systems*, xi, 4.

25. Fosdick, *European Police Systems*, 59–61, 78–79; Keller, *Triumph of Order*, 133.

26. "Criminal Identification," *Police Bulletin* 1, no. 6 (June 1915): 12.

27. "Criminal Identification," *Police Bulletin* 1, no. 6 (June 1915): 12.

28. "Criminal Identification," *Police Bulletin* 1, no. 6 (June 1915): 12; Lauer, *Creditworthy*, 17.

29. "Criminal Identification Continued," *Police Bulletin* 1, no. 11 (November 1915): 7.

30. Woods, *Crime Prevention*, 1–2, 22.

31. Woods, *Crime Prevention*, 32 (emphasis added).

32. Woods, *Crime Prevention*, 38, 64, 72.

33. Woods, "Problem of the Black Hand," 47

34. "The Enforcement of the Law: A Police View of the Law," unpublished manuscript.

35. "Boddy, Caught in Philadelphia, Admits He Killed Detectives," *Daily News*, January 10, 1922, 1–2; Du Bois, "Boddy," 199.

36. Du Bois, "Boddy," 199.

37. "Enright Admits Crime Wave in City," *Brooklyn Daily Eagle*, December 19, 1920, 5.

38. Becker and Wetzell, eds., *Criminals and Their Scientists*; Rafter, *Creating Born Criminals*; Rafter, ed., *The Origins of Criminology*.

39. Lyon, "Race Betterment and the Crime Doctors," 887, 889; Gault, "Race Improvement through Social Inheritance," 166. For thorough explorations of the gendered

and racial violence of sterilization, see Ordover, *American Eugenics*; Lira, *Laboratory of Deficiency*; Canaday, *Straight State*, 30.

40. "Classes in Foreign Languages," *Police Bulletin* 1, no. 6 (June 1915): 3; "Classes for Police in South Brooklyn High School," *Police Bulletin* 1, no. 9 (September 1915): 2.; "Law Course for Policemen at Columbia University," *Police Bulletin* 3, no. 2 (February 1917): 1.

41. Y. Takahashi to August Vollmer, December 15, 1935.

42. Brunk, "What Courses Should Be Taught Prospective Policemen at the University of California?"

43. John O'Connell to August Vollmer, December 11, 1935; John O'Connell to August Vollmer, November 15, 1933; Brunk, "What Courses Should Be Taught Prospective Policemen at the University of California?"

44. Becker and Wetzell, eds., *Criminals and Their Scientists*, 7; Rafter, *Creating Born Criminals*, 113. For a good exploration of the nature of police expertise, see Lvovsky, "Rethinking Police Expertise"; Czitrom, *New York Exposed*, 40–41.

45. Scott, *Seeing Like a State*, 320; Lyon, "Race Betterment and the Crime Doctors," 887; Rafter, *Born Criminals*, 161–62.

Conclusion

1. Keh, "A Park Is Renewed, the Better to Honor the Hero in Its Name," *New York Times*, October 13, 2009.

2. Freedman, "New York Race Tension Is Rising Despite Gains," *New York Times*, March 29, 1987, 1.

3. Weichselbaum, "Harlem Intersection Renamed for NYPD Pioneer Samuel Battle Who Integrated Police," *New York Daily News*, August 4, 2009.

4. New York Civil Liberties Union, "Stop-and-Frisk Data."

5. Wilson, *Cop Knowledge*, 65.

6. Malcolm, "Cities Try Out New Approach in Police Work," *New York Times*, March 29, 1989, A14; Kelling and Wilson, "Broken Windows," *Atlantic*, March 1982.

7. McGirr, *The War on Alcohol*, 69.

8. McGirr, *The War on Alcohol*, 5.

9. National Commission on Law Observance and Enforcement, *Report on the Enforcement of the Prohibition Law of the United States* (January 7, 1931), 162; Muhammad, *Condemnation of Blackness*, 54.

10. National Commission on Law Observance and Enforcement, *Report on the Enforcement of the Prohibition Law of the United States* (January 7, 1931), 162–65.

11. See Malka, *Men of Mobtown*.

12. Roediger, *Working toward Whiteness*; T. Guglielmo, *White on Arrival*, 7–8.

13. Apuzzo and Goldstein, "New York Drops Unit That Spied on Muslims," *New York Times*, April 15, 2014. For a detailed investigation into NYPD wiretapping surveillance in the Arthur Woods era, see Hochman, *The Listeners*.

14. Dienst, McHugh, Ing, and Neubert, "I-Team: NYPD Embeds Intelligence Officers in 13 Cities Overseas Since 9/11," *NBC New York*, November 14, 2016.

15. Musgrave, Meagher, and Dance, "Pentagon Finally Details Its Weapons-for-Cops Giveaway"; Delehanty, Mewhirter, Welch, and Wilks, "Militarization and Police Violence," 3; Vitale, *End of Policing*, 4.

16. Cummings and Kokenes, "Kerik Gets Four Years of Felony Charges," CNN, February 18, 2010.

BIBLIOGRAPHY

Archives

Bancroft Library, University of California, Berkeley

Brunk, Paul S. "What Courses Should Be Taught Prospective Policemen at the University of California?" Box 36. August Vollmer Papers.

O'Connell, John, to August Vollmer. December 11, 1935. NYPD Folder, Box 24.

O'Connell, John, to August Vollmer. November 15, 1933. NYPD Folder, Box 24.

Takahashi, Y., to August Vollmer. December 15, 1935. Box 29.

Columbia University Archives (New York, NY)

Battle, Samuel J. "The Reminiscences of Samuel J. Battle." Interview by John Kelley, February 1960. Columbia University Oral History Office.

Herbert Hoover Presidential Library, Manuscript Collections (West Branch, IA)

"Black Hand Confessions." 1910. From Box 1, Lawrence Richie Papers.

Library of Congress, Manuscript Division (Washington, DC)

THEODORE ROOSEVELT PAPERS

"Awful Possibility under Our Blue Laws." July 15, 1895. Cartoon. *New York World*. Scrapbook, Reel 454.

"The Combination Was Too Much for the Cops." Cartoon. *New York Recorder*, July 12, 1895. Scrapbook, Reel 454.

Greene, Francis V., to Theodore Roosevelt. December 26, 1902. Theodore Roosevelt Digital Library, Dickinson State University. https://www.theodorerooseveltcenter.org/Research/Digital-Library/Record?libID=039938.

Hay, John, to Theodore Roosevelt. July 27, 1898. Reel 2.

Roosevelt, Theodore. "America for Americans." Speech delivered in St. Louis, Missouri, May 31, 1916.

Roosevelt, Theodore, to Alphonse Major, Esq. January 28, 1896. Reel 412.

Roosevelt, Theodore, to G. Fraser, Esq., British Consulate General. August 11, 1896. Reel 412.

Roosevelt, Theodore, to Sir Cecil Spring Rice. August 5, 1896. Reel 415.

"Roosevelt Takes a Night Tour: President of the Police Board Out to See How the City Is Guarded: Surprises Many Shirks." *New York Herald*, June 8, 1895. Scrapbook, Reel 454.

ARTHUR WOODS PAPERS

Bingham, Theodore, to Arthur Woods. April 12, 1907. Reel 1.

"The Enforcement of the Law: A Police View of the Law." Unpublished manuscript. Reel 1.

Menkel, William. "Police Preparedness in New York." *American Review of Reviews*, August 1916. Scrapbook, Reel 2, 203–5.

"New York Police Are Becoming More Militaristic." *The Call*, October 18, 1916. Scrapbook, Reel 2.

O'Brien, Frank M. "New York's New Police." *Munsey's Magazine*, August 1916. Scrapbook, Reel 2.

"Police Diet Squad to Show How to Live on 25c. a Day." *New York American*, January 5, 1917. Scrapbook, Reel 2.

"Police Rookies Brave Cents a Day Diet Test." *New York Tribune*, January 5, 1917. Scrapbook, Reel 2.

"Police Start Diet Squad." *Sun*, January 4, 1917. Scrapbook, Reel 2.

Report. December 21, 1915. Reel 1.

"Rollo's Rambles." *New York American*, December 1–14, 1914. Scrapbook, Reel 1.

"3,000 Police-Soldiers Parade in Fifth Avenue, Winning Plaudits from Military Achievement." *New York Herald*, October 18, 1916. Scrapbook, Reel 2.

"Wrist Watch for Police." *New York Times*, September 2, 1917. Scrapbook, Reel 2.

Lloyd Sealy Library, John Jay College of Criminal Justice, City University of New York

Trial Transcripts of the County of New York, 1883–1927.

People of New York v. Dora Miadowicz. 1911. Trial 1373, 6–7.

People of New York v. Francesco Sansone. 1910. Trial 1171.

People of New York v. George Glucksman. 1909. Trial 1046.

People of New York v. Robert Jefferson. 1905. Reel 488, 1905.

People v. Francesco Purpura. 1909. Trial 1170. Criminal Trial Transcripts of New York County Collection.

People v. Leon Jung. 1911. Trial 1385. Criminal Trial Transcripts of New York County Collection.

People v. Leonardo Broncado. 1905. Criminal Trial Transcripts of New York County Collection, 22.

Trial Transcripts of the County of New York, 1883–1927.

New York City Municipal Archives

Civil Service Roster for the City of New York. 1902–1908. New York City Municipal Archives.

District Attorney to Police Commissioner William McAdoo. December 27, 1904. New York District Attorney Letters, Roll 22.

District Attorney to William McAdoo, Commissioner of the NYPD. June 22, 1904. New York District Attorney Letters, Roll 22.

New York District Attorney Case File 42841/1903.

Report of the Municipal Civil Service Commissioner Investigation of Promotions From Sergeant to Captain in the Police Department of the City of New York. June 19, 1901. Papers of Mayor Van Wyck, Box 10, Folder 109.

York, Bernard, to Mayor Robert Van Wyck. May 23, 1899. Papers of Mayor Van Wyck, Box 10, Folder 109.

New York Public Library, Manuscripts and Archives Division (New York, NY)

FRANCIS VINTON GREENE PAPERS

Alger, Russell A., to Francis Vinton Greene. November 12, 1898. Box 4, Folder, November 1898.

Corbin, H. C., Adjutant General. "Special Order 240." October 11, 1898. Washington, D.C. Box 4, Folder, October 1898.

Corbin, H. C., Adjutant General. "Special Order 307." December 30, 1898. Box 4, Folder, December 1898.

Corbin, H. C., to Francis Vinton Greene. December 2, 1898. Box 4, Folder, December 1898.

Roosevelt, Theodore, to Francis Vinton Greene. January 21, 1903. Box 1, Folder, Roosevelt Correspondence.

Sherman, P. Tecumseh, to Francis Vinton Greene. May 12, 1891. Box 2, Sherman Folder.

Sherman, William Tecumseh, to Francis Vinton Greene. July 28, 1878. Box 2, Sherman Folder.

Sherman, William Tecumseh, to Francis Vinton Greene. January 13, 1878. Box 2, Sherman Folder.

Sherman, William Tecumseh, to Francis Vinton Greene. October 23, 1877. Box 2, Sherman Folder.

Upton, Emory, to Francis Vinton Greene. August 18, 1877. Box 2, Upton Folder.

Upton, Emory, to Francis Vinton Greene. October 3, 1879. Box 2, Upton Folder.

NYPD Museum (New York, NY)

"Collection of death threats and threatening notes left on Petrosino's door, 1907–1909." Joseph Petrosino Papers.

Original Italian Squad, 1904. Photo collage believed to have been created between 1909 and 1910. Joseph Petrosino Papers.

Yale University (New Haven, CT)

BEINECKE RARE BOOK AND MANUSCRIPT COLLECTION, YALE UNIVERSITY
Battle, Samuel, to Langston Hughes. 1946. Langston Hughes Papers, Box 275, Folder 4527.

Bishop, William Henry, to Assistant Secretary of State, April 18, 1908, 1. Box 1, Folder 3, William Henry Bishop Papers (MS 83).

Bishop, William Henry, to Assistant Secretary of State. March 20, 1909. Box 4, Folder 21, William Henry Bishop Papers (MS 83).

Bishop, William Henry, to Assistant Secretary of State. March 20, 1909. Box 4, Folder 22, William Henry Bishop Papers (MS 83).

Bishop, William Henry, to Professor Rallo, March 6, 1909. Box 4, Folder 21, William Henry Bishop Papers (MS 83).

Bishop, William Henry, to the Commander of the SS *Minerva*, January 4, 1909. Box 3, Folder 15, William Henry Bishop Papers (MS 83).

Bishop, William Henry, to Tuohy, March 1909. Box 4, Folder 22, William Henry Bishop Papers (MS 83).

"GI'imponenti funerali del luogotenente Petrosino." Box 4, Folder 23, William Henry Bishop Papers (MS 83).

Vice Consul in Charge to the American Red Cross Society. May 1, 1909. Box 4, Folder 22, William Henry Bishop Papers (MS 83).

Woods, Arthur. "The Problem of the Black Hand." *McClure's Magazine*, May 1909, 43. Box 4, Folder 22, William Henry Bishop Papers (MS 83).

Newspapers

(Untitled.) *Tammany Times*, May 11, 1895.

"Address to the Diet Squad." *Police Bulletin* 3, no. 3 (March 1917).

"Aflano Will Be Deported." *Chattanooga Daily Times*, April 23, 1907.

After the Battle." *Sun*, November 8, 1894.

"The American and Foreign Anti-Slavery Society." *New York Herald*, May 12, 1852.

"Among The Victims . . ." *Tammany Times*, September 14, 1895.

"Another Colored Policeman." *Evening World*, April 25, 1892.

Apuzzo, Matt, and Joseph Goldstein. "New York Drops Unit That Spied on Muslims." *New York Times*, April 15, 2014.

"Arrests in Palermo." *New York Tribune*, March 18, 1909.

"Arrests without Evidence." *Sun*, August 4, 1904.

"Assassinated: Superintendent of Police David C. Hennessey Victim of the Vendetta." *Times-Picayune*, October 16, 1890.

"August Vollmer Suicide on Coast: Criminologist Shoots Himself in Berkeley—Was Pioneer in Scientific Detection." *New York Times*, November 5, 1955.

"Ban Will Let Thaw Roam at Will: Mitchel to Police 'Club the Gunmen.'" *Evening World*, January 12, 1914, 1.

"Battle Thanks Friends through *Age*." *New York Age*, July 20, 1911.

"Bingham Makes a Speech." *New York Times*, April 19, 1906.

"Bingham Takes Office." *New York Times*, January 2, 1906.

"Bingham vs. The Black Hand." *Sun*, February 7, 1908.

"The Black Hand." *International Gazette*, April 6, 1907.

"Blame Italian Police." *New York Tribune*, March 14, 1909.

"Boddy, Caught in Philadelphia, Admits He Killed Detectives." *Daily News*, January 10, 1922.

"Bomb Squad Joined With the Italian." *New York Times*, February 5, 1922.

"Brought Police Dogs Here." *New York Tribune*, April 4, 1914.

"Captain Williams Questioned: He Says He Takes No Bribes." *Sun*, October 14, 1885.

"Capt. Williams Promoted." *New York Times*, August 10, 1887.

"Career of Petrosino: Full of Thrilling Adventure and Brilliant Achievement." *New York Tribune*, March 14, 1909.

"Chief Byrnes Retired: He Served over 32 Years on the New-York Police Force." *New York Times*, May 28, 1895.

"Chinese Police: A Queer System of Espionage in the Oriental Quarter of San Francisco." *Democrat and Chronicle*, November 22, 1896.

"Chinese Prisoners Let Go." *Sun*, February 14, 1905.

"Classes for Police in South Brooklyn High School." *Police Bulletin* 1, no. 9 (September 1915).

"Classes in Foreign Languages." *Police Bulletin* 1, no. 6 (June 1915).

"Commissioner Bingham." *New York Times*, January 7, 1906.

"Common Sense Is to Be the Keynote of the New Police Head." *New York Times*, January 11, 1914.

"Cops Begin at Noon on 8 Cent Feasts." *Sun*, January 8, 1917.

"Counterfeiters Guilty; Get Heavy Sentences." *Brooklyn Daily Eagle*, February 20, 1910.

"Criminal Identification." *Police Bulletin* 1, no. 6 (June 1915).

"Criminal Identification Continued." *Police Bulletin* 1, no. 11 (November 1915).

"Crusade to Restore Italian Detectives to Be Started Here." *Brooklyn Daily Eagle*, July 12, 1911.

"Daniel F. Tiemann Elected Mayor by over 3,000 Majority." *New York Times*, December 2, 1857.

"De Palo Will Be Brought Back." *Brooklyn Daily Eagle*, April 26, 1905.

"Detective is Real Thief: Chinatown Writes to M'adoo Begging for Mercy." *Sun*, April 4, 1905.

"District Attorney Files His Report on Italian Lynching." *Times-Picayune*, April 29, 1891.

"District Attorney Swan Order Inquiry Into Brutal Murder of Richard Hill by the Police." *New York Age*, May 31, 1917.

"The Draft." *New York Herald*, July 25, 1863.

"Eight Killed in Fight Riots." *New York Times*, June 5, 1910.

"Elsie Siegel's Slayer Fled." *New York Times*, December 9, 1911.

"Enright Admits Crime Wave in City; Adopts Woods Plan." *Brooklyn Daily Eagle*, December 19, 1920.

"Entraps Bandits: Earns Promotion." *Star Gazette*, March 8, 1912.

"Every Policeman a Card Indexer." *New York Times*, August 18, 1916.

"Fairness to Mr. McKay." *New York Times*, February 21, 1914.

"Farewell to Williams: Retired from the Police Force at His Own Request: Rumors that Byrnes Will Withdraw Next." *New York Times*, May 25, 1895.

"Fat Policemen Hurt in Spill." *Evening World*, January 13, 1903.

"Fat Policemen Must Walk." *New York Tribune*, May 4, 1905.

"Favor Negro Police." *New York Age*, March 21, 1910.

"Fifty Wounded, Forty Arrested." *Buffalo Evening News*, August 16, 1900.

"Filing Data on Criminals." *Police Bulletin* 2, no. 5 (May 1916).

"A Filipino Ambush." *Brooklyn Daily Eagle*, April 24, 1899.

"Filipino Methods." *Statesman Journal*, March 12, 1902.

"A Filipino's Blade for Wanger." *Bucks County Gazette*, July 5, 1900.

"Fine Police Exhibit." *Times Democrat*, June 18, 1904.

"Finger Prints Blab." *A.H.T.A. Weekly News*, June 9, 1904.

"First Negro Named For City's Police." *New York Times*, June 29, 1911.

"Flynn Revolutionizes the Detective Bureau." *New York Tribune*, November 18, 1910.

"Foot Troubles: Their Cause and Prevention." *Police Bulletin* 1, no. 7 (July 1915).

"Four Held for Straus Murder." *Sun*, January 11, 1914.

"Fourth of July." *New York Tribune*, July 6, 1857.

Freedman, Samuel. "New York Race Tension Is Rising Despite Gains." *New York Times*, March 29, 1987.

"Gangsters Need Clubbing." *Brooklyn Daily Eagle*, October 12, 1916.

"Gen. Francis V. Greene Named to Head Police." *Brooklyn Daily Eagle*, December 23, 1902.

"Goethals Will Stay, Unless Forced Out." *New York Times*, January 24, 1914.

Guariglia, Matthew. "'Blue Lives' Do Matter—And That's the Problem." *Washington Post*, November 20, 2017.

"Harlem Murder Full of Mystery." *New York Age*, March 20, 1913.

"Heroic Rescuers Afloat." *New York Times*, June 16, 1904.

"His Whiskers Fooled Sara." *Pittsburgh Press*, December 12, 1904.

"Home Defense Men in San Juan Hill Riot." *New York Tribune*, May 27, 1917.

"Hoover Aide Warns Irish-Americans." *New York Tribune*, November 4, 1917.

"Horace Was a Poet Piker." *Evening World*, July 17, 1919.

"Indicted for Barrel Murder." *New York Times*, June 26, 1903.

"Italian Crime and Police Incompetence: Detectives of the Force Seem Utterly Unable to Unearth 'Black Hand' Conspirators." *New York Tribune*, August 21, 1904.

"Italian Criminals." *Argus-Leader*, February 22, 1908.

"Italians United against Black Hand." *Buffalo Commercial*, February 7, 1908.

"Italians Who Were Deported." *New York Times*, March 19, 1909.

"Jews Will Vote as Americans, Says Rabbi Schulman." *New York Tribune*, November 4, 1917.

Keh, Andrew. "A Park Is Renewed, the Better to Honor the Hero in Its Name." *New York Times*, October 13, 2009.

"Kidnappers May Return Stolen Boy to Parents." *Brooklyn Daily Eagle*, August 13, 1904.

"Late Riots." *New York Tribune*, July 7, 1857.

"Law Course for Policemen at Columbia University." *Police Bulletin* 3, no. 2 (February 1917).

"Laying for Taft in the Philippines." *New York Age*, August 10, 1905.

"Local Board Calls Public Hearing on the Chinatown Park Plan." *Evening World*, March 6, 1906.

"Made Detective Sergeants." *Brooklyn Daily Eagle*, August 6, 1901.

Malcolm, Andrew H. "Cities Try Out New Approach in Police Work." *New York Times*, March 29, 1989.

"Man in Barrel War Tortured, then Murdered." *Evening World*, April 14, 1903.

"The Master of the Club: Captain Williams on Trial for Failing to Suppress Gambling." *Brooklyn Daily Eagle*, February 13, 1885.

"The Mayor's Rebellion." *New York Tribune*, June 18, 1857.

"McCullagh's Police Plan for Havana." *New York Times*, December 17, 1898.

"Missouri Negroes Slated: Demand that Pre-election Patronage Promises Be Kept— Negro Police." *New York Age*, September 16, 1909.

"Miss White Says 'Straight-Line' Dresses Aid Morality, and That Danger and Demoralization Lurk in Curves." *Evening World*, September 12, 1907.

"M'Kay's Resignation Kept Quiet by Mayor for Several Days." *Evening World*, April 1, 1914.

"The Mob in New York." *New York Times*, July 14, 1863.

"Most Criminal Nation on Earth, Says Rev. Peters." *Evening World*, August 10, 1907.

"Mysteries of New York's Chinatown." *Buffalo Courier*, July 4, 1909.

"Negroes Demand Justice." *New-York Tribune*, September 13, 1900.

"Negroes in a Riot on San Juan Hill." *New York Times*, November 29, 1907.

"Negroes' Public Protest." *New York Times*, September 13, 1900.

"Negro Police for New York." *New York Age*, August 5, 1909.

"Negro Policeman Hazed by Silence." *New York Times*, August 17, 1911.

"The New Mayor's Third Day." *New York Times*, January 4, 1895.

"The News." *New York Herald*, January 14, 1860.

"New Secret Service to Fight Black Hand." *New York Times*, February 20, 1909.

"New Spirit of the New York Police Force." *Sun*, August 23, 1914.

"New York City Has a Colored Police Officer." *New York Age*, June 29, 1911.

"New York Police Brutality." *New York Age*, July 27, 1905.

"New York's Chinese Policeman a Hero." *Capital Times*, July 25, 1923.

"No Clubbing Still Mitchel's Orders." *Sun*, October 16, 1917.

"No Clue to Sack Murder." *Brooklyn Daily Eagle*, July 29, 1902.

"No Job Too Big." *New York Age*, July 20, 1911.

"Officer Holmes Assigned to 28th District." *New York Age*, October 16, 1913.

"Officials Cooperate to Punish Police." *New York Age*, June 7, 1917.

"Only Chinese Policeman Passes Up Assignment to Chinatown." *El Paso Herald*, May 5, 1909.

"On the Force: Commissioner Hayden Appoints Wiley G. Overton." *Brooklyn Daily Eagle*, March 5, 1891.

"The 'Other McAdoo,' Meaning Tammany's New Police Commissioner." *Democrat and Chronicle*, January 3, 1904.

"Our Fat Policemen." *New York Times*, February 2, 1899.

"Oust Bingham, Gaynor Urges." *New York Times*, June 2, 1909.

"Owens Picture to Remain." *Brooklyn Citizen*, March 29, 1903.

"Paid $500 to Schmittberger." *New York Times*, October 12, 1894.

"Partridge Resigns." *Democrat and Chronicle*, December 13, 1902.

Pickens, William. "Racialism of Crime." *New York Age*, January 14, 1922.

"Pinkerton Man to Aid State." *Philadelphia Inquirer*, May 2, 1902.

"Police Are Certain They Have Slayers." *Evening World*, April 16, 1903.

"The Police Board." *Times Democrat*, February 15, 1900.

"Police Club Big Anarchist Mob." *Sun*, April 5, 1914.

"Police Club Mob in Cloak Strike Riot." *New York Tribune*, July 27, 1916.

"The Police Club Should Be Used Freely in Dealing with 'Gunmen' and 'Heelers.'" *New York Times*, January 27, 1914.

"The Police Library." *Police Bulletin* 1, no. 8 (August 1915).

"Police List of Victims." *New York Times*, June 23, 1904.

"Police Matrons at Last: Now the City Will Soon Have the Needed Reform." *Evening World*, March 21, 1891.

"Police Officer Battle Now on Regular Duty: Not Sent to Harlem." *New York Age*, August 3, 1911.

"Police Quell Race Riot." *New York Times*, June 14, 1903.

"The Police Situation." *New York Times*, November 4, 1907.

"Police the Police." *New York Tribune*, October 28, 1915.

"The Preparatory School for Promotion to Sergeant." *Police Bulletin* 1, no. 6 (June 1915).

"Quick Shakeup by Greene in Police Department." *Brooklyn Daily Eagle*, March 13, 1903.

"Quiet on San Juan Hill." *New York Times*, July 19, 1905.

"Race Riot on the West Side." *New York Times*, August 16, 1900.

"Removal of Bingham." *Chattanooga News*, July 2, 1909.

"Roosevelt." *Tammany Times*, January 25, 1897.

"Roosevelt Will Accept." *Democrat and Chronicle*, April 24, 1895.

"San Juan Hill Riots after Bellboy's Ball." *New York Times*, September 13, 1906.

"Scare of Caruso." *New York Tribune*, March 5, 1910.

"A Secret Service Squad to Hunt the Black Hand." *New York Times*, December 20, 1906.

"Sheehan Out, Andrews In: The Young Soldier Appointed Police Commissioner by Mayor Strong." *Evening World*, February 14, 1895.

"Slain Man in a Barrel; May Be a Brooklyn Crime." *Brooklyn Daily Eagle*, April 14, 1903.

"Slash and Beat Black Hand's Foe." *Chicago Daily Tribune*, May 2, 1909.

"Slashed Wife With Stiletto." *Brooklyn Daily Eagle*, May 23, 1906.

"Soldiers All the Time." *Police Bulletin* 1, no. 11 (November 1915).

"Stabbed with a Stiletto: Italians Quarrel about the Assassination of King Humbert." *New York Tribune*, September 3, 1900.

"Stab Chicago's Petrosino." *Sun*, May 2, 1909.

"Stiletto Should be Banished." *Evening World*, March 21, 1894.

"Subject of Negro Police." *New York Age*, August 19, 1909.

"Suspects Knew Bendetto, the Barrel Victim." *Evening World*, April 20, 1903.

"Tear Down the Dens of Chinatown and Make a Park of New York's Darkest Spot." *Evening World*, February 28, 1906.

"Terror of the Black Hand." *Nebraska State Journal*, September 2, 1904.

"Theodore A. Bingham." *Buffalo Enquirer*, May 14, 1908.

"To Greet His Soldier Son." *New York Times*, June 10, 1902.

"Told by Negro's Prisoners." *Sun*, March 22, 1906.

"Transport Service to Manilla." *St. Louis Globe-Democrat*, February 15, 1900.

"Try Again to Kill Longabardi." *Chicago Daily Tribune*, January 23, 1910.

"Used Teeth and Stiletto." *Brooklyn Daily Eagle*, July 1, 1904.

"Virtues of Fat Policemen." *New York Times*, February 5, 1899.

"Waldo Will Make Fat Policemen Train." *Evening World*, August 28, 1913.

"War Mementoes." *Daily Herald*, June 19, 1900.

"Warned of Petrosino Death: Pittsburgh Detective Says He Told Him Months Ago He Would Be Killed." *New York Tribune*, March 14, 1909.

"War on the Black Hand." *Alexandria Gazette*, June 16, 1909.

Weichselbaum, Simone. "Harlem Intersection Renamed for NYPD Pioneer Samuel Battle Who Integrated Police." *New York Daily News*, August 4, 2009.

"West Side Race Troubles." *New York Times*, February 23, 1901.

"Who Wrote Dynamite Letter: Police Having a Hard Time with Cunard Pier Bomb." *Sun*, May 11, 1903.

"Williams, 'Ex-Czar' of Tenderloin, Dies." *New York Times*, March 26, 1917.

"Will Not Take Examination." *New York Age*, September 2, 1909.

"Wooden Leg Swings in New Crime Wave." *Evening World*, August 5, 1908.

"Work of Police Is Discussed by Woods." *New York Age*, November 1, 1917.

Books and Articles

Agar, Jon. *The Government Machine: A Revolutionary History of the Computer*. Cambridge, MA: MIT Press, 2003.

Agee, Christopher Lowen. *The Streets of San Francisco: Policing and the Creation of a Cosmopolitan Liberal Politics, 1950–1972*. Chicago: University of Chicago Press, 2014.

Agyepong, Tera Eva. *The Criminalization of Black Children: Race, Gender, and Delinquency in Chicago's Juvenile Justice System, 1899–1945*. Chapel Hill: University of North Carolina Press, 2018.

Alexander, James. *Blue Coats, Black Skin: The Black Experience in the New York City Police Department since 1891*. Hicksville, NY: Exposition Press, 1978.

Anderson, David M., and David Killingray, eds. *Policing the Empire: Government, Authority and Control, 1830–1940*. Manchester, UK: Manchester University Press, 1991.

Anderson, Margo. "The Language of Class in Twentieth-Century America." *Social Science History* 12, no. 4 (Winter 1988): 349–75.

Anbinder, Tyler. *City of Dreams: The 400-Year Epic History of Immigrant New York.* New York: Mariner, 2017.

Anbinder, Tyler. *Five Points: The 19th-Century New York City Neighborhood That Invented Tap Dance, Stole Elections, and Became the World's Most Notorious Slum.* New York: Free Press, 2001.

Appier, Janis. *Policing Women: The Sexual Politics of Law Enforcement and the LAPD.* Philadelphia: Temple University Press, 1998.

Arnold, David. *Police Power and Colonial Rule, Madras 1859–1947.* New York: Oxford University Press, 1986.

Balto, Simon. *Occupied Territory: Policing Black Chicago from Red Summer to Black Power.* Chapel Hill: University of North Carolina Press, 2019.

Baptist, Edward. *The Half Has Never Been Told: Slavery and the Making of American Capitalism.* New York: Basic Books, 2014.

Barnes, David. *The Draft Riots in New York, July 1863: The Metropolitan Police; Their Services During the Riot Week.* New York: Baker and Godwin, 1863.

Barrett, James. *The Irish Way: Becoming American in the Multiethnic City.* New York: Penguin, 2013.

Beachy, Robert. *Gay Berlin: Birthplace of a Modern Identity.* New York: Vintage, 2014.

Becker, Peter and Richard F. Wetzell, eds. *Criminals and Their Scientists: The History of Criminology in International Perspective.* New York: Cambridge University Press, 2006.

Bederman, Gail. *Manliness and Civilization: A Cultural History of Gender and Race in the United States, 1880–1917.* Chicago: University of Chicago Press, 1995.

Bender, Daniel. *American Abyss: Savagery and Civilization in the Age of Industry.* Ithaca, NY: Cornell University Press, 2011.

Bender, Daniel. *Sweated Work, Weak Bodies: Anti-sweatshop Campaigns and Languages of Labor.* New Brunswick, NJ: Rutgers University Press, 2004.

Benton-Cohen, Katherine. *Inventing the Immigration Problem: The Dillingham Commission and Its Legacy.* Cambridge, MA: Harvard University Press, 2018.

Beredo, Cheryl. *Import of the Archive: U.S. Colonial Rule of the Philippines and the Making of American Archival History.* Sacramento, CA: Litwin Books, 2013.

Bingham, Theodore. "Foreign Criminal in New York." *North American Review* 188, no. 634 (September 1908): 383–94.

Bingham, Theodore. *The Girl That Disappears.* Boston: Gorham Press, 1911.

Bingham, Theodore. "How to Give New York the Best Police Force in the World." *North American Review* 187, no. 630 (May 1908): 702–11.

Blair, Cynthia M. *I've Got to Make My Livin': Black Women's Sex Work in Turn-of-the-Century Chicago.* Chicago: University of Chicago Press, 2010.

Bolton, H. W., ed. *History of the Second Regiment Illinois Volunteer Infantry from Organization to Muster-Out.* Chicago: R. R. Donnelley and Sons, 1899.

Brandt, Allen M. *No Magic Bullet: A Social History of Venereal Disease in the United States Since 1880*. New York: Oxford University Press, 1985.

Briggs, Laura. *Reproducing Empire: Race, Sex, Science, and U.S. Imperialism in Puerto Rico*. Berkeley: University of California Press, 2002.

Brown, Elspeth. *The Corporate Eye: Photography and the Rationalization of American Commercial Culture, 1884–1929*. Baltimore, MD: Johns Hopkins University Press, 2005.

Browne, Arthur. *One Righteous Man: Samuel Battle and the Shattering of the Color Line in New York*. Boston: Beacon, 2015.

Browne, Simone. *Dark Matters: On the Surveillance of Blackness*. Durham, NC: Duke University Press, 2015.

Brownson, Orestes A. "Catholics and the Anti-draft Riots." *Brownson's Quarterly Review* 4 (October 1863).

Broxmeyer, Jeffrey D. *Electoral Capitalism: The Party System in New York's Gilded Age*. Philadelphia: University of Pennsylvania Press, 2020.

Burrows, Edwin G., and Mike Wallace. *Gotham: A History of New York City to 1898*. New York: Oxford University Press, 1998.

Burrows, J. C. "The Need of National Legislation against Anarchism." *North American Review* 173, no. 541 (December 1901): 727–45.

Burton, William L. *Melting Pot Soldiers: The Union's Ethnic Regiments*. Ames: Iowa State University Press, 1988.

Busey, Samuel C. *Immigration: Its Evils and Consequences*. New York: De Witt and Davenport, 1856.

Cahalane, Cornelius. *Police Practice and Procedure*. New York: E. P. Dutton, 1914.

Canaday, Margot. *The Straight State: Sexuality and Citizenship in Twentieth-Century America*. Princeton, NJ: Princeton University Press, 2011.

Canaday, Margot, Nancy F. Cott, and Robert O. Self, eds. *Intimate States: Gender, Sexuality and Governance in Modern US History*. Chicago: University of Chicago Press, 2021.

Capozzola, Christopher. *Bound by War: How the United States and the Philippines Built America's First Pacific Century*. New York: Basic Books, 2020.

Capozzola, Christopher. *Uncle Sam Wants You: World War I and the Making of the Modern American Citizen*. New York: Oxford University Press, 2008.

Carey, Arthur. *Memoirs of a Murder Man*. New York: Doubleday, Doran, and Company, 1930.

Carlson, Robert. *The Americanization Syndrome: A Quest for Conformity*. New York: St. Martin's, 1987.

Carson, Mina. *Settlement Folk: Social Thought and the American Settlement Movement, 1885–1930*. Chicago: University of Chicago Press, 1990.

Carter, Julian. *The Heart of Whiteness: Normal Sexuality and Race in America, 1880–1940*. Durham, NC: Duke University Press, 2007.

Chandler, Alfred. *The Visible Hand: The Managerial Revolution in American Business*. Cambridge, MA: Belknap Press of Harvard University Press, 1977.

Chandler, Alfred, and James Cortada, eds. *A Nation Transformed by Information: How Information Has Shaped the United States from Colonial Times to the Present*. New York: Oxford University Press, 2000.

Chauncey, George. *Gay New York: Gender, Urban Culture, and the Making of the Gay Male World, 1890–1940*. New York: Basic Books, 1994.

Childs, Dennis. *Slaves of the State: Black Incarceration from the Chain Gang to the Penitentiary*. Minneapolis: University of Minnesota Press, 2015.

Clement, Elizabeth Alice. *Love for Sale: Courting, Treating, and Prostitution in New York City, 1900–1945*. Chapel Hill: University of North Carolina Press, 2006.

Cohen, Lizabeth. *Making a New Deal: Industrial Workers in Chicago, 1919–1939*. New York: Cambridge University Press, 1990.

Cohen, Patricia Cline. *The Murder of Helen Jewett*. New York: Vintage, 1998.

Cole, Simon. *Suspect Identities: A History of Fingerprinting and Criminal Identification*. Cambridge. MA: Harvard University Press, 2002.

Corbin, H. C., to General E. S. Otis, Manila, December 21, 1898. In *Correspondence Relating to the War With Spain*, vol. 2. Washington, DC: Center of Military History, United States Army, 1993.

Crofton, A. F. B. "Identifying Criminals." *The Cosmopolitan* 20, no.1 (November 1895): 37–39.

Cronon, William. *Nature's Metropolis: Chicago and the Great West*. New York: W. W. Norton, 1992.

Crosby, Howard. "Crime and Punishment in New York." *North American Review* 133, no. 297 (August 1881): 167–75.

Cummings, Julian, and Chris Kokenes. "Kerik Gets Four Years of Felony Charges." CNN, February 18, 2010. http://www.cnn.com/2010/CRIME/02/18/kerik .sentence/index.html.

Czitrom, Daniel. *New York Exposed: The Gilded Age Police Scandal That Launched the Progressive Era*. New York: Oxford University Press, 2016.

D'Amato, Gaetano. "The 'Black Hand' Myth." *North American Review* 187, no. 629 (April 1908): 543–49.

Davis, John. *Conflict and Control: Law and Order in Nineteenth-Century Italy*. Atlantic Highlands, NJ: Humanities Press International, 1988.

Deflem, Mathieu. *Policing World Society: Historical Foundations of International Police Cooperation*. New York: Oxford University Press, 2002.

Delehanty, Casey, Jack Mewhirter, Ryan Welch, and Jason Wilks. "Militarization and Police Violence: The Case of the 1033 Program." *Research and Politics* 4, no. 2 (April–June 2017): 1–7.

Derrida, Jacques. *Writing and Difference*. Chicago: University of Chicago Press, 1978. First published 1967.

DeSalvo, Louise. "Color: White/Complexion: Dark." In *Are Italians White? How Race Is Made in America*, edited by Jennifer Guglielmo and Salvatore Salerno, 17–28. New York: Routledge, 2003.

Devins, John Bancroft. *An Observation of the Philippines*. New York: American Tract Society, 1905.

Dickens, Charles. *American Notes and Pictures from Italy: A Reprint of the First Editions*. London: Macmillan, 1925.

Dienst, Jonathan, Rich McHugh, Nancy Ing, and Michelle Neubert. "I-Team: NYPD Embeds Intelligence Officers in 13 Cities Overseas Since 9/11." *NBC New York*, November 14, 2016. https://www.nbcnewyork.com/news/local/NYPD -Stationed-Overseas-Increasing-Global-Terror-Threat-401186455.html.

Diner, Hasia. "The Encounter between Jews and America in the Gilded Age and Progressive Era." *Journal of the Gilded Age and Progressive Era* 11, no. 1 (January 2012): 3–25.

Dphrepaulezz, Omar H. "'The Right Sort of White Men': General Leonard Wood and the U.S. Army in the Southern Philippines, 1898–1906." PhD diss., University of Connecticut, 2013.

Du Bois, W. E. B. "Boddy." *The Crisis*, March 1922.

Du Bois, W. E. B. "Social Uplift." *The Crisis*, August 1911.

Duggan, Lisa. *Sapphic Slashers: Sex, Violence, and American Modernity*. Durham, NC: Duke University Press, 2000.

Dulaney, W. Marvin. *Black Police in America*. Bloomington: Indiana University Press, 1996.

Edwards, Laura. *A Legal History of the Civil War and Reconstruction: A Nation of Rights*. New York: Cambridge University Press, 2015.

Ellis, Mark W. "Reservation *Akicitas*: The Pine Ridge Indian Police, 1879–1885." *South Dakota History* 29, no. 3 (1999): 185–210.

Emsley, Clive. *Crime Police and Penal Policy: European Experiences 1750–1940*. New York: Oxford University Press, 2013.

Emsley, Clive. *Gendarmes and the State in Nineteenth-Century Europe*. New York: Oxford University Press, 1999.

Emsley, Clive, and Barbara Weinberger, eds. *Policing Western Europe: Politics, Professionalism, and Public Order, 1850–1940*. Westport, CT: Greenwood Press, 1991.

Escoffier, Jeffrey, Whitney Strub, and Jeffrey Patrick Colgan. "The Comstock Apparatus." In *Intimate States: Gender, Sexuality, and Governance in Modern US History*, edited by Margot Canaday, Nancy F. Cott, and Robert O. Self, 41–64. Chicago: University of Chicago Press, 2021.

Evens, Elizabeth. "Plainclothes Policewomen on the Trail: NYPD Undercover Investigations of Abortionists and Queer Women, 1913–1926." *Modern American History* 4, no. 1 (2021): 49–66. https://doi.org/10.1017/mah.2020.22.

Felker-Kantor, Max. *Policing Los Angeles: Race, Resistance, and the Rise of the LAPD*. Chapel Hill: University of North Carolina Press, 2018.

Fiaschetti, Michael, and Prosper Buranelli. *You Gotta Be Rough: The Adventures of Detective Fiaschetti of the Italian Squad*. New York: Doubleday, 1930.

Finn, Jonathan. *Capturing the Criminal Image: From Mug Shot to Surveillance Society*. Minneapolis: University of Minnesota Press, 2009.

Fischer, Anne Gray. *The Streets Belong to Us: Sex, Race, and Police Power from Segregation to Gentrification*. Chapel Hill: University of North Carolina Press, 2022.

Fishman, J. E. *Dynamite: A Concise History of the NYPD Bomb Squad*. New York: Verbitrage, 2013.

Flowe, Douglas. "'Drug-Mad Negroes': African Americans, Drug Use, and the Law in Progressive Era New York City." *Journal of the Gilded Age and Progressive Era* 20, no. 4 (October 2021): 503–22.

Flowe, Douglas. *Uncontrollable Blackness: African American Men and Criminality in Jim Crow New York*. Chapel Hill: University of North Carolina Press, 2020.

Foner, Eric. *Gateway to Freedom: The Hidden History of the Underground Railroad*. New York: W. W. Norton, 2016.

Fosdick, Raymond. *American Police Systems*. New York: Century, 1921.

Fosdick, Raymond. *European Police Systems*. New York: Century, 1915.

Fosdick, Raymond. "The Passing of the Bertillon System of Identification." *Journal of the American Institute of Criminal Law and Criminology* 6, no. 3 (September 1915): 363–69.

Foucault, Michel. *Discipline and Punish: The Birth of the Prison*. New York: Vintage, 1975.

Fronc, Jennifer. *New York Undercover: Private Surveillance in the Progressive Era*. Chicago: University of Chicago Press, 2009.

Fulton, Robert A. *Moroland: The History of Uncle Sam and the Moros 1899–1920*. Bend, OR: Tumalo Creek Press, 2007.

Gabaccia, Donna R. "Race, Nation, Hyphen: Italian-Americans and American Multiculturalism in Comparative Perspective." In *Are Italians White? How Race Is Made in America*, edited by Jennifer Guglielmo and Salvatore Salerno, 44–59. New York: Routledge, 2003.

Gage, Beverly. *The Day Wall Street Exploded: A Story of America in Its First Age of Terror*. New York: Oxford University Press, 2010.

Gardner, Charles. *The Doctor and the Devil, or Midnight Adventures of Dr. Parkhurst*. New York: Vanguard, 1894.

Gault, Robert. "Race Improvement through Social Inheritance." *Journal of the American Institute of Criminal Law and Criminology* 3, no. 2 (1912): 165–67.

Gilfoyle, Timothy. *City of Eros: New York City, Prostitution, and the Commercialization of Sex, 1790–1920*. New York: W. W. Norton, 1992.

Gilmore, Ruth Wilson. *Golden Gulag: Prisons, Surplus, Crisis, and Opposition in Globalizing California*. Berkeley: University of California Press, 2007.

Ginzburg, Carlo. *Clues, Myths, and the Historical Method*. Translated by John and Anne C. Tedeschi. Baltimore, MD: Johns Hopkins University Press, 2013. First English translation published in the United States in 1989.

Go, Julian. "The Imperial Origins of American Policing: Militarization and Imperial Feedback in the Early 20th Century." *American Journal of Sociology* 125, no. 5 (March 2020): 1193–254.

Goodman, Adam. *The Deportation Machine: America's Long History of Expelling Immigrants*. Princeton, NJ: Princeton University Press, 2020.

Gordon, Michael. *The Orange Riots: Irish Political Violence in New York City, 1870 and 1871*. Ithaca, NY: Cornell University Press, 1993.

Gross, Kali. *Colored Amazons: Crime, Violence, and Black Women in the City of Brotherly Love, 1880–1910*. Durham, NC: Duke University Press, 2006.

Guariglia, Matthew. "Facial Recognition Technology Is the New Rogues' Gallery." *Slate*, February 17, 2020.

Guariglia, Matthew. "Wrench in the Deportation: Louis F. Post's Objection to Mechanized Red Scare Bureaucracy." *Journal of American Ethnic History* 38, no. 1 (Fall 2018): 62–77.

Guernsey, Alfred and Henry Alden. *Harper's Pictorial History of the Civil War*. Vol. 2. New York: Harper and Brothers, 1866.

Guglielmo, Jennifer. "Introduction: White Lies, Dark Truths." In *Are Italians White? How Race Is Made in America*, edited by Jennifer Guglielmo and Salvatore Salerno, 1–14. New York: Routledge, 2003.

Guglielmo, Jennifer. *Living the Revolution: Italian Women's Resistance and Radicalism in New York City, 1880–1945*. Chapel Hill: University of North Carolina Press, 2010.

Guglielmo, Jennifer, and Salvatore Salerno, eds. *Are Italians White? How Race Is Made in America*. New York: Routledge, 2003.

Guglielmo, Thomas. *White on Arrival: Italians, Race, Color, and Power in Chicago, 1890–1945*. New York: Oxford University Press, 2000.

Hadden, Sally. *Slave Patrols: Law and Violence in Virginia and the Carolinas*. Cambridge, MA: Harvard University Press, 2001.

Haley, Sarah. *No Mercy Here: Gender, Punishment, and the Making of Jim Crow Modernity*. New York: Oxford University Press, 2016.

Hall, Stuart, Chas Critcher, Tony Jefferson, John Clarke, and Brian Roberts. *Policing the Crisis: Mugging, the State, and Law and Order*. 2nd ed. New York: Palgrave Macmillan, 2013. First published 1978.

Harlan, Louis R., ed. *The Booker T. Washington Papers*. Vol. 3. Urbana: University of Illinois Press, 1974.

Harring, Sidney. *Policing a Class Society: The Experience of American Cities, 1865–1915*. 2nd ed. Chicago: Haymarket Books, 2017.

Harris, Leslie M. *In the Shadow of Slavery: African Americans in New York City, 1626–1863*. Chicago: University of Chicago Press, 2003.

Heap, Chad. *Slumming: Sexual and Racial Encounters in American Night Life, 1885–1940*. Chicago: University of Chicago Press, 2009.

Heclo, Hugh. *Modern Social Politics in Britain and Sweden: From Relief to Income Maintenance*. New Haven, CT: Yale University Press, 1974.

Hernández, Kelly Lytle. *Bad Mexicans: Race, Empire and Revolution in the Borderlands*. New York: W. W. Norton, 2022.

Hernández, Kelly Lytle. *City of Inmates: Conquest, Rebellion, and the Rise of Human Caging in Los Angeles, 1771–1965*. Chapel Hill: University of North Carolina Press, 2017.

Hernández, Kelly Lytle. *Migra! A History of the U.S. Border Patrol.* Berkeley: University of California Press, 2010.

Hicks, Cheryl. *Talk with You Like a Woman: African American Women, Justice, and Reform in New York, 1890–1935.* Chapel Hill: University of North Carolina Press, 2010.

Higginbotham, Evelyn Brooks. *Righteous Discontent: The Women's Movement in the Black Baptist Church, 1880–1920.* Cambridge, MA: Harvard University Press, 1993.

Hinton, Elizabeth. *From the War on Poverty to the War on Crime: The Making of Mass Incarceration in America.* Cambridge, MA: Harvard University Press, 2016.

Hirota, Hidetaka. *Expelling the Poor: Atlantic Seaboard States and the 19th-Century Origins of American Immigration Policy.* New York: Oxford University Press, 2017.

Hochman, Brian. *The Listeners: A History of Wiretapping in the United States.* Cambridge, MA: Harvard University Press, 2022.

Hoff, John Van R. *Report of the Superior Board of Health of Porto Rico.* USPRMG, June 30, 1900.

Hughes, Steven. *Crime, Disorder and the Risorgimento: The Politics of Policing in Bologna.* New York: Cambridge University Press, 1994.

Ignatiev, Noel. *How the Irish Became White.* New York: Routledge, 1995.

Igo, Sarah. *The Averaged American: Surveys, Citizens, and the Making of a Mass Public.* Cambridge, MA: Harvard University Press, 2007.

Igo, Sarah. *The Known Citizen: A History of Privacy in Modern America.* Cambridge, MA: Harvard University Press, 2018.

Jacobsen, Annie. *First Platoon: A Story of Modern War in the Age of Identity Dominance.* New York: Dutton, 2021.

Jacobson, Matthew Frye. *Barbarian Virtues: The United States Encounters Foreign Peoples at Home and Abroad, 1876–1917.* New York: Hill and Wang, 2000.

Jacobson, Matthew Frye. *Whiteness of a Different Color: European Immigrants and the Alchemy of Race.* Cambridge, MA: Harvard University Press, 1998.

Jensen, Richard Bach. *Liberty and Order: The Theory and Practice of Italian Public Security Police, 1848 to the Crisis of the 1890s.* New York: Garland Publishing, 1991.

Johnson, James Weldon. *Black Manhattan.* New York: Knopf, 1930.

Johnson, Marilynn. *Street Justice: A History of Police Violence in New York City.* Boston: Beacon, 2003.

Joyce, Patrick. *The Rule of Freedom: Liberalism and the Modern City.* New York: Verso, 2003.

Jung, Moon-Ho. *Menace to Empire: Anticolonial Solidarities and the Transpacific Origins of the US Security State.* Berkeley: University of California Press, 2022.

Kafka, Ben. *The Demon of Writing: Powers and Failures of Paperwork.* Cambridge, MA: Zone Books, 2012.

Keller, Lisa. *Triumph of Order: Democracy and Public Space in New York and London.* New York: Columbia University Press, 2009.

Kelling, George L., and James Q. Wilson. "Broken Windows: The Police and Neighborhood Safety." *Atlantic,* March 1982.

Kohler-Hausmann, Julilly. *Getting Tough: Welfare and Imprisonment in 1970s America.* Princeton, NJ: Princeton University Press, 2017.

Kornmann, Andrea Marie. *Our Police.* New York: J. J. Little, 1887.

Kornweibel, Theodore. *"Investigate Everything": Federal Efforts to Ensure Black Loyalty During World War I.* Bloomington: Indiana University Press, 2002.

Kornweibel, Theodore. *Seeing Red: Federal Campaigns against Black Militancy, 1919–1925.* Bloomington: Indiana University Press, 1998.

Kramer, Paul A. *The Blood of Government: Race, Empire, the United States, and the Philippines.* Chapel Hill: University of North Carolina Press, 2006.

Kraut, Julia Rose. *Threat of Dissent: A History of Ideological Exclusion and Deportation in the United States.* Cambridge, MA: Harvard University Press, 2020.

Lambert, Léopold, and Ruth Wilson Gilmore. "Making Abolition Geography in California's Central Valley." *Funambulist,* January–February 2019. https:// thefunambulist.net/magazine/21-space-activism/interview-making-abolition -geography-california-central-valley-ruth-wilson-gilmore.

Lauer, Josh. *Creditworthy: A History of Consumer Surveillance and Financial Identity in America.* New York: Columbia University Press, 2017.

Lebrón, Marisol. *Policing Life and Death: Race, Violence, and Resistance in Puerto Rico.* Berkeley: University of California Press, 2019.

Lee, Erika. *At America's Gates: Chinese Immigration During the Exclusion Era, 1882–1943.* Chapel Hill: University of North Carolina Press, 2003.

Lepore, Jill. *New York Burning: Liberty, Slavery, and Conspiracy in Eighteenth-Century Manhattan.* New York: Vintage, 2015.

Levett, Allan Edward. "Centralization of City Police in the Nineteenth Century United States." PhD diss., University of Michigan, 1975.

Lew-Williams, Beth. *The Chinese Must Go: Violence, Exclusion, and the Making of the Alien Race.* Cambridge, MA: Harvard University Press, 2018.

Linn, Brian McAllister. *The U.S. Army and Counterinsurgency in the Philippine War, 1899–1902.* Chapel Hill: University of North Carolina Press, 2000.

Lira, Natalie. *Laboratory of Deficiency: Sterilization and Confinement in California, 1900–1950s.* Berkeley: University of California Press, 2022.

Lodge, Henry Cabot. "The Restriction of Immigration." *North American Review* 152, no. 410 (January 1891): 27–36.

Lombroso, Cesare. *Crime, Its Causes and Remedies.* Translated by Henry Horton. Boston: Little, Brown, 1911.

Lombroso, Cesare. "Illustrative Studies in Criminal Anthropology: The Physiognomy of the Anarchists" *Monist* (1890): 336–43.

López, Ian Haney. *White by Law: The Legal Construction of Race.* New York: NYU Press, 2006.

Lowe, Lisa. *The Intimacies of Four Continents.* Durham, NC: Duke University Press, 2015.

Lüdtke, Alf. *Police and State in Prussia, 1815–1850.* New York: Cambridge University Press, 1989.

Lui, Mary Ting Yi. *The Chinatown Trunk Mystery: Murder, Miscegenation, and Other Dangerous Encounters in Turn-of-the-Century New York City*. Princeton, NJ: Princeton University Press, 2005.

Lvovsky, Anna. "Rethinking Police Expertise." *Yale Law Journal* 131, no. 2 (November 2021): 475–572.

Lvovsky, Anna. *Vice Patrol: Cops, Courts, and the Struggle over Urban Gay Life before Stonewall*. Chicago: University of Chicago Press, 2021.

Lyon, F. Emory. "Race Betterment and the Crime Doctors." *Journal of the American Institute of Criminal Law and Criminology* 5, no. 6 (1915): 887–91.

MacArthur, Arthur. *Annual Report of Major General Arthur MacArthur*. Vol. 2. Manila: US Army, 1900. https://catalog.hathitrust.org/Record/100159850.

Malka, Adam. *The Men of Mobtown: Policing Baltimore in the Age of Slavery and Emancipation*. Chapel Hill: University of North Carolina Press, 2018.

Marinari, Maddalena. *Unwanted: Italian and Jewish Mobilization against Restrictive Immigration Laws, 1882–1965*. Chapel Hill: University of North Carolina Press, 2020.

Marks, George P., ed. *The Black Press Views American Imperialism*. New York: Arno Press and the *New York Times*, 1971.

May, Samuel. *The Fugitive Slave Law and Its Victims*. New York: American Anti-Slavery Society, 1861.

McAdoo, William. *Guarding a Great City*. New York: Harper and Brothers, 1906.

McCallum, Jack. *Leonard Wood: Rough Rider, Surgeon, Architect of American Imperialism*. New York: NYU Press, 2005.

McCoy, Alfred. *Policing America's Empire: The United States, the Philippines, and the Rise of the Surveillance State*. Madison: University of Wisconsin Press, 2009.

McCrossen, Alexis. *Marking Modern Times: A History of Clocks, Watches, and Other Timekeepers in American Life*. Chicago: University of Chicago Press, 2013.

McGirr, Lisa. *The War on Alcohol: Prohibition and the Rise of the American State*. New York: W. W. Norton, 2016.

"Memorabilia: A Hero's Story." *Spring 3100*, July/August 1990, 10.

Miller, Wilbur. *Cops and Bobbies: Police Authority in New York and London, 1830–1870*. Chicago: University of Chicago Press, 1973.

Molina, Natalia. *How Race Is Made in America: Immigration, Citizenship, and the Historical Power of Racial Scripts*. Berkeley: University of California Press, 2014.

Monkkonen, Eric. *Police in Urban America, 1860–1920*. New York: Cambridge University Press, 1981.

Moore, Colin D. *American Imperialism and the State, 1893–1921*. New York: Cambridge University Press, 2017.

Moore, Louis. *I Fight for a Living: Boxing and the Battle for Black Manhood, 1880–1915*. Urbana: University of Illinois Press, 2017.

Moran, Rachel Louise. *Governing Bodies: American Politics and the Shaping of the Modern Physique*. Philadelphia: University of Pennsylvania Press, 2018.

Morgan, Appleton. "What Shall We Do With the 'Dago?'" *Popular Science* 38 (December 1890).

Moss, Frank ed. *Story of the Riot*. New York: Citizens' Protective League, 1900.

Muhammad, Khalil Gibran. *The Condemnation of Blackness: Race, Crime, and the Making of Modern Urban America*. Cambridge, MA: Harvard University Press, 2010.

Mumford, Kevin. *Interzones: Black/White Sex Districts in Chicago and New York in the Early Twentieth Century*. New York: Columbia University Press, 1997.

Murakawa, Naomi. *The First Civil Right: How Liberals Built Prison America*. New York: Oxford University Press, 2014.

Murphy, Kevin. *Political Manhood: Red Bloods, Mollycoddles, and the Politics of Progressive Era Reform*. New York: Columbia University Press, 2008.

Musgrave, Shawn, Meagher, Tom, and Gabriel Dance. "The Pentagon Finally Details Its Weapons-for-Cops Giveaway." *Marshall Project*, December 3, 2014. https://www.themarshallproject.org/2014/12/03/the-pentagon-finally-details-its-weapons-for-cops-giveaway.

Nadel, Stanley. *Little Germany: Ethnicity, Religion, and Class in New York City, 1845–1880*. Urbana: University of Illinois Press, 1990.

Nast, Thomas. "The American River Ganges." *Harper's Weekly*, September 30, 1871.

Nast, Thomas. "Charge of the Police on the Rioters of the 'Tribune' Office." In *Harper's Pictorial History of the Civil War*, vol. 2., edited by Alfred Guernsey and Henry Alden. New York: Harper and Brothers, 1866.

National Commission on Law Observance and Enforcement. *Report on the Enforcement of the Prohibition Law of the United States*. Washington, DC: Government Publishing Office, 1931.

New York City Police Department. *Report of the Police Department of the City of New York for the Year Ending December 31, 1895/1905/1906/1908*. New York: Martin B. Brown Company Printers, 1896–1909.

New York Civil Liberties Union. "Stop-and-Frisk Data." https://www.nyclu.org/en/stop-and-frisk-data.

New York (State) Senate. *Report and Proceedings of the Senate Committee Appointed to Investigate the Police Department of the City of New York*. 5 vols. Albany, NY: James B. Lyon, 1895.

Ngai, Mae M. *Impossible Subjects: Illegal Aliens and the Making of Modern America*. Princeton, NJ: Princeton University Press, 2003.

Nitti, Francesco. "Italian Anarchists." *North American Review* 167, no. 504 (November 1898): 598–608.

Odem, Mary. *Delinquent Daughters: Protecting and Policing Adolescent Female Sexuality in the United States*. Chapel Hill: University of North Carolina Press, 1995.

Öfele, Martin W. *True Sons of the Republic: European Immigrants in the Union Army*. Westport, CT: Praeger, 2008.

Oliver, Willard. *August Vollmer: The Father of American Policing*. Durham, NC: Carolina Academic Press, 2017.

O'Malley, Brendan P. "Protecting the Stranger: The Origins of US Immigration Regulation in Nineteenth-Century New York." PhD diss., City University of New York, 2015.

Ordover, Nancy. *American Eugenics: Race, Queer Anatomy, and the Science of Nationalism*. Minneapolis: University of Minnesota Press, 2003.

Parkhurst, Rev. Charles H. *Our Fight with Tammany*. New York: Charles Scribner's Sons, 1895.

Peel, Robert. *Principles of Law Enforcement*. 1829. https://archive.org/details /principles-of-law-enforcement-peel/mode/1.

Pegler-Gordon, Anna. *In Sight of America: Photography and the Development of U.S. Immigration Policy*. Berkeley: University of California Press, 2009.

Pennsylvania State Federation of Labor. *The American Cossack*. 1911. Reprint, New York: Arno Press and *New York Times*, 1971.

Pick, Daniel. Faces of Degeneration: A European Disorder, c. 1848–1918. New York: Cambridge University Press, 1989.

Pitts, Jennifer. *A Turn to Empire: The Rise of Imperial Liberalism in Britain and France*. Princeton, NJ: Princeton University Press, 2005.

Pliley, Jessica. *Policing Sexuality: The Mann Act and the Making of the FBI*. Cambridge, MA: Harvard University Press, 2014.

Rafter, Nicole Hahn. *Creating Born Criminals*. Urbana: University of Illinois Press, 1997.

Rafter, Nicole, ed. *The Origins of Criminology: A Reader*. New York: Routledge, 2009.

Reports of the Taft Philippine Commission. Washington, DC: Government Printing Office, 1901.

Richardson, James. *The New York Police: Colonial Times to 1901*. New York: Oxford University Press, 1970.

Ripley, William Z. *The Races of Europe: A Sociological Study*. New York: D. Appleton and Company, 1899.

Ripley, William Z. *A Selected Bibliography of the Anthropology and Ethnology of Europe*. New York: D. Appleton and Company, 1899.

Robertson, Craig. *The Passport in America: The History of a Document*. New York: Oxford University Press, 2010.

Robertson, Stephen. "Harlem Undercover: Vice Investigators, Race, and Prostitution, 1910–1930." *Journal of Urban History* 35, no. 4 (May 2009): 486–504. https:// doi.org/10.1177/0096144209333370.

Rodgers, Daniel. *Atlantic Crossings: Social Politics in a Progressive Era*. Cambridge, MA: Belknap Press of Harvard University Press, 1998.

Roediger, David. *Working toward Whiteness: How America's Immigrants Become White*. New York: Basic Books, 2006.

Roosevelt, Theodore. "Administering the New York Police Force." *Atlantic Monthly*, September 1897.

Roosevelt, Theodore. "The Ethnology of the Police." *Munsey's Magazine*, June 1897.

Roosevelt, Theodore. "Municipal Administration: The New York Police Force." *Atlantic Monthly*, September 1897.

Rosenwaike, Ira. *Population History of New York City*. Syracuse, NY: Syracuse University Press, 1972.

Ross, Luana. *Inventing the Savage: The Social Construction of Native American Criminality*. Austin: University of Texas Press, 1998.

Sacks, Marcy S. *Before Harlem: The Black Experience in New York City before World War I*. Philadelphia: University of Pennsylvania Press, 2006.

Schrader, Stuart. *Badges without Borders: How Global Counterinsurgency Transformed American Policing*. Berkeley: University of California Press, 2019.

Schrag, Zachary. *The Fires of Philadelphia: Citizen-Soldiers, Nativists, and the 1844 Riots over the Soul of a Nation*. New York: Pegasus Books, 2021.

Schulz, Dorothy Moses. *From Social Worker to Crime Fighter: Women in United States Municipal Policing*. Westport, CT: Praeger, 1995.

Scott, James C. *Domination and the Arts of Resistance: Hidden Transcripts*. New Haven, CT: Yale University Press, 1990.

Scott, James C. *Seeing Like a State: How Certain Schemes to Improve the Human Condition Have Failed*. New Haven, CT: Yale University Press, 1999.

Seigel, Micol. *Violence Work: State Power and the Limits of Police*. Durham, NC: Duke University Press, 2018.

Singh, Nikhil Pal. *Race and America's Long War*. Berkeley: University of California Press, 2017.

Singh, Nikhil Pal. "The Whiteness of Police." *American Quarterly* 66, no. 4 (2009): 1091–99.

Singha, Radhika. "Settle, Mobilize, Verify: Identification Practices in Colonial India." *Studies in History* 16, no. 2 (2000): 151–98.

Skowronek, Stephen. *Building a New American State: The Expansion of National Administrative Capacities, 1877–1920*. New York: Cambridge University Press, 1982.

Slotkin, Richard. *Lost Battalions: The Great War and the Crisis of American Nationality*. New York: Holt, 2005.

Smith, Carl. *Urban Disorder and the Shape of Belief: The Great Chicago Fire, the Haymarket Bomb, and the Model Town of Pullman*. Chicago: University of Chicago Press, 1995.

Sohi, Seema. *Echoes of Mutiny: Race, Surveillance and Indian Anticolonialism in North America*. Oxford: Oxford University Press, 2014.

Somerville, Siobhan B. *Queering the Color Line: Race and the Invention of Homosexuality in American Culture*. Durham, NC: Duke University Press, 2000.

Spencer, Elaine Glovka. *Police and the Social Order in German Cities: The Düsseldorf District, 1848–1914*. DeKalb: Northern Illinois University Press, 1992.

Stansell, Christine. *City of Women: Sex and Class in New York, 1789–1860*. New York: Knopf, 1986.

Stein, Melissa N. *Measuring Manhood: Race and the Science of Masculinity, 1830–1934*. Minneapolis: University of Minnesota Press, 2015.

Stern, Scott. *The Trials of Nina McCall: Sex, Surveillance, and the Decades-Long Government Plan to Imprison "Promiscuous" Women*. Boston: Beacon, 2018.

Stoddard, William Osborn. *The Volcano under the City*. New York: Fords, Howard, and Hulbert, 1887.

Stoler, Ann Laura. *Along the Archival Grain: Epistemic Anxieties and Colonial Common Sense*. Princeton, NJ: Princeton University Press, 2009.

Stowell, David O. *Streets, Railroads, and the Great Strike of 1877*. Chicago: Chicago University Press, 1999.

Suddler, Carl. *Presumed Criminal: Black Youth and the Justice System in Postwar New York*. New York: NYU Press, 2019.

Taylor, Clarence. *Fight the Power: African Americans and the Long History of Police Brutality in New York City*. NYU Press, 2019.

Taylor, Frederick W. *On the Art of Cutting Metals*. New York: American Society of Mechanical Engineers, 1906.

Thale, Christopher. "The Informal World of Police Patrol: New York City in the Early Twentieth Century." *Journal of Urban History* 33, no. 2 (January 2007): 183–216. https://doi.org/10.1177/0096144206290384.

Thompson, Courtney E. *An Organ of Murder: Crime, Violence, and Phrenology in Nineteenth-Century America*. New Brunswick, NJ: Rutgers University Press, 2021.

Thompson, Heather Ann. "Why Mass Incarceration Matters: Rethinking Crisis, Decline, and Transformation in Postwar American History." *Journal of American History* 97, no. 3 (December 2010): 703–34. https://doi.org/10.1093/jahist/97.3.703.

Thornbrough, Emma Lou. *T. Thomas Fortune: Militant Journalist*. Chicago: University of Chicago Press, 1972.

Tilley, Helen. *Africa as a Living Laboratory: Empire, Development, and the Problem of Scientific Knowledge, 1870–1950*. Chicago: University of Chicago Press, 2011.

Tunney, Thomas, and Paul Merrick Hollister. *Throttled! The Detection of German and Anarchist Bomb Plotters*. Boston: Small, Maynard and Company, 1919.

Turner, George Kibbe. "The Daughters of the Poor: A Plain Story of the Development of New York City as the Leading Centre of the White Slave Trade of the World, under Tammany Hall." *McClure's Magazine* 34 (November 1909).

United States Army. *General Orders and Circulars Issued from Office of the U.S. Military Governor in the Philippine Islands*. Manila: US Army, 1900.

United States Congress. *Report of the Select Committee on Immigration and Naturalization: And Testimony Taken by the Committee on Immigration of the Senate and the Select Committee on Immigration and Naturalization of the House of Representatives under Concurrent Resolution of March 12, 1890*. Washington, DC: Government Printing Office, 1891.

United States Department of Commerce and Labor. *Report of the United States Commission of Investigation Upon the Disaster to the Steamer "General Slocum."* October 8, 1904. Washington, DC: Government Printing Office, 1904.

Unterman, Katherine. *Uncle Sam's Policemen: The Pursuit of Fugitives Across Borders.* Cambridge, MA: Harvard University Press, 2015.

Verdery, Katherine. *My Life as a Spy: Investigation in a Secret Police File.* Durham, NC: Duke University Press, 2018.

Vitale, Alex. *The End of Policing.* New York: Verso, 2017.

Vollmer, August, and Alfred Parker. *Crime and the State Police.* Berkeley: University of California Press, 1934.

Von Skal, George. *History of German Immigration in the United States and Successful German-Americans and Their Descendants.* New York: Fred T. Smiley Printing and Publishing Company, 1910.

Walling, George W. *Recollections of a New York Chief of Police.* New York: Claxton Book Concern, 1887.

Washington, Booker T. "Address before the Cotton States and International Exhibition." 1895. In *The Booker T. Washington Papers,* vol. 3, 583–87. Edited by Louis R. Harlan. Urbana: University of Illinois Press, 1974.

Washington, Booker T. "Negro Crime and Strong Drink." *Journal of the American Institute of Criminal Law and Criminology* 3, no. 3 (1912): 384–92.

Watkins-Owens, Irma. *Blood Relations: Caribbean Immigrants and the Harlem Community, 1900–1930.* Bloomington: Indiana University Press, 1996.

Weld, Kirsten. *Paper Cadavers: The Archives of Dictatorship in Guatemala.* Durham, NC: Duke University Press, 2014.

Wexler, Laura. *Tender Violence: Domestic Visions in an Age of U.S. Imperialism.* Chapel Hill: University of North Carolina Press, 2000.

Wild, Mark. *Street Meeting: Multiethnic Neighborhoods in Early Twentieth-Century Los Angeles.* Berkley: University of California Press, 2005.

Wilder, Craig Steven. *A Covenant with Color: Race and Social Power in Brooklyn.* New York: Columbia University Press, 2001.

Wilkerson, Isabel. *The Warmth of Other Suns: The Epic Story of America's Great Migration.* New York: Random House, 2010.

Willard, Frances. "Annual Address before the National Woman's Christian Temperance Union at Its Twenty-First Convention in Cleveland, Ohio." November 16–21, 1894. https://babel.hathitrust.org/cgi/pt?id=umn.31951002070100f&view=1up&seq=1.

Willemse, Cornelius. *Behind the Green Lights.* New York: Knopf, 1931.

Willemse, Cornelius. *A Cop Remembers.* New York: Dutton, 1933.

Willis, Henry Parker. *Our Philippine Problem: A Study of American Colonial Policy.* New York: Henry Holt, 1905.

Willrich, Michael. *Pox: An American History.* New York: Penguin Press, 2011.

Wilson, Christopher P. *Cop Knowledge: Police Power and Cultural Narrative in Twentieth-Century America.* Chicago: University of Chicago Press, 2000.

Wu, Ellen D. *The Color of Success: Asian Americans and the Origins of the Model Minority.* Princeton, NJ: Princeton University Press, 2014.

Yates, JoAnne. *Control through Communication: The Rise of System in American Management.* Baltimore, MD: Johns Hopkins University Press, 1989.

cultural gaps, 2–3, 8, 89, 109, 115
cultural identity, 101, 203
cultural institutions, 14
cultural knowledge, 4, 8, 35, 48, 67, 70, 81–82, 93, 98–99, 105, 120–21, 142, 154, 156, 170

Democratic Party, 7, 26, 30–31, 34, 52, 55, 64, 71, 99, 143
Diet Squad, 167, 169–70

East Harlem, 9
economic mobility, 11, 13, 16, 113, 141–42
Emigrant Squad, 31
ethnic difference, 4, 73, 203
ethnic groups, 8, 11, 80, 87, 137
ethnic knowledge, 47–48, 81, 136, 154, 196
Europe: and American experiences, 49–50, 129; and anarchists, 37; civilization, 54; and emigration, 11–14, 49–50, 69, 72, 117–18, 129, 132, 155, 179, 191, 194, 204, 222n1; and empires, 19, 81, 180, 187; and European Jews, 101, 112; and immigrant officers, 48, 96; and imperialism, 6; and information management, 21; and police institutions, 3, 20, 74, 82, 84, 152, 155, 175, 177, 184, 188; and race, 11, 67–68; and racial science, 109; and technology, 6, 187; and warfare, 75; and whiteness, 179; and women, 47, 124; and World War I, 170
Evening World, 1, 87, 107–8, 123, 158, 176
exclusion, 3–4, 14, 65

fat men, 168–72
federal government, 7, 63, 89–90, 134, 174, 202
federal immigration administration, 4, 109
federal immigration policy, 5, 95, 109
federal slavery enforcement, 33–34
federal soldiers, 75, 136
Five Points, 28–29, 31, 46
Fosdick, Raymond, 6, 8–10, 12, 21, 154, 156–57, 160, 177, 184, 188–90, 202
Fugitive Slave Act, 35

gambling, 46, 48–49, 51–53, 60, 88–89, 98, 102, 150, 202
Germans: as Americans, 173; Democrats, 30–31; German Tenth Ward, 31; immigrants to the United States, 7, 11, 19, 25, 32, 37, 55, 61, 68, 73, 84, 129, 147, 149, 172; language, 101–4, 147, 151, 161; model of policing, 188–90; neighborhoods, 7; New Yorkers, 29, 100–101; patrolmen, 105; police officers, 19–20, 27, 46, 65–66, 68, 104, 106, 142, 161, 171; spies, 155; theaters, 28; women, 47; working-class, 26, 34; and World War I, 173–74
German Squad, 8, 20, 93, 99–100, 103–6, 137
global knowledge networks, 17, 176
governance, 43, 177–78, 201; American, 12–13, 78, 80, 104; civic, 136; colonial, 17, 73–74, 76, 177–78; hierarchical, 115; liberal, 76; military governance, 83; municipal, 8, 12, 51, 187, 206; racial, 37, 72, 81; urban, 55
Greene, Francis Vinton, 8, 19, 71–72, 74–79, 82–84, 88, 89, 101, 104, 120–21, 168

Harlem, 121, 140, 148–50, 152, 154, 159, 200
Haymarket Massacre, 128
Hennessey, David, 117, 128
Henry, Guy, 86
Home Guards, 166
homosocial spaces, 63, 95–96

immigrants: and abolitionism, 34; activism, 108; Americanized, 19; arrests of, 2; Asian, 14, 104, 119; and assimilation, 12, 96; belonging, 194; and Black Americans, 34; in Brooklyn, 27; bureaucracy, 31; Catholic, 166; Chinese, 2, 7, 13–14, 48, 56, 215n8; communities, 5–6, 8, 11–12, 49, 94–96, 100–102, 114, 120, 142, 147, 156, 167, 179, 196; control of, 114, 144, 196; and corruption, 61; crime, 6, 10, 87, 94, 109, 122–24, 128, 134, 155, 191; and criminalization, 15, 160; cultures, 154; Dutch, 99; Eastern European, 69, 104, 194; and emigration reasons, 9; European, 11–14,

New Yorkers, 176; American born, 108, 119; Anglo, 30, 36, 42, 62, 104, 109; Black, 9–10, 13, 19, 25, 33–35, 39, 48–49, 91, 96, 113, 135–42, 144, 149, 167, 171, 173, 193, 200, 204; Chinese, 11, 14, 29, 46, 113; and crime, 107; foreign-born, 109, 119, 156; German, 11, 20, 29, 104, 173; immigrant, 5, 32, 36, 110, 156; Irish, 11, 28, 36, 42, 50, 55, 127, 172, 214n40; Italian, 121; lower-middle-class, 57; native-born, 32; nativist, 37; policing of, 73, 170, 185, 215n8; and race relations, 199–200; and racial difference, 25; upper-class, 14, 37, 39, 47, 60; white, 14, 49, 96; working-class, 15, 45, 159

New York Times, 41, 53, 63, 83, 91, 130, 134, 146–47, 157, 167, 201

nonwhite men, 2, 47–48, 95–96

organized crime, 129, 132

patrolmen, 45–46, 48, 51, 60–61, 63, 65, 69, 83, 121, 134, 141, 154, 160, 162, 166, 173, 185, 192

personal knowledge, 18, 69

Petrosino, Joseph, 20, 111, 114–15, 120–22, 124–26, 128–32, 142–43, 147–48, 151, 191, 199–201

Philippines, 6, 19, 71–73, 75–79, 81–83, 85–88, 90, 118, 157, 183, 206; Filipino independence, 72, 76, 85, 89; Filipino society, 72, 77–80, 82; Filipino soldiers, 76, 87, 105

police brutality, 18–20, 26, 45, 53, 55, 59–60, 87, 91–92, 97, 135–36, 139–40, 149, 159–60, 174

Police Bulletin, 162–63, 165, 167–68, 171

police "civil war" (1857), 27, 30–31

Police Practice and Procedure, 153–54, 156, 159, 162, 164, 165–66

police reform, 20, 51, 56, 59–60, 64, 142, 158, 162, 166–68, 186, 190

policing: and ability, 68; and academic knowledge, 170; and algorithms, 18; American-style, 45, 84, 94; Anglo-Saxon, 118; bad, 56; of Black citizens, 137–40,

145; and the carceral state, 15–16; and Chinese immigrants, 14–15, 48, 102; coercive, 47; colonial, 79, 82–86, 89, 109, 121; "common sense," 157; community, 201; and criminality, 45; and detective work, 62; ethnic, 8, 12, 18–20, 93–94, 99, 141, 145, 199; European models of, 74, 175, 187–88, 190; as a family business, 42–43; and fighting, 40; fugitive slave, 34; good, 45, 56, 62–64, 70, 73, 115, 148, 151, 156, 197; of immigrant communities, 95, 102, 123, 137, 153, 155–56; and imperialism, 22; and inhumanity, 35; innovations in, 84; and Irish officers, 55, 127; of Italian people, 107, 111, 114, 119, 122; labor of, 125; London-style, 7, 25, 82; as a machine, 22–23; and masculinity, 44, 46, 58; methods of, 3, 12, 18, 60, 63, 161, 165–66, 177–78, 202, 205–6; and militarization, 196, 206; modern, 4, 74, 99, 158; morals, 47, 97, 120, 142; of multiracial communities, 100–102, 195–96; native, 19, 109, 151, 172, 178; and nostalgia, 214n45; and power relationships, 3–4; predictive, 18; proactive, 190; problems of, 195, 203; Progressive Era, 202; and prostitution, 48, 95; and public opinion, 14, 168; quality-of-life, 16, 200; and race, 1, 6, 8, 11, 17, 23, 25, 33, 43, 213n35; race-based, 102, 144; race-blind, 134, 176, 206; race-conscious, 143; and racial hierarchies, 68; reforms of, 21, 70; as a science, 3; skills, 40; standardization, 173; and surveillance, 4–5, 82, 94; and technocracy, 17, 192, 198; and Theodore Roosevelt, 62–64, 67–68, 105–6, 147–48; urban, 72; and violence, 27, 30, 59, 159; wartime, 165; and whiteness, 193–94; and women, 56; and xenophobia, 14

popular knowledge, 25, 197

"potential" criminality, 33

Progressive Era, 2, 5; and academic knowledge, 156; and anti-vice groups, 150, 187; and bureaucracy, 67; and the carceral state, 18; and categorization, 67; and Europe, 187; and men, 115; and moral

violence, 2, 4, 40–41, 47, 54, 57, 65, 72, 75, 95–96, 157, 159, 171, 174; Americanized, 88; anti-Black, 90–91; criminal, 27; domestic, 202; ethnic, 26; exclusionary, 142; extralegal, 90; hypermasculine, 50; inclusionary, 142; informal, 174; interpolice, 33; Italian, 115–19; legitimate, 30, 110; military, 71; mob, 36, 39, 135, 143, 204; police, 10, 12–13, 22, 136–37, 140, 149, 165, 211n5, 212n28; political, 7, 214n40; racial, 3, 5, 16, 29, 35, 37–38, 90, 92, 136, 140–41, 165, 167, 197, 232n39; state, 5, 9–10, 23, 16–17, 42, 55, 77, 79, 91, 139, 209; suppression of, 31–32; threat of, 78; unrestrained, 188; unsanctioned, 44; workers, 3, 34
Vollmer, August, 84, 178, 196–97

Waldo, Rhinelander, 132–33, 146–47, 168
Walling, George, 32–33, 35–36, 39–40, 45–48, 50, 53, 59
war on crime, 16
war on drugs, 16
Washington, Booker T., 140–42
Washington, DC, 5, 63, 75, 77, 178, 191

whiteness, 1, 11–12; and assimilation, 12–13; and belonging, 32; and Blackness, 16, 39–40; consolidation of, 41, 61, 179; and immigrants, 55, 179, 204; and Italians, 113, 132, 141; and masculinity, 49, 65, 173; middle-class, 194; and mobility, 62; and policing, 13, 59, 194; privileges of, 113, 135; and racial state-building, 19; white men, 64–65, 86, 97, 119, 186; white women, 2, 9, 47
Willemse, Cornelius, 91, 93, 99–104, 151
witnesses, 2, 60–61, 91, 98, 101, 120, 127, 131, 134, 177, 185
women's rights, 155
Woods, Arthur, 21, 134, 151–53, 156–62, 165, 168, 170, 173, 177, 185, 187, 190–93, 202
working-class white men, 40, 119
World Police Congress, 5
World War I, 8, 134, 153–55, 165, 169–70, 172–75, 177, 187, 196, 202
World War II, 15, 72, 230n2

xenophobia, 2, 5, 7–8, 14, 40, 95–96, 108, 116, 123, 132, 165, 172, 196